The Cocaine War

The Cocaine War
in Context: Drugs and Politics

Belén Boville

Translated from Spanish by
Lorena Terando

Algora Publishing
New York

ISBN: 0-87586-293-4 (softcover)
ISBN: 0-87586-294-2 (hardcover)
ISBN: 0-87586-295-0 (ebook)

Library of Congress Cataloging-in-Publication Data

Boville Luca de Tena, Belén.
  [Guerra de la cocaína. English]
  The cocaine war in context : drugs and politics / Belén Boville ; [translated to
English by Lorena Terando].
     p. cm.
  Translation of: La guerra de la cocaína : drogas, cocaína y medio ambiente.
  Includes bibliographical references and index.
  ISBN 0-87586-293-4 (pbk. : alk. paper) — ISBN 0-87586-294-2 (hard cover :
alk. paper) — ISBN 0-87586-295-0 (ebook)
  1. Narcotics, Control of—Latin America. 2. Narcotics, Control of—United
States. 3. Cocaine industry—Latin America. 4. Cocaine habit—United States.
5. Drug traffic—Latin America. 6. Drug traffic—United States. I. Title.

HV5840.L3B6913 2004
363.45—dc22

2004006340

Printed in the United States

From darkness into light,
Thank you, José Antonio

Acknowledgements

This book is the result of several years of research including my dissertation for the Universidad Complutense doctoral program (entitled *Las relaciones interamericanas ante la lucha contra la droga*, or "Inter-American Relations in the War Against Drugs," 1994), and the doctorate degree conferred on me by the Agencia Española de Cooperación's program Problemas y perspectives en la integración de América Latina (Problems and Perspectives in Latin American Integration). My 1996 master's degree in environmental education and my experiences as an environmental journalist and member of a movement of NGOs seeking a more respectful world have further exposed me to the depth of today's environmental problems.

In addition, I am grateful for the counsel of: Antonio Escohotado (Professor of Sociology at UNED), María Novo (Dean of Environmental Education at UNED-UNESCO), Celestino de Arenal (Dean of International Law and International Relations at the Universidad Complutense), Manuel Gutierrez Estévez (Dean of Anthropology at the Universidad Complutense), Gustavo Palomares (Dean of Political Science at the Universidad Complutense), Juan Ossio (Dean of Andean Anthropology at the Universidad La Católica in Lima), Alberto Van Klaveren (Professor of International Law at the Universidad de Chile) and Joseph. S. Tulchin (Director of the Latin American Program at the Woodrow Wilson Center); in Spain, for the collaboration of those in the Center for Peace Research (Centro de Investigaciones para la Paz - CIP), the Spanish Agency for International Cooperation, the Ortega y Gasset Foundation, the Washington Irving Cultural Center in Madrid and the Embassies of Colombia, Perú and Bolivia; in the US and Latin America, for the cooperation of Mauricio Mamani, Mario Argandoña, Hugo Cabieses, Ricardo Soberón, Baldomero Cáceres, Róger Rumrrill, José Mesa y Teresa Gisbert, the Embassies of Spain and the United Status in Perú, the Peruvian Minister of Health Mr. Costa Bauer, ENACO, CEDIB, COINCOCA, the Permanent Assembly for Human Rights in Cochabamba (Bolivia) and Ricardo Vargas (CINEP); in Europe for the cooperation of Joep Omen (ENCOD), Martin Jelsma, Virginia Montañés and all the members of the Transnational Institute of Amsterdam team.

I also thank María Luisa Luca de Tena and the Lohmann family for their logistical support, and Marisa Guiulfo and her children for their kindness and dedication. Finally, this research was only possible thanks to the unwavering support and patience of my husband, José Antonio Navalón.

TABLE OF CONTENTS

INTRODUCTION

While the younger generation was nursing a hang-over from the free and creative scene in the late 1980s, we began to feel the effects of a dual process that ten years later would place us smack dab in the middle of globalization. On the one hand, we saw the puritan neo-liberalism that first cropped up under Reagan had caused the traffic in of all sorts of goods to spread worldwide; on the other hand we witnessed the fall of communist societies, accompanied by the proliferation and consolidation of criminal organizations during the transition to savage capitalism.

Contrary to the popular paradigm, we saw proof at every hand that this is an inter-dependent world characterized by a range of economic, social and environmental problems more than by any one political ideology. Thus a period began which demanded an extraordinary effort from all of us: faced with the free competition of the markets (for both job and goods), there was more pressure, more stress (environmental and personal) and more competition among individuals, and companies, and countries.

At the end of the 1980s all of these complex relationships were more obvious than ever, and young people watched, bewildered, as consumer products multiplied vertiginously — including drugs, which were very much in demand in a heterogeneous society in need of escape mechanisms; policies intended to limit or stop drug consumption and trafficking multiplied vertiginously, too.

Between 1988 and 1998 the world witnessed a slow abandonment of ideologies and an accommodation to neo-liberalism and globalism, where every country is attempting to position itself advantageously in the race for production and consumption. The progressive sectors are aware of the complexity of this new scenario and of a new threat in the form of an ecological crisis. The specific physical problems caused by ecological imbalances are immediate consequences of our unsustainable model of society. To the schizophrenia of this international race to make more, sell more, and have more we can add specific problems caused by (and for) countries that are producers of illegal drugs. The producers place all kinds of natural and synthetic drugs on the consumers' plates. The world financial system accedes to the informal and criminal dimensions of the economy by guaranteeing banking secrets of other countries, many of which become exotic financial paradises. Rules are created, and rules are bent, to foster the capitalist idol of the free exchange of goods and services.

Behind this welter of illegal activities is the might of the bureaucratic institutions that control them. Financial institutions play a role, but so do technology and criminal, police and military organizations.

The 21st century will see nations reaching for a new model of society, a model which takes into account the many environmental problems linked to the current economic model and which proposes transformation toward sustainability.[1] Scientists, based on projections begun in the middle of the 20th century[2], highlight the dire need for a change in the current productive system if we want to

---

1. This concept is based on the *Brundtland Report* (1987) and serves as a process which harmoniously combines development and respect for the environment. Sustainable development is that which satisfies the needs of the present without endangering the capability of future generations to satisfy their own needs.

2. Informe del Club de Roma (1972 — 1976) and Informe Meadows de la Sociedad Sostenible, in Meadows O. and Randesers, J.D., *Más allá de los límites del crecimiento*, Editorial El País, 1993.

avoid the collapse of life on our planet. Among the most serious problems affecting the human and natural environments is the current world policy against drugs. This policy, debuted in 1988 with the Vienna Convention, celebrated its fifteenth anniversary in 2003. But it has never evaluated its own enormous impact, which includes environmental consequences as well as increased growth of illegal drug production and consumption. The last UN General Assembly Special Session dedicated to the drug problem was held in New York in 1998. So far, nothing has changed since then.

The 1998 plan remains an obvious failure. That was a landmark in the creation of an international drug policy, mainly because it brought into relief the irrational immobility of the official institutions. The UN was confronted with the dynamism and openness of civil society symbolized by small NGOs and an outstanding group of intellectuals and scientists. Among them are several Nobel prize winners who signed a manifesto for a diametrically different plan, because "the war on drugs currently waged worldwide may actually be causing more harm than drug abuse itself." The punitive measures ostensibly designed to control drugs have fueled illegal trafficking instead, moving US$40 billion a year. This "strengthens criminal organizations, corrupts governments and stimulates violence by distorting economic markets and society values."

To the series of failures resulting from the war on drugs, we may add the epidemics of AIDS, hepatitis and other contagious diseases, human rights violations, attacks on the environment and the diversion of funds that were needed for investment in health and education. The trust placed in the United Nations when it pleaded for the "emphasis placed on punishment to yield to common sense, science, public health and human rights" turned this supranational mechanism into an important player in orienting international drug policies. Thus, one must know what has caused concern about drug consumption to spread from its US origin to the rest of the countries that make up the United Nations. And one must see why the punitive focus, the focus on control over supply and production, has historically been the priority instead of controlling consumption (or demand) — an issue that has only been considered internationally since 1990.

That a concrete vanguard of thinkers would formally request a diametrical change in the drug policy of our political authorities in favor of regulation and controlled release mechanisms, coupled with the paradigm shift on the ecological crisis taking place in most universities and world research centers, invite us to develop a political analysis of the drug problem and its associated policies. It poses a serious environmental problem and is very important to the relations of inter-dependence that mark today's foreign policies for the countries involved.

This paradigm shift means analyzing reality from a theory of systems and the paradigm of complexity.[3] Indeed, the process of drug-trafficking and the international relations that sustain and fight it are overwhelmingly complex. This is why it is necessary to understand the international system as a whole, elements in interaction — economic, political, natural, geographic and social — the enormously complex and inter-dependent political reality.

A systematic focus is thus not only a theory of reality, but also a theory of action. Einstein's modern physics marked the importance of globalization and understanding nature as a whole instead of in fragments, as well as the multiple relations of inter-dependence. This has had fundamental consequences in the organization of the scientific model and in the perception and study of the political reality, overcoming the traditional vision of the State as the only actor. In this sense, the scientific/determinist paradigm that has fostered the development of science and technology from the dawn of the Enlightenment to the limitless spaces of our era begins to fail in its analysis of reality. It keeps the realms of knowledge in parcels; it impedes an analysis of the whole and poses knowledge as the limitless dominion of man, unaffected by chance or chaos. The fragmented scientific method that made the development of the sciences and technology possible in the first place is now impeding the

---

3. Wagensberg, Jorge, *Ideas sobre la complejidad del mundo*, Metatemas, Tusquets, 1994.

development of the global science that Einstein conceived of as a broad vision born of complexity. The politics that analyze and confront this problem embody a determinist vision of knowledge and an interventionist vision of man in nature. Our faith that we can resolve problems through science is related to our belief in man's ability to perfect himself. This feeds into a notion in the political realm where health, physical hygiene and morality are determining factors in establishing a political philosophy.

In the case of drug trafficking, the complexity of the problem and the different environmental, social, economic and political aspects require a partial analysis of every component, without losing sight of the overall view. A simultaneous analysis of the micro and the macro is only possible through an interdisciplinary analysis limited to one geopolitical space. An analysis of the US (the originator of all policies against drugs) and Latin America (the main supplier of cocaine) and their relations based on the cocaine problem can be taken as a model of how the great power behaves with respect to its general drug policy. This may reveal the real possibilities offered by regulating policies.

The need for a concrete referent to theoretical approximations and the visible reality of a plant that links the First and the Third worlds through the crystalline substance that is cocaine invites us on an intellectual journey into the world organized around the coca leaf. The intellectual tools of several scientific disciplines — International Relations, Anthropology, History, Sociology, Economy, Political Science, Pharmacology and Pharmaco-dynamics — will help us in our quest.

Though the contemporary phenomenon of drugs is a social, economic and political problem often dissected to form two opposing societies (the producing society vs. the consuming society), the policies of the 1990s overcame this static, simplistic vision. The truth is rather that of a constantly moving and evolving inter-dependent process which does not distinguish between societies but affects industrialized and developing countries alike. The phenomenon of drug trafficking and consumption itself, which is the most dynamic and flexible phenomenon known to date and is highly sensitive to the dictates of international politics as well as those of its own environment, can be analyzed using thermodynamic laws that study change as a way to scientifically interpret an overwhelmingly disturbing process. The environmental paradigm, or the paradigm of complexity, allows for an interpretation of the world that is adapted to the new reigning schemas of econo-political and social relations of neo-liberalism, and simultaneously supposes epistemological novelty as it critically dissects the system while contributing suggestions that adjust coherently to interdependence. This implies a radical critique of current anti-drug polices which are only continuations of older policies and which homogenize the socio-cultural reality of humanity. The current policies are based on ethnocentrism and the political cosmo-vision of the Cold War; they adapt the ideological confrontation of that time to a world that is much more complex and dynamic, to a reality that has many different shades.

Behind the bi-polar confrontation, the new order is characterized by a superpower, the US, which marks the pace of international relations and powerfully influences the economic environment, propagating its culture and its model for civilization. Since the US is the world's main drug consumer and is historically the country in which all anti-drug policies began, it is important to analyze its relations with its Latin American neighbors.

Since the coca leaf originated in the Andes Mountains (where the indigenous culture has revolved around this traditional resource for more than 3,500 years), and since cocaine is the most-traded drug in the hemisphere, it is interesting to note the different environments of the coca/cocaine process and to begin to distinguish the ecosystems and their interrelations. Illegal trafficking is mainly organized around cocaine and is not, as many have attempted to demonstrate, a closed and hierarchical structure or vertically integrated criminal world. Quite to the contrary; the coca/cocaine process and the economic complex of narco-trafficking is an open system in constant flux and must, like a living ecosystem, form a level of organization with participants who co-exist and react with each other and who are influenced by the space in which they move (physical, political, economic and social space).

Current anti-drug policies focus on cocaine, just as in other times they focused on opiates, alcohol or hemp derivatives. The clear orientation of the Vienna Convention (1988) was to repress the coca/cocaine complex and to grant a special role to American hemispheric relations. US/Latin American relations, though discontinuous and not at all homogenous, show the interactions among internal factors and their influence on the development of the phenomenon. They also show interactions among countries because the formulation of a determined US policy, domestic or international, has serious repercussions in Central and Southern America.

US/Latin American relations and their differences with respect to anti-drug policies symbolize the North/South confrontation overall: a broad confrontation, or environmental conflict, between the industrialized world and the developing world that demonstrates their diametrically opposing views on environmental issues. While for the North it is a question of quality of life, for the South the environmental problematic is inextricably linked to development. Globalization and neo-liberalism have widened the gap between developed and developing countries and the result is a flagrant contradiction: a prosperous industrialized center seeking creativity and the satisfaction of new needs in diversity, and a periphery that is engrossed in a daily struggle for survival, generating great instability in the system. This is manifested in drug consumption and narco-trafficking. Fundamentally, the first can be applied to the developed countries, and the second, to the South.[4]

The gap between the North and the South, far from narrowing, is increasing, as are tensions. Faced with the impossibility of a head-on confrontation and given the weakness of the less-developed countries,

4. Rensselaer, W., "Tráfico de drogas y países en desarrollo," pp. 15 — 31, in Tokatlian y otros, *Economía y política del narcotráfico*, CEREC, Universidad de los Andes, Bogotá, 1990.

the conflicts are carried out locally, indirectly, partially. They are low-intensity conflicts which often denote resource and related structural problems which generate social tensions and fear of injustice. Within this problematic are inscribed the fight against drugs and the unstoppable corrupting power of narco-trafficking.

The policies of the 1980s have been modified since the Conservative Revolution under Reagan first promulgated purely anti-supply policies that viewed the drug problem as a Latino connivance. Thus began a series of policies to militarize the problem — leading to present-day policies derived from the 1990 UN plan. This plan considers the issue more equitably, and the producers as well as the consumers assume responsibilities that translate into military cooperation. This allows for prohibition, economic cooperation in infrastructures and agricultural development, and education and health cooperation for the prevention and treatment of addicts, which facilitates consensus in the war against drugs.

The increasingly broad economic gaps and the structural impediments for the integration of less-developed economies, along with restrictions on legal immigration, have propelled the growth of a criminal economy in the South. This is why the current anti-drug policy, the opulence of the developed world and its transformation into stable economies do not resolve the problem, rather they stimulate the participation of organized crime and its extension and growth. Drugs are now the main — and quite considerable — source of financing of the criminal organizations[5] which constantly reproduce in favorable environments, like plagues.

The environmental paradigm, with an ecological or systematic focus, has the peculiarity of being an ideological alternative in the political sense, since it supplies analytic description of contemporary society using beliefs about the human condition and the prescription of the analyzed society, and a program for political action.[6] In this

---

5. Garzón, Baltasar y Megías, Eusebio, *Narco*, Colecció Gregori Mayans, Editorial Germanis, Valencia, 1997.

6. Dobson, Andrew, '*Green Political Thought*' Routledge Ed. 1995..

sense, and even if a Green political program is in fact not very realistic, it would imply a much more radical change than that of the Bolshevik Revolution. It still brings to life alternatives that are compatible with the current system and which could be imposed slowly as a sort of cultural and educational revolution, constantly expanding through new ways of eating and medicating, to include the recovery of the man-nature relationship through the extension of ecologically safe crops and homeopathic or natural medicine. Within this possible context is the regulation of natural substances with many medicinal, nutritional and even industrial values, such as the coca leaf or hemp derivatives.

Advancing in the knowledge of traditional Andean cultures and the resource of coca is, then, indispensable. Until the current narco-trafficking boom with its obvious transformation of Andean societies, coca has historically been considered a treasure, the sacred plant of the Incas integrated into the original spaces of deep America. However, this controversial cultural resource has dragged along a religious, socio-economic and political polemic. A greater cultural relativism and the adoption of an anthropological perspective would show us the Andean cosmo-vision and allow us to recognize and admire the many nutritional, medicinal, economic, social and ritual virtues of coca, making it an economic and political resource that, with more appropriate regulation,[7] could inspire a new era of relations, a new international order more harmonious and in accordance with environmental ethics and the concepts of sustainable development confirmed at the Rio Summit (1992) as an apt medium for the necessary development of a substantial part of the planet, without altering the base of resources that sustain life.

---

7. Another psychotropic substance, found in the hemp plant, begs a similar historical and socioeconomic analysis and is likewise a suitable candidate for appropriate regulation. In addition, it is the basis of a decentralized economy, consistent with the principles of ecologist thinking and defended, in that sense, by many who support ecologically responsible commerce. At the same time — like coca — it favors a return to the countryside and ecologically-sound agriculture, and it renews the distorted relations of man with nature as it recovers a resource that formed an important part of traditional and family medicine.

CHAPTER I. THE ORIGIN OF DRUG POLICIES

Drugs have accompanied humans throughout history as a vital part of their natural environment and a fundamental component of different cultures. Drugs and their multiple uses have allowed humans to proliferate and improve their well-being.

Drugs can calm, sedate, stimulate or aid in approaching divinity in the long, dark night of time, or when faced with the unknown and the fear of natural phenomena. Drugs are essentially cultural elements, and, as such, throughout history they have been rejected or accepted according to the uses and customs of the receiving culture. The adoption of different drugs by a society is a slow process, similar to adapting new foods and new agricultural crops. Because drugs were useful as a food, stimulant, medicine or hallucinogen, they gradually came to be cultivated and consumed in places far from their original environments, in processes of ecological adaptation to the new environmental surroundings and following the same dynamics of any other socially-used plant.

This slow "acclimatization" has often meant restrictions and cultural, political or religious controls. In Europe and its early colonies, the more exceptional cases of drug control came about during the Inquisition when the threat of death accompanied any deviation from orthodox thinking, including all pagan rites (which anything outside of the mystic experience of Catholicism was considered to be). Pagan rites, satanic rites, and their mingling with popular medical practices following ancient tradition, provoked atrocious persecution by the Church and executions were public shows of pain and death, intended to deter anyone else from deviating from the approved social and religious norms. The use of potent hallucinogens enveloped the witch era (between medieval and modern times) in an aura of magic and mystery;[8] it is the closest historical antecedent to the current anti-drug crusade.

Though cultural control of new drugs has existed throughout history, at the end of the 19th century experimenting with new drugs coincided with a phase of industrial acceleration, the advent of the first large scale systems of sales and marketing, and the regulation of professional sectors linked to health. Here, at the threshold of scientific modernity, popular medicine was enlivened by a disorderly proliferation of home remedies, preparations of new and potent medicines, promoted by university professionals (or those who claimed to be), witchdoctors, traveling salesmen, apothecaries and small businesses. All sorts of products were manufactured and dispensed by diverse sales and marketing systems with no government control. Indeed, the State was barely fulfilling social functions and was just beginning to regulate and order professions, products and foods. The State in those days did not assume any of today's medical responsibilities; hospitals were mostly run by various Churches and charity organizations. Family medicine was handled by professional doctors, pharmacists and women; the latter were the repositories of oral and domestic cultures and some were very knowledgeable about the therapeutic value of plants and medicinal preparations to alleviate pain, anxiety and common illnesses. These women, steeped in local lore, are synonymous with the agrarian societies that depended on their popular wisdom — which was all but lost during the massive migrations from the country to the city that followed industrialization.

---

8. Caro Baroja, Julio. *Las brujas y su mundo*, Alianza Editorial, 1986.

Starting in the mid-19th century, within this open panorama, new medicines and administrative methods arose. Some were as noteworthy as muscular or intravenous injections, which increased the potency of the substance administered. At that time, drugs and their cultural and domestic control scarcely caused health problems, let alone social problems. Society was familiar with people growing different plants and using natural concoctions. Though many of the drugs in use could generate serious dependency problems, especially opium and natural opiates, the great majority of dependent consumers were middle-aged and their dependence was usually either related to their work as health professionals or was the result of a prolonged medical treatment. Eighty to one hundred per cent of these consumers continued to be dependent for three to four decades without many problems, until the mid 1920s when the first controls for non-medicinal uses of opiates led to the prohibition of maintenance therapies and the clinics which supplied them.

If for so many centuries drugs were both remedy and poison, and the individual and personal control of their administration and consumption had not caused problems beyond those related to experimenting new drugs, why then did 20th century society gradually decide it had to control these substances? What were the cultural and political patterns that led to control, restriction and, finally, prohibition? Why were some drugs pursued while others were freely available? Why were some natural drugs that had been adapted to the customs of 19th century society later withdrawn? How was today's prohibition shaped and to what degree are policies that are supposedly formulated for problem reduction related to consumption?

Coherent responses are needed to an international situation; current policy is a far cry from addressing the real problems of drug consumption. This policy has been a priority throughout nearly the entire 20th century and includes controls over production, trafficking and the distribution of natural drugs; but it completely ignores problems arising from consumption.

1. A US Preoccupation

The first drug controls were established in the 19th century, to regulate substances derived from the scientific explosion that began with the Enlightenment. The first regulations were fiscal and were unrelated to moral considerations. The State established norms and responsibilities for the production and distribution of the substances, since there was no type of state encroachment on issues in the private domain.

What we today consider "drug policies" originated in the US, which from the early 20th century drove the social and legislative initiative and international support for drug control. Faced with a growing population that seemed unable to manage its own habits, the US responded by promoting puritanical notions in an effort to stem a growing problem of alcoholism and drug use. Before morphine and heroin were available in concentrated forms, and before the hypodermic syringe came into use (19th century), there was very little drug problem to be controlled. Now, technology had gotten ahead of self-discipline, and since there was money to be made, there were enthusiastic vendors distributing supplies.

A counter effort was therefore made, labeling any type of dependence or non-medicinal consumption a vice, an attack on individual dignity and the moral integrity of society. This rhetoric and this attitude took hold in American socio-political history, uncomfortably, alongside that great tolerance of innovative life-styles and cultures that was one of the country's greatest appeals. In a highly complex and varied society, the drug issue and the related issue of alcohol were associated with the clash between puritanical traditions on one hand and the different cultural patterns of certain immigrant groups, but also with varied forms of entertainment and artistic creation. The social preoccupation with the consumption of drugs became a political preoccupation with their production and international trade as a method of controlling domestic consumption. This explains the exterior dynamism and functional and geo-strategic nature of drug control policies which, given the dominant role played by the US, are an important part of international relations as well as a pragmatic form of world government.

Puritanism: The Empire's Answer to Too Much Technological Success

Drug policies resulted from a historical process parallel to the creation and consolidation of a new US nation as the first world power, which began with the political independence of the thirteen colonies. It developed thanks to an efficient security/diplomacy system which guaranteed foreign trade, and was consolidated through social and cultural control of a varied, multi-racial population.

Political, economic and cultural factors contributed to creating the hegemonic power. Drug control policies are just one dimension of a broad program designed by the dominant group to resolve the many divergent cultural tensions of a multi-ethnic population that was a product of successive waves of African, European, Asian and Latin American immigrants.

The anti-drug policy — like alcohol prohibition in the 1920s — was a mechanism for social, economic and cultural control. The philosophical, political and religious bases of the US explain the subsequent vigor of highly moralizing policies to this day.

The founding fathers were grounded in a considerable religious and moralist element and a deep, democratic conviction: they fervently believed the democratic republic was the best form of government. But they also believed they were chosen by God, which granted them a confidence and legitimacy not unlike the absolute monarchs they had left behind. It also led them to believe that "the American revolution began a great experiment which would be the model for the rest of the world to follow."[9] The coherence of the

---

9. Gilbert, F., *To the Farewell Address. Ideas of Early American Foreign Policy*, Princeton University Press, New Jersey, 1961.

historical project that linked capitalism, democracy and the so-called Protestant work ethic was the key to the powerful and expansive US society.

The religious element was shaped as the most important cultural element: puritanical moralism was the basic cultural expression of the protestant society that ruled the nation from the beginning. "Manifest Destiny," which established the expansionist vocation of the new nation, shaped the US redemptionist vision, demonstrated in a kind of "messianic hegemony." The expansionist period that began with Independence translated into rapid economic growth, political strengthening and territorial expansion toward the West. This was when the principles of hemispheric hegemony and its foreign policy were established, which appropriated and applied the traditional policies of the British Crown. For theorists of the British Empire, the magnitude of the nation and its prosperity were the products of economic progress and a security/diplomacy system that guaranteed the control and navigation of the seas for foreign trade. Trade and defense were inextricably linked later by the theorists of imperialism, while religion and the utopian ideal of a democratic society were part of its colonizing stamp. Puritanism and patriotism were thus synchronized in an aggressive formula, laying the groundwork for Imperialism.

The profound economic transformation of the US after the Civil War was obvious. Perhaps less obvious to us from today's perspective are some of the social transformations wrought by those technological and economic breakthroughs. It was only in the 19th century that distilled liquors became readily available, so that drunkenness rose dramatically. In response, temperance movements arose as communities sought to limit the damage. Industrialization and the accumulation of capital allowed meant that the country was evolving from a principally agrarian nation to an industrial and urban lifestyle, and the uprooted populace lost many of its traditional anchors. Meanwhile, there was high demographic growth due to massive

European migration. The US went from expansionism to imperialism when it hit its "natural borders" in 1890.

The annexation of the Philippines and the Cuba protectorate, after the Spanish/American War, demonstrated the international behavior that the US would repeat again and again throughout the century. (Cuba, as the largest West Indies island, is of paramount geo-strategic importance for the control of the Caribbean. It was occupied by the US from 1899 to 1902, and remained a US protectorate until 1934, which meant Washington had tight control over laws and administrations and gave the US rights to economic and business intervention. It also gave the US access to new criminal sectors related to the development of the island's tourist industry.)

At the same time, the increasingly prohibitionist policies in the US began to redefine American conduct that had been normal as criminal, and this led to the formation and expansion of large sectors of illegal activity and the highly-organized drug trafficking which supplied widespread domestic consumption.

The Immorality of Drugs

After the US occupied the Philippines, the temperance movement and pressure from the US missionaries to prohibit non-medicinal uses of opium explain the subsequent events and the evolution of a network of laws, treaties and international conventions on drugs that inaugurated the new century.[10] The Philippines archipelago was a haven for drug smugglers and any effort to curtail the trade in opium and its derivative, morphine, would have to include it. The US Congress sought to outlaw the use of opium in the

---

10. See Musto, David F. *The American Disease: Origins of Narcotics Control.* NY: Oxford UP, 1987. Notes and page references correspond to the Spanish version, for how the Philippines were occupied and opium intervention, the origin of prohibitionist policies, and the beginning of the entire US drug control process. Regarding Cuba, from the 1920s, the Italian-American mafia worked hand in hand with the ever-present US secret service to run operations using the strategically placed island as a base. See Cirules, Enrique. *El imperio de La Habana*, Habana: Ediciones Casa de las Américas, 1993.

Philippines altogether, and this reflects growing concern over domestic drug use as well.

Measures against opium, cocaine and alcohol were part of a social environment marked by a growing rejection of any degree of drunkenness or drug dependence. The increasing emphasis on restraint and the increasing influence of the conservative religious sectors on the media led to a gradual rejection of all substances used for recreational purposes. This explains the progressive control of opium and opiate imports and the extension of prohibitionist measures to other substances like cocaine and even alcohol, which were also the main ingredients for many medicines and tonics that were available without a doctor's prescription. This was when the first "drug free" establishments were established and popularized — *soda fountains* that concocted all kinds of natural, non-alcoholic and caffeine-, cocaine- and opiate-free beverages and tonics. Cocaine-free Coca-Cola was already one of the most popular soft drinks and the company one of the staunchest supporters of prohibitionist legislation.[11]

It was in tune with this restrictive social climate that President Theodore Roosevelt, in 1903, prohibited non-medicinal uses of opium in the Philippines, which affected the large population of Chinese immigrants in the US as well as people in the Philippines. The Chinese had been lured to the US as disciplined and cheap labor to help construct the trans-continental railroad. The break in their

---

11. Coca-Cola's secret formula contained the natural extract of the coca leaf and the African cola nut, a mixture popularly known as *dope* (drug dose). In 1903, widespread anti-drug public opinion, many trials, the accumulation of testimonials, the adverse reaction of the press and the sale of the bottled soft drink among the Black population all prompted the company to eliminate the extract of cocaine and substitute it with caffeine. All other alkaloids of the coca leaf remained. The skillful business policy of voluntarily removing the cocaine before the Pure and Food Drug Act was passed in 1906 (regulating food and drugs and requiring product labeling to inform consumers of any opiates, cocaine, cannabis, alcohol or other psychoactive ingredients) and the doubts that the drink would continue to sell in the more puritanical sectors led Coca-Cola to enthusiastically defend the law as a way of ending competition. Later and in the 1930s, the philanthropic foundation created by Coca-Cola also used monetary contributions to anti-narcotics agencies in its political and commercial strategy. See Pendergast, Mark. *"For God, Country and Coca-Cola.* Revised New Edition. Basic Books 2002. Notes refer to the Spanish version.

opium flow sparked serious disturbances in New York and San Francisco. A law exempting the Chinese labor force from the prohibition was passed, but not before China responded to the perceived harassment, which had come on top of very severe abuses of its people, with a boycott of US goods. That boycott, enthusiastically sustained by residents in China, provoked an overwhelming response from American merchants and industrialists, in turn, who called for the deployment of the Marines to the Far East.

The critical diplomatic and trade situation encouraged the US to seek support for its original drug policy. They requested an international conference to help China with its "fight against opium." The conference also, and above all, legitimized US measures and alleviated trade tensions. This required repressive national legislation to save face in the Shanghai Opium Convention (1909), the immediate predecessor to The Hague, or the Opium, Convention. Thus a moralistic urge to temperance, geopolitical needs, and the demands of Evangelical and Episcopalian missionaries worked together in a dynamic of cultural and commercial control to gradually arrive at the prohibition of any "non-medicinal" use of opium in 1908 and the creation of an inspection committee.

Prohibitionist Laws with No Parliamentary Debate

The moralizing rationale and racial prejudices of a multi-racial society determined the control of international drug trade and production was the predecessor of what has become characteristic of the entire history of drug prohibition. Accords were automatically adopted, in international conferences, with no debate in national parliaments. There was no discussion for the public; prohibitionist measures and their scope were handed down from the top. The first and perhaps most dramatic event in this line of history was the International Opium Conference in The Hague, which was ratified by a few countries in 1912.

The leading role of the US in The Hague and its legislative initiatives was shaped in the Harrison Narcotics Act (1914), which granted the Federal Government power and authority over states in drug issues. With the implementation of Article VI of the Constitution, which establishes that international treaties signed by the US take priority over any State law, the Federal government appropriated an issue that until then had been handled as a question of health and considered under the jurisdiction of individual states. From then on it was in the hands of the Federal government and acquired a special geo-political function.

Specifically, this first law restricted opium, morphine, heroin and cocaine to exclusively medicinal purposes. It required the registration of people and laboratories dealing with opium and the coca leaf, establishing the first penal sanctions.

Falling in step with the US, other nations adopted the prohibitionist provisions of The Hague Agreement; it was incorporated into the Treaty of Versailles ending World War I. As a result, most of the leading governments subscribed willy-nilly to the clauses that had been agreed to by a few in 1912[12].

Many of these laws violate constitutional principles and blatantly contradict fundamental human rights. Yet they were adopted in most cases with no discussion and are the source of very serious national and international conflicts and disturbances. This automatic mechanism, which skirts the complexity of the legislative process and the discussion on the scope and consequences of prohibitionist measures, arose from an era that blindly trusted positive progress and failed to adequately envision the dramatic consequences. This automatism has led to numerous widespread effects that were not intended. Still, the mistake has not yet been

---

12. The fundamental precept of The Hague Conference is Article 20, establishing that the signatories "may dictate laws or regulations to punish the illegal possession of raw or processed opium, morphine, cocaine and their salts:" Escohotado, Antonio. *Historia de las drogas*. III volumes. Madrid: Alianza Editorial, 1989. After the first international conference, the intervention of the highest institutions like the League of Nations and later the United Nations legitimized the measures. But they have never taken up the specific problems of these legislations in complete debates over such a complex issue. Comisión Andina de Juristas. *Drogas y control penal en los Andes. Deseos, utopias y efectos perversos*. Lima, 1994.

officially recognized, and the dynamic that was begun then persists now.

With the Harrison Narcotic Act, the US began a powerful prohibitionist phase by attempting to implicate other nations. But through the Treaty of Versailles the international anti-drug movement had shifted its locus to the League of Nations, which would eventually be dragged into US-imposed restrictive positions.

In the US, the policy of maintaining addicts was beginning to be questioned. What had been considered a normal, socially-accepted approach took on tones of immorality, a vice that imprisoned the addict and enriched unscrupulous doctors and pharmacists who over-prescribed potent formulas and encouraged users. The transformation process was slow and involved the debate on addiction as an illness and the possibility for a cure, in addition to bureaucratic issues of responsibility in the many administrative and professional sectors. Repression of drug use in maintenance programs was explained by the long-expressed fear of ethnic minorities and immigrants, as well as by the generalized belief that drugs encouraged anti-social, criminal behavior.

All this was synthesized in widespread social alarm, gathering every insecurity, fear and prejudice in the social crisis of the period between the wars. "Drug use was weakening the nation then, and it was related to other non-US influences that could dissolve societal links".[13] This was when drug trafficking was first linked to criminal behavior, terrorism and the revolutionary influence of Bolshevik communism. There was a tendency to exaggerate and over-estimate the number of drug-related crimes, which sky-rocketed in the mid-1920s because of the ban on maintenance therapies and clinics. The ban meant that morphine and heroin addicts who had been provided access to the drugs they needed, on a controlled basis, now had to get their product through the already burgeoning black markets. Thus began a period when greater prohibition meant higher crime rates: a dramatic equation that still persists.[14]

---

13. Musto, op. cit. p. 164, 1993.

2. INTERNATIONAL DRUG CONTROL

The initial control of drug production and trade in the US created controversy among Europeans, who thought it was a mistake to penalize private consumption since it would automatically generate a black market. The fact that throughout the 20th century the drug policy slowly spread to other countries is an illustration of the common belief in the power of law and order to promote national and international harmony. The application and extension of these laws to all nations also demonstrated US power before the League of Nations, as well as its vocation as a superpower.

Drug Diplomacy

Diplomacy, trade and health factors have influenced drug control policy. US interest in controlling opium in Asia was determined by its need to make a space for itself among the colonial powers. US control of opium in the Philippines was unilateral; other colonial powers accepted opium consumption as something that did not do too much harm. Indeed, they combined pragmatism and tolerance and established several monopolies with fiscal impositions in both French and British colonies, almost until World War II.

Notwithstanding its nature as a health issue, concerning both physical and emotional well-being, the drug issue has since its inception been driven by the institution that directs US international and foreign policy: the State Department. This is a clear indication of the direction, objectives and strategies that led not to the control of consumption or the resolution of health problems, but to control of

---

14. Violations of the Harrison Narcotics Acts shot up after the 1919 Supreme Court decision against maintenance clinics. Musto, op. cit. p. 214, note 6, 1993.

1916:	1,900	1921:	4,300	1925:	10,300
1917:	1,100	1922	6,700	1926:	10,300
1918:	1,300	1923:	7,200	1927:	8,900
1919:	2,400	1924:	10,300	1928:	8,700
1920:	3,900				

drug production, trade and distribution. The diplomatic and political aims of those seeking to control the drug trade have been ambiguous from the start. Yet, also from the start, the medical and scientific population had a very different vision of the value of drugs and their uses, and noted that it would be more rational to educate the public instead of eliminating drugs. As we shall see, there will always be arguments in favor of control of demand and use within the anti-supply strategy, though politicians often seem oblivious to that argument.

With the implementation of the Treaty of Versailles, prohibitionism began to mature. International efforts at drug control between the world wars did not impress the US; it did not trust that the League of Nations could implement controls over opium. The US Senate voted in 1919 not to join the League, and this is considered the beginning of the US isolationist phase. A desire to tighten its hemispheric control induced the US to develop more rigid controls which would later drag the rest of the countries along with it.

The addictive nature of opiates, the continued lack of efficient scientific treatment for addiction and the absolute ignorance of the moralists brought about the prohibition of these substances with no substitute or effective treatment. Since abrupt withdrawal could lead to painful withdrawal and even death. This was why it was necessary to trust in the forces of order to enforce the law. This immediately generated contraband inside the US from producing nations and their intermediaries. The trend spread from there to China and elsewhere.

Illegal drug trafficking continued in spite of international law. The US, unable to stop the trafficking and distanced from the League of Nations, increased in its distrust and stepped up controls over the sources of opium and the coca leaf. The Europeans reproached strict control of trafficking and criticized the US position against suppliers, pointing out that it was irresponsible consumption, after all, that was the problem.

US "Intolerance" and European "Incomprehension"

European countries believe that high rates of drug use in the US are a product of its culture — the tensions of life under competition in every phase, the wealth and abundance that invite indulgence, and other factors.

In the 1920s, the US preferred to name international drug control as the solution to US abuse problems — because it blamed other nations. After all, by sending in so great a supply of drugs, weren't they causing high US usage? Every region or continent was considered dangerous because of some specific drug: South America = cocaine; Europe = morphine and heroin; Asia = opium; Africa = hashish.

For a self-sufficient, growing nation, it was much easier to attribute drug abuse problems to the conspiring of alleged enemies rather than examining domestic causes, including the tensions endemic to a multi-cultural society. Thus, we have the anti-supply strategy which, furthermore, linked drug use to ethnic and racial minorities.

In 1923, just four years after the Volstead Act (the National Prohibition Act) took effect, Congress proclaimed that the only way to stop drug addiction was to control production. This supported the theory that the US government was unable to control the domestic drug and alcohol black markets; it seemed the only solution was to control them at the source.

The anti-supply strategy enjoyed support because of what happened after World War I and during World War II. Drug use decreased, a phenomenon that was attributed to decreased supply since there was no international transportation during the wars. This led the US to defend a strategy of international drug control that is still in place. First came the strict regulation of legitimate uses, and then the unilateral use of force, all the while prioritizing the needs of international policy and certain aspects of national security.

The US deplored international drug control as it was approached by the League of Nations, yet maintained its strong position with the rest of the countries until World War II. The US made its position very clear at all times, including its distance from the system, as it did not adopt the League's conditions. This pressure was sometimes very subtle. If the US did not accept normalized relations with the League, the entire international drug control movement (begun by US initiative, after all) would appear to lack legitimacy.

Prohibitionist Policies Promote Crime

Resentment and isolation also served so the US could organize anti-drug policies on the domestic legal and bureaucratic levels.[15] Inspection and control were considered increasingly important, so it emphasized repressive aspects, handily supported by the social moment of intolerance toward alcohol and drugs.

The unification of both controls in one single agency, the Prohibition Unit, aggravated political corruption and gangsterism. The unification gave mafias intensive training in alcohol, narcotics and buying political and legal protection for nearly a decade; this would prove useful in the future. Successive agency scandals favored the creation of an independent agency in 1930: the Federal Narcotics Bureau (FNB). It unified domestic policy and foreign representation and is the oldest predecessor of today's "Drug Czar."

Meanwhile, at the 1931 Geneva Conference, the League of Nations followed the US example and passed drug controls and regulations with quota systems and country-needs evaluations. New organizations were in charge of the control.[16] This made it the earliest predecessor of today's international drug control system. By 1931, there was a global predisposition to make the drug issue one of public

---

15. The repressive measure caused a notable increase in addicted prisoners and resulting harassment in federal prisons. The problems were different from traditional prison problems: poor sanitary conditions, no chance of rehabilitation and drug trafficking. There was also damaging association with other criminals. In 1928, 22% of the prison population was in for violating drug laws, 15% for addiction. Musto, op. cit., p. 234. Today in the US, one-third of all arrested and three-fourths of those jailed have violated drug laws. Wacquant, Loïc. "El encierro de las "clases peligrosas en Estados Unidos," *Le Monde Diplomatique.* August — September, 1998.

16. The first express prohibitions were for diacetylmorphine, opium and coca leaf alkaloids. The 1948 supplementary protocol established a mechanism for international organizations to add or withdraw substances.

order. The Volstead Act was repealed in 1933 but organized crime, which had grown strong on smuggling and bootlegging activity, kept on growing.

The extension of crime and corruption coincided with (and probably aggravated) the depression in the legal economy that followed the 1929 stock market crash. This submerged the country in a decade-long crisis with a quarter of the workforce unemployed and many left homeless. Unemployment in a time of crisis and criminal proliferation added to the mistrust of cheap labor from Mexico, which quickly slid from social rejection to ethnic and cultural rejection. Using this resentment as one of its tools, the US created a fear and distaste for marijuana (which was associated with Mexico), and, in 1936, attempted to pass an international law in the League of Nations to control the cultivation of marijuana and other hemp derivatives, and the poppy. When this was not possible, it established restrictive domestic legislation, prioritizing fiscal considerations. It indirectly made marijuana more expensive and impractical terms illegal by establishing a federal fiscal tax (the transfer tax) and bureaucratic requirements that hampered dealers — a very indirect campaign attacking drug use.

3.   POSTWAR SCHIZOPHRENIC DUALISM

After World War II, the US rose as a hegemonic power and reorganized the entire international system, from military alliances to the various agencies of the newly formed United Nations. As far as the complex world of drugs and consumption, production and prohibition, a new stage was begun (though it was subordinated to the needs of national security, which set as its first priority the containment of communism). It combined severe intolerance of drugs and the use of drug trafficking by the secret services themselves.

Harsh McCarthyism

This was when the severest legal sanctions for anti-drug law violators were established, including the death penalty.[17] Intolerance permeated postwar ideology, as illustrated most graphically by McCarthyism. The radicalization of legalist postures was a result of the postwar climate exalting the "Red menace." Thus were repeated the same fears in the cosmo-vision and mentality of the average American as during the between-war period, and a parallel was established between the political conspiring of communists and socialists and the moral conspiring of those who betrayed the nation with immoral drug use. This same scheme has been repeated over and over again, as we shall see with the "Latino drug conspiracy" and subsequent accusations aimed at the narco-guerrilla.

This period of intolerance and severe penalization coincided with postwar efforts to re-organize for the new era, and the creation of the United Nations (its charter was officially ratified on October 24, 1945) was one dimension of that.

The United States spearheaded the passage of the UN Single Convention on Narcotics (1961). While the United Nations promoted the movement against natural drugs, producer countries were given instruments which legitimized the disappearance of original crops, like the report issued by the UN Commission of Enquiry on the coca leaf.

The UN Commission on Narcotic Drugs Coca Leaf Study (1950)

The desire to entirely wipe out cocaine extended into a desire to wipe out the coca plant from which the drug is derived. Official institutions began to equate "cocaism" to "cocainism" after the investigations of the Commission on Narcotic Drugs (1950). The UN Study on the Coca Leaf in Bolivia and Peru was implemented. It was based on two essential goals: the study of chewing and the study of

---

17. The Boggs Act (1951), or the law of minimum-required sentences, and the 1956 Narcotics Control Act, or PL 728, which included capital punishment.

the possible limitation of the production and distribution of cocaine. South America was dependent on the great triumphant power, after the war, and had little say in such matters. The studies on chewing and its effects were prejudiced from the start; well before they were begun, they it was understood that their outcome would be used to limit consumption and production. In the case of marijuana and the coca leaf, bureaucratic excesses were committed, attributing human degeneration to the two drugs when in fact the primitive living conditions and general poverty clearly played the major role in determining the condition of the local consumers.

Predictably, these seriously prejudiced goals, the ethnocentric mentality of the time and the unscientific methodology[18] resulted in a Report that called for the complete obliteration of coca leaf crops, even for the traditional consumer who was not producing cocaine. The study's conclusions were adopted by the World Health Organization (WHO). Its 1952 and 1953 decisions and that of its Expert Committee on Drug Dependence decided against the coca leaf because it was "addictive." Shortly thereafter, the Single Convention on Narcotic Drugs (1961) highlighted the traditional coca leaf as a product to be eradicated within 25 years, starting in 1964. This is a paradox since the same Convention made an exception for industrial uses of cocaine-free coca, like the flavoring in Coca-Cola, thereby assigning legal use and a worldwide monopoly of the coca leaf to a US multinational corporation, through Article 27.

The 1961 Single Convention on Natural Drugs

This 1961 Convention, held in New York (and the 1971 Convention on Psychotropic Substances) unified and universalized international legislation and control strategies. It also universalized

---

18. It was a completely inadequate methodology. Cultural tests for illiterate Peruvian prisoners were designed for literate Europeans and all tests were done with cocaine, extending the results to cocaine addiction as well as coca addiction. Ossio, Juan et. al., *La coca… tradición, rito, identidad*, Instituto Indigenista Interamericano, Mexico, 1989; and Grinspoon, Lester and Bakalar, J.B., *Cocaine: A Drug and its Social Evolution*. Basic Books, 1985.

the series of scientific, semantic, pharmacological and legal incongruities that had been allowed to develop — a general confusion of terms and concepts surrounding natural and synthetic drugs, and such subjective issues as drug habits and addictions. The inability to define the concepts of drug, narcotic, narcotic drugs and psychotropic drugs and addiction[19] was exacerbated by the subjective creation of lists classifying drugs not by pharmo-dynamic effect or chemical composition, but by their alleged "addiction level."

The lists lumped together traditional "narcotic drugs" (i.e. opium, morphine, heroin, cocaine, hemp and the coca leaf) and other natural substances used by the "counter-culture," according to Antonio Escohotado.[20] These substances do not present major addiction problems — especially compared to Lists II and IV, which include amphetamines, barbiturates, synthetic narcotics and stimulants (crude imitations of opiates and cocaine), which sometimes cause high addiction levels and side effects. While List I (all naturally-produced substances) is "prohibited for any use except by duly authorized medical or scientific establishments with very limited ends and under direct government control," making it impossible to legally produce or circulate them even for scientific research, List II and IV substances can be manufactured, exported, imported, distributed and stored as each signatory country deems "appropriate." Not only is the production of List I items prohibited, but related raw material crops are also prohibited. That means that all poppy, coca and opium plants had to be destroyed, event though they had uses other than the production of drugs. In 1971, amphetamines and barbiturates were included in the prohibition, but by that time they had already been legally substituted by lesser tranquilizers such as benzodiazepines and ansiolytic agents made in laboratories

---

19. The coca leaf and cocaine were initially described as narcotics and then as psychotropics, though they are clearly stimulants. Today there still has not been an official correction to explain the error in naming.

20.DET, DMHP, DMT, LSD, mescaline, psylocine, psylocibine, parahexyl, STP (DOM) and THC (tetrahydrocannabitriol, the main activant in hemp). Escohotado, Antonio, op. cit., vol. 3, pp. 111 — 123, 1989; and Escohotado, Antonio, *El libro de los venenos*, Mondadori, 1990.

throughout the industrialized world. The exhaustive limitations and controls over natural products (opium and its derivatives, the coca leaf and cocaine) coupled with the unfettered production, circulation and distribution of industrial substitutes, tranquilizers and stimulants, hurt Third World economies which were barred from selling their products and forced to import commercial substitutes. (Industrialized nations tend to consider synthetic drugs "non-abusive," as Escohotado comments.) The Third World complained, of course, and proposed price controls for synthetic drugs sales, but their interests were not the primary concern of those driving these developments.

The Reactions of Scientists and Young People

In the US, reaction to the intolerance for drugs in those years was not long in coming. Medical and pharmacological professionals and those who were potential users for "illicit ends" both rejected this extreme inflexibility. Beginning in the 1960s, the medical and legal fields confronted the official policy and objected to the fact that medical issue had been made into a criminal one. They pressed for sociological and scientific, i.e. medical, treatments of the problem of addiction, recalling the earlier systems of treating addicts and offering maintenance clinics (where methadone or other hopefully less harmful and less expensive substances were made available to heroin addicts, for example, to help them wean themselves from destructive habits). Government officials began in a piecemeal fashion to dismantle some of the most restrictive laws. Some criminal sentences were reduced, and there was an increase in research on addiction and abuse. The drug issue was reassigned to the Justice, Health, Education and Welfare Departments.

Changes in the way official institutions approached the drug issue "humanized" it. There was a shift in the 1960s and 1970s from the radical position that drugs were a criminal and anti-social issue to the view that they were an issue of sociology and medicine. This change in attitude percolated down to the man in the street as a new degree of tolerance for drug use and abuse. A climate was generated in which the use of marijuana became acceptable in many circles. Simultaneously, there was a massive inflow of drugs into the country. The fight against communism in the Far East was funded by supporting groups that financed themselves by producing and trafficking heroin.

Whereas the previous generations had established worldwide use of tobacco and alcohol, the generation that came of age during the 1960s and the dubious war being waged in Vietnam and its neighbors revolted against the establishment (which they considered to encompass all levels of government and the traditions of their own social groups) and their revolt included an increase in drug use. This in turn led to a broad, generalized increase in the acceptance and use of certain drugs, which soon were not limited to fringes of society. The legal statutes and general consensus came to be more tolerant of marijuana. Originally declared illegal and painted as a cultural emblem of the despised Mexican laborers, the acceptance of marijuana influenced the perception of and general tolerance toward other drugs at the time.

Then, as with many drugs, enormous exaggerations of the dangerous effects of marijuana were promoted and it was strongly suggested that smoking it went hand in hand with criminal behavior. The sparse facts to support such assertions discredited the claims, so that other warnings about drugs also fell under suspicion. This led to increased tolerance among young people, at least, for other drugs that had also been painted as terribly dangerous.

Starting in 1967, confronted with the spread of marijuana use, the heroin epidemic and the paucity of drug raids, the drug policy was re-organized with a dual objective: repression and prevention. While the Democrats (looking for the "youth vote") emphasized prevention, the Republican era inaugurated by Nixon began forming a state structure to repress the spread of consumption and "worrisome" tolerance. The National Institute on Drug Abuse (NIDA) and the Drug Enforcement Administration (DEA) were established. The country prepared for the recovery of its vital and traditional pulse, characterized by the "Republican revolution" and Reagan's anti-drug crusade, as we will see.

Chapter II. The Coca Leaf vs. Cocaine

The quasi-colonial religious, geo-strategic motives of the United States at the beginning of the 20th century, in an unsavory combination with the profit motives of those who knew that this was a very lucrative trade, prompted efforts to control opium production and trafficking. By the end of the century, the political and geo-strategic needs of the superpower prompted it to pursue cocaine and its source, the coca leaf, with pointed urgency. Cocaine, relegated to a status similar to that of opium, morphine and heroin since the beginning of drug controls, still played a special role in the 1980s.

We must understand the coca leaf and its main alkaloid to understand the crusade in its full dimensions. The original plant has been fully integrated into the Andean culture for millennia, yet in a brief century and a half of cocaine use, its reputation has gone from that of a panacea to something that is "evil." In its demise, cocaine has irrevocably dragged the coca leaf down with it.

The pharmacological characteristics, varied uses, and evolution of practices and attitudes relating to coca leaf and cocaine use demonstrate that the current persecution is driven by politics rather than the well-being of those who are directly affected.

1. COCAINE IN THE ANDES

The coca plant is a flowering shrub of the *Erythroxylaceae* family, with alternating oval and whole leaves, little white flowers and small, red berries. There are between 75 and 250 species of *Erythroxylaceae*, the most common being *Erytroxylon coca lam* and the *Erytroxylon novogranatense*, which are grown in the Andes for traditional use, medicines, infusions, soft drinks and to make into cocaine. The plant produces seventeen alkaloids, of which cocaine is the widest known. Coca alkaloids have various benefits for health, but the pharmaco-dynamics of the lesser alkaloids have barely been studied. Cocaine has been considered the coca's main alkaloid because it is a stimulant that works on the human central nervous system to alleviate hunger and fatigue, which is its main attraction for indigenous Andean people and for users in the more developed countries.

Coca originates in the Valle del Cauca and is known throughout South America. It is grown from the Caribbean Sea to Central America to the Amazon basin. The oldest archeological remains date it to 1500 BC on the central and southern coasts of Peru, which would suggest that the peoples of the high plateau probably knew it before then.[21] The first testimonials mentioning its cultivation date from *La Conquista*, the Spanish conquest of the Americas. Coca was part of the vertical ecological system of the steep Andes Mountains. An altitude of between 500 and 1,200 meters and a tropical climate are needed for its cultivation. It was cultivated early on by the self-sufficient peasant communities of the highlands, the *ayllu*, which were largely based on collective agriculture.

Indigenous Consumption

The indigenous methods of consumption generally entail mixing the juice of the coca leaf with calcareous (lime) substances, then

---

21.Carter, William and Mauricio Mamani, *Coca en Bolivia*, Editorial Juventud, La Paz, Bolivia, 1986.

chewing the leaves and absorbing the active ingredients through the lining of the mouth and by swallowing, which allows for slow and progressive absorption. This turns cocaine into ecgonine, increasing the beneficiary effects of the alkaloid. A user places a leaf in his cheek, rolls it up with his tongue and at the same time bites it, releasing the alkaline substance and obtaining the desired effect. This is followed by placing new leaves over the previous leaves. The *llujt'a*, an alkaline ball which accompanies and compliments the *acullico*[22] of the coca, fulfills a social function along with the coca leaf. When one practices *acullico*, the mouth becomes a laboratory where this ball undergoes hydrolysis of in less than five seconds, making 0.05% of the cocaine, turning it into ecgonine and other alkaloids that assume different functions which do not damage the organism. This is why it is impossible to find cocaine in the bloodstream of the experienced *acullicador*, or chewer[23].

Traditional consumers take in between 80 and 100 grams of coca leaf a day, three to five times a day, selecting the sweetest and least damaged leaves and rejecting the bitter, black ones for their high cocaine content.[24] They put approximately 900 milligrams of cocaine in their mouths a day, and every pinch contains between 150 to 200 milligrams of alkaloid. Yet, the way they consume it, which mixes saliva, the juices of the coca leaf and alkaloids, significantly reduces the incorporation of the alkaloids. This beneficial form of consumption has extended throughout history in the Andean ecosystem and part of the Amazon ecosystem. In eastern Bolivia, the lime ball has been substituted with industrial bicarbonate; it is not known when this recipe was discovered and the custom was

---

22. *Acullicar, chacchar, pijchear, pegar* are Spanish words indicating methods of chewing coca.

23. Burchard, Roderick E. 'Coca y trueque de alimentos' in Alberti, G. and Mayer, E., *Reciprocidad e intercambio en los Andes peruanos*, pp 209-251, Instituto de Estudios Peruanos, Lima, Peru, 1974. Ossio Acuña, *op. cit.* in Chapter I, p. 261 Mamani, Mauricio. 'El jilaqata en el coqueo en los Andes' in *Revista del Museo de Etnografía y Folklor*, number 4, 1991.

24. In Peru's Empresa Nacional de la Coca (ENACO), coca leaves are classified into three groups. The most damaged and highest in cocaine content are passed over by the traditional consumer, and are therefore destined for export as flavoring for Coca-Cola, i.e. for legal cocaine. (Personal visit, ENACO, Quillabamba and Lima, January 1998).

assumed.[25] In Brazil, the *Ipadú* variety is mixed with the ashes of the *Crecopia* plant.

The adaptation to the Amazon environment demonstrates how cultivation and consumption depend on the natural ecosystem. In the Amazon, the quantities are small because of the jungle's high humidity and the subsequent rapid decomposition. This requires easy availability of the leaf and the continuous creation of new crops.[26] Consumption has also spread to the Argentine central Andes. In addition to the typical peasant consumption, a broad sector of wage workers — miners and plantation workers — consume coca, as they do in Bolivia, as well as a large sector of the urban population. The most curious case is that of the elites of the Argentine provinces of Salta and Jujuy, who have perfectly adapted consumption to the different social conventions. There is an innovative mixture of Western lifestyle with some Andean customs, like the public consumption of the coca leaf at important soccer games or other events.

There is no consensus between historians and coca experts about consumption during the Inca period and Spanish domination: was coca consumed by the entire population, albeit with social differences,[27] or was it a privilege exclusive to the Incas[28]? For anthropologist Mauricio Mamani, the notion that the Incas had a monopoly on coca use is a historical fallacy fed by ethnocentrism and

---

25. There is a mixed form of indigenous consumption adapted to urban life: a small bag of *mate de coca* tea is placed in the mouth with a little bit of sodium bicarbonate, obtaining the same effects as *acullico* (Personal experiment following the directions and invitations of Baldomero Cáceres).

26. This Amazon variety is produced by alternating coca crops with manioc or yucca, which are abandoned almost every four years. Authorities interpret this as the continual creation of new plantations, camouflaged among legal plants. Henman, Anthony Richard. "Tradición y represión: dos experiencias en América del Sur." García Sayán, Diego, ed., *Coca, cocaína y narcotráfico. Laberinto en los Andes*, Comisión Andina de Juristas, Lima, Peru, 1989.

27. Gagliano, Joseph A., "The Coca Debate in Colonial Peru," in *The Americas, XX*, pp. 43 — 63, Academy of American Franciscan History, Maryland, July 1963.

28. Peña Begue, Remedios. "El uso de la coca en América según la legislación colonial y republicana," in *Revista Española de Antropología Americana*, pp. 179 — 204, volume 6, Facultad de Filosofía y Letras, Universidad Complutense, Madrid, 1971; and "El uso de la coca entre los incas," in *Revista Española de Antropología Americana*, pp. 277 — 304, volume 7:1, Facultad de Filosofía y Letras, Universidad Complutense, Madrid, 1972.

the dark myths attributed to the plant. We do know that the coca leaf was a delicacy used as an offering and for many remedies, and during the Inca epoch it was held in high esteem and used as money, forming an important part of tribute payments made within the Inca realm. The common man had access to coca, which was grown in archipelagos or colonies, through his contribution to community work.

The mercantalist character of the colonies was the great stimulus to massive coca consumption. The Americas were colonized for money, after all. Food production was left by the wayside as workers were conscripted to extract the precious metals demanded by the Iberian powers. As food became scarce, coca consumption greatly expanded. The energizing and stimulating power of the coca leaf and its high nutritive value made it an ideal food substitute; it increased miner productivity and circumvented costly and complex food supply systems. This was a critical boost, as most of the indigenous work force was assigned to mining gold and silver.

Colonial exploitation and prejudices about coca use in shaman rites meant confrontations between missionaries and planters. For the planters, coca was business, a fiscal resource for greater mining and crop productivity over and above the dramatic living conditions of the indigenous people. Viceroy legislation in the mid 16th century, intended to reduce the high death rate of *Camayos* (skilled workers) testifies to the shocking conditions of exploitation and "environmental" diseases the local people endured, as they were forced to migrate from the high sierra to the tropics with no thought for their adaptation. The new legal requirement — to limit the workers' time on the plantations to 24 days per month with a minimum salary, the establishment of rest on Sundays and holidays, the provision of food on a daily basis and on holidays, and even the provision of food and coca for the return trip, and the later measure in favor of coca use — demonstrate that coca was used as a food substitute or supplement on a daily basis. In such cases it was a remedy and relief to assist the hapless natives in their transition through many elevations and climates, not a poison or invigorating drug in the slave regime[29] that the Spaniards established after the Conquest. Still, evangelizers considered it the devil's work[30] and this prompted several councils in Lima (1551–1772), though the prohibitionist virulence eventually decreased given the planters' pragmatism. The debate which occupied the religious and civil authorities since the Conquest would be resolved by the Council of the Indies, which determined that the habit had to be tolerated because of the dependence the Indians had on it.

Indigenous consumption later suffered the brunt of the Peruvian leaders who viewed coca chewing as colonial, a symbol of Spanish exploitation. It is true that the coca was a food substitute in the times of scarcity, and that it increased work productivity; but according to coca experts and defenders, such as Baldomero Cáceres, before the official indigenism of the 1940s. it was much easier to blame the Indian for his own misery than to do an exhaustive study on the causes for underdevelopment. This same official policy of indigenism, complete with ethnocentric prejudices, was the instigator for the 1950 UN coca study which had very negative consequences for the Andean culture.

---

29. Viceroy legislation of the Marquis of Cañete (1555 - 1560), Francisco de Toledo (1567 - 1581), and the royal dispositions of Felipe II, Matienzo, Juan de, *Gobierno del Peru, obra escrita en el siglo CVI* (Buenos Aires, 1910). Cited by Gagliano, *op. cit.* pp. 47 - 49, 1963. These regulations were completed by the royal orders of Felipe II dated 23.XII.1560, which prohibited forced labor on plantations; 1563, which protected women and children from forced labor; 18.X.1569, which allowed coca use by the Indians, prohibited idolatrous or ceremonial use and recommended the improvement of the workers' standard of living (also 11.VI. 1573 and 6.VII574) in *Recopilación de leyes de los reynos de Indias...* (ed. rev., 3 volumes, Madrid, 1943). The determination of Francisco de Toledo established research mechanisms to determine the causes of the high mortality rate and controls for ensuring that planters abided by the law. See Toledo, "Ordenanzas de la coca" in *Gobernantes del Peru, cartas y papeles, siglo XVI*, documents of the Archives of the Indies, ed. Roberto Levillier (14 volumes, Madrid, 1921 - 1926, VIII, 14, 18 - 19; cited by Gagliano, *op. cit.* p. 51, 1963).

30. Juan de Solórzano Pereyra, *Política indiana...* (1647), ed. F.R. Valenzuela (5 Volumes, Madrid, 1930), I, Book II, Chapter X, page 214, cited by Gagliano, *op. cit.*, page 62, 1963. The ecclesiastic servants did not believe in mental dependence, but rather that since it was a diabolical plant, the Indians just imagined that they obtained vigor and well-being from the coca, which made them dependent on it.

Profane and Religious Uses

The coca has always been considered "the sacred plant of the Incas." It was not just an object for offerings, but also something much more profound and linked to the existence of the Andean. The coca, though needed for work, was not simply a consumer good required for daily subsistence; it served much more complex purposes. It offered personal gratification and pleasure, which granted it greater social use and fluidity and made it a unique and treasured good. Thus it was an apt offering for the gods, along with gold, silver, sea shells, *chicha* (a local drink), llamas and guinea pigs. But coca was an aid, above all, for work. The stimulating effect that gives it such renown is due largely to the cocaine in it (although there have been few studies on the other alkaloids).

The effect of cocaine, or ecgonine, works against fatigue by increasing glucose in the blood and redistributing it through different vascular beds via vasoconstriction. It also increases the effectiveness of cardiac contraction and lung ventilation because of its effect on the respiratory center and its direct effect on the bronchial muscles.

Chewing coca is also an important indigenous characteristic. It grants the individual joining the group and the culture the most identity because, among other things, he is a habitual coca consumer. The social value of the coca is very important: it is chewed in community to affirm friendship links when solidarity and support from others are needed. The testimonials of numerous interviewees by Carter and Mamani (1986) demonstrate this point:

> People, when they care about each other, know how to offer a chew. First we chew a bit to thank each other and right after we start to chat (Atiliano Pérez).

And the testimony of another neighbor highlights its polyvalent and necessary nature:

> The coca is used in everything. When we chat with someone, first there's the handful of coca. And when we go to work, we have to ask for

a favor with an offer of a chew. Right afterwards we ask if we can work. This is the custom; otherwise we couldn't get anything (Alejandro Ollisco).

Coca is one of the main ingredients in indigenous medicine, the main officiator of which is the shaman, who has religious, medicinal and divining attributes. The various therapeutic applications of coca have to do with this multiplicity. Coca-reading offers diagnostic and prognostic ways to find the source of an ill and its possible remedy. Its curative features include anesthetic, vasoconstrictor and stimulant to the central nervous system, all joined together in the self-suggestive capacity of the remedy in its traditional context. Coca is used in various preparations in infusions, poultices, dyes and is chewed with lime. Common illnesses (toothache, indigestion, rheumatism, wounds and diarrheas) are cured at home and, in many cases, daily chewing serves a preventative function. Thus, in the Andean region coca has been an essential element in the family medicine chest, just as in some Asian areas opium has been the medicine par excellence. Only in cases of more complex illnesses or in complicated problems that we would call psychological ("evil eye," "scares," etc.) did people resort to the shaman, who used ancestral knowledge and special preparations to ritualize coca consumption, along with other elements.

Early chroniclers noted with surprise that the Indians enjoyed very good dental health (toothaches and cavities were rare) and that prevention was prominent in Peru during the Republic, which decreased as acculturation progressed. Coca became useful to the *criolla* population for addressing skin problems, dental health and the common cold. It began to be used by doctors in Lima as an ingredient in many mixtures and infusions, though chewing was still frowned upon as being part of primitive indigenous traditions. Hipólito Unanue, Antonio Julián and Manuel Atanasio Fuentes were the most fervent admirers of the Andean plant and its disseminators in the 19th century in the Europe, which surrendered in admiration of the stimulating and energizing effects of its main alkaloid.

The Dissemination of Coca Among Scientists

Starting in the 18th century, the scientific expeditions of the Enlightenment became interested in the coca bush and sent samples to Europe. The interest Europe would have in coca was expressed from Peru, in particular for the army on polar expeditions and in colder areas of the European continent. The most notable coca proponent was the Jesuit Antonio Julián, who was clearly mercantalist in his orientation. He thought it was a magnificent stimulant that could substitute for coffee and tea, and which, if organized into a monopoly by the Spanish crown, could mean relief for the embattled Treasury as well as an enormous source of income. But all of these reasons for promoting it did not mean that anyone had a greater understanding of coca, its wide diffusion or even the scientific nature of its properties.

Starting with the independence of the American colonies and the arrival of travelers from all over Europe, more began to be known about coca. The main supporter and first propagandist for the Andean plant was Paolo Mantegazza, an Italian doctor who practiced in Peru for many years. When he returned to Europe he wrote an enthusiastic article extolling the virtues of the plant. This translated into its use among chemists, pharmacists and doctors, who began to experiment with and prescribe it. Gaedcke (1855) worked to synthesize the different alkaloids, starting with the extract of the coca leaf, Niemann (1860) isolated the main alkaloid, or cocaine; and Lossen (1862) established the definitive chemical formula. They confirmed the growing interest among scientists and doctors in coca and cocaine.

2. COCAINE

The history of cocaine, from discovery to now, has been closely linked to that of similar drugs or stimulants. In the history of drugs, the decision about which were consumed while others were forgotten depended on many factors, such as the disposition of substitutes, ease in obtaining them, sociological value, social prestige, pharmaco-dynamic effects, legislation, relations among administrators (doctors, pharmacists, witch doctors, chemists) and others. Its legal situation marked the rhythm of its consumption. In the case of cocaine, consumption is closely linked to the availability of substitutes. Current control over ingredients needed to make the coca leaf into an alkaloid has generated a sub-product: base or crack, the consumption of which is even more controversial.

Chemistry, Pharmaco-Dynamics and Similarity to Amphetamines

Coca leaf, with all its alkaloids, is very different from cocaine alone, its main and most famous alkaloid. Cocaine is a white, organic, crystalline compound — $C_{17}H_{21}NO_4$ — which is bitter, water soluble and reacts with acids by forming salts.

When taken by a human, cocaine directly penetrates the central nervous system through the bloodstream, creating a pleasant feeling. Its most immediate effects are anesthesia and stimulant. Cocaine can block the electric flow through nerve cells, providing the local anesthesia. The stimulant is the result of a chemical interference or modification in the synapse, or where two neurons connect.

Cocaine and other drugs — like caffeine and amphetamines — can reinforce norepinephrines, or molecules or amino acids in the central nervous system. Since cocaine, amphetamines and caffeine all intervene in the hypothalamus (the center which regulates appetite, thirst, sleepiness, sexual arousal and emotions), in the ascendant reticular activation system (which functions upon stimulation and guides vigilance and attention), and in the nerve lines (which reach the hypothalamus and the ascendant reticular activation system in the cerebellum, where conceptualization and memory are produced), their pharmaco-dynamic effects on the central nervous system are quite similar. Thence the tendency to use them, depending on the historical moment and their availability or prohibition. However, they are very different chemical or pharmacological substances.

There are only slight differences in how cocaine and amphetamines work on the central nervous system. The main difference is in how the organism responds. For example, there is exceptionally high tolerance to amphetamines and risks of physical and psychic deterioration of the heart, liver and kidneys, and genetic birth defects. Any deterioration from cocaine is due to abuse (kidney failure, malnutrition, psychic fatigue from insomnia, paranoia and persecution delirium). Cocaine has no withdrawal syndrome, unlike amphetamines (depression or psychic collapse), nor do users develop such a tolerance that they have to use increasing dosages.

While the methods of consuming the coca leaf make abusing it difficult and labor-intensive, the concentration of the alkaloid in the chlorohydrin, along with the fact that it can be injected or sniffed, make possible both moderation and abuse, chronic or occasional use. Its flexibility is why it has been used for medicinal purposes as a local anesthetic for gastric, asthma and nasal congestion relief, a mild laxative and a diuretic. It has been used to enhance concentration for specific tasks, to improve vigilance, to alleviate fatigue and depression, and as a festive or recreational stimulant to increase and invigorate mental resilience resulting in talkativeness and confidence.[31]

Freud found the substance was very valuable for medicinal and recreational purposes, administered intravenously in conveniently inter-spaced small doses (subcutaneous injections of 30 to 50 mg). This induces euphoria and vigor in many people, while higher doses create anxiety, physical discomfort and behavioral chaos. Taken intravenously, the drug acts immediately, creating stupor. This lasts about four to five minutes and is followed by intense anxiety and some exhaustion, requiring more injections; but the dose needed to avoid falling into total depression with convulsions and hyperactivity requires the counter-ingestion of a sedative. This is why shooting cocaine is normally accompanied by soothing and sedating opiates.

---

31. An outline of the various forms of consumption may be found in: Escohotado, Antonio. *Historia general de las drogas.* Espasa, Madrid, 1998.

This is the nineteenth century "morphino-cocainism" mentioned in the scientific literature of the time, which attributed the main problems to the effects of cocaine. This type of use today is rather rare, unless the user is a disturbed person seeking a "minute of madness," according to Escohotado.

Now, consumption and effects similar to those resulting from morphine-mania occur because of problems in measuring doses, even if it is inhaled. The fact that "normal" doses look small can make people think they will get a better high with a larger dose, so they consume more. But higher doses can produce uncomfortable feelings of rigidity (the rigors), which leads to the use of large quantities of alcohol or other depressants in compensation. Alcohol and depressants let the user consume more cocaine, calling for greater sedation, and all this is often accompanied by an endless chain of cigarettes. Exhausted, in the end the user winds up needing sleeping pills. This unpleasant scenario is all too frequent in recreational use and, like the heroin-cocaine combination, it is not healthy — even if it does not suffer the stigma of morphine-mania.

The Uses of Coca and Cocaine in the 19th Century

From the middle of the 19th century (when cocaine was first marginalized) to today, coca and cocaine have been used in many different ways for medicinal and recreational purposes. The downfall of cocaine and its progressive limitation even for medicinal purposes, which dragged coca down along with it, has deprived humanity of the scientific study of both substances and reduced its use to the black market, which supplies our nightmare in highly adulterated products. But until then, coca and cocaine were both useful in developed countries and were adapted culturally to daily diets and rites.

The coca plant was used in many different ways: to fight fatigue, stomach problems, sexual impotence and frigidity, hysteria, migraines, throat problems, depression and addiction to opium and heroin. Cocaine's therapeutic value was highlighted as a local anesthetic for ophthalmology and dentistry. Its use was also encouraged for armies as a food substitute and stimulant.

Between 1864 (when cocaine was isolated and formulated) and 1906, with the first US controls and the advent of product labeling, cocaine attained great popularity. It was sold directly in offices and bars, by mail and door-to-door; marketing had carried it to every US home. Legal pharmaceutical companies sold cocaine, the extract of coca and coca leaves in syrups, tonics, liqueurs, capsules, tablets, hypodermic needles, cigars, cigarettes and nose powders. It was sponsored by medical foundations and prescribed by all US doctors as a cure-all. Then, it was declared illegal.

Freud's research, which took shape in *Uber Coca* (1884), is very important to the widespread medical use of cocaine. He experimented with himself, animals and patients[32]. Freud discovered many uses for cocaine in psychiatry and promoted cocaine therapy for addiction to morphine, a therapy which essentially turned morphine addicts into cocaine addicts. That provoked its discredit among researchers and many cocaine research projects were abandoned. Freud is one of very few who have done in depth studies on the substance. Though Freud defended himself against his colleagues' attacks by establishing a difference between oral and intravenous ingestion, the generalization of cocaine as an anesthesia had already created some alarm about its high toxicity in determined applications and high doses.

In 1899, Einhorn discovered Novocain, a synthetic anesthesia which reduced the dangers of cocaine. You could say that at the end of the 19th century the scientific prestige of cocaine began a nose-dive. Yet, its popularity with the public at large was increasing, and many products with coca and cocaine as a stimulant and tonic appeared, such as the famous Mariani Wine and Elixir (its creator prided

---

32. Five articles were also published between 1864 and 1867. Objectively, these are the only non-prejudiced studies on cocaine. In 1973 the establishment of the National Institute on Drug Abuse (NIDA) marked the beginning of extensive research worldwide to demonstrate how terrible drug consumption was rather than the potential or nature of the drugs themselves. In 1995 the OMSS-UNICRI study confirmed the dearth of studies on moderate consumption and its effects.

himself on his intellectual curiosity about the plant), and other elixirs or beverages (alcoholic or otherwise) which mixed coca or cocaine with other ingredients, such as Parke Davis' Coca Cordial, Metcalf's Coca Wine, Coca Beef Tonic and Coca-Cola, which included small quantities of cocaine until 1903[33].

Cocaine and Social Control over African-Americans

At the turn of the 20th century, coinciding with the growing discredit of cocaine among doctors and scientists and with the regulation, bureaucratization and the increase in State responsibilities, liberal systems leaned toward the regulation of many social issues. This process coincided with the organization of professions into more formal colleges and associations defending their interests and fields of action. This process of organization and responsibility was a determining factor in the evolution of the consumption of coca, cocaine and other drugs, since the growing tendency to legislate on issues of all sorts went from a merely fiscal process to one that included consumption and, later, one that was restrictive and prohibitionist. In the 20th century, in many countries the State assumed responsibility for the health as well as the morality of the individual. For any gentleman of the 19th century, such a notion would have been taken as a serious violation of personal space, but it was progressively adopted — without debate — throughout the developed world.

In the case of cocaine, its popularity at every level and its widespread consumption among the African-American population immediately after the abolition of slavery generated anti-racist sentiments and scandal in the most puritan sectors. It was already the preferred drug of African-Americans, musicians, dancers and artists

---

33. Pendergrast, op. cit., 1993. Pendergrast assured us that it was the extract of coca and cola, the famous article 5, while Gagliano (op. cit., cf. *The Coca-Cola Company. Opinions, Orders, Injunctions and Decrees Relating to Unfair Competition and Infringement of Trade Mark*, 3 volumes, Vol. I, page 3, St. Louis, 1929 — 1939) and Escohotado (op. cit., 1990) say that it was pure cocaine until 1903 and then later it was the extract of the coca with all the other alkaloids except cocaine.

— the free and creative sectors, specifically those which questioned class-based society and racism. Coinciding with the campaign to impose morality, which attacked cocaine, alcohol and opiates with equal passion, Black Americans were immediately linked to cocaine abuse and its consumption, and suspicions of cocaine abuse were linked to any crime committed by a Black.

Taking advantage of the morphine and opium prohibition that the US promoted internationally through its Philippine colony, cocaine was also included in The Hague Convention (1912), applied in 1914 in the US for the prohibition of cocaine, morphine, heroin and opium (The Harrison Law). Shortly thereafter, alcohol was under attack (in some states, temperance movements had already been developing for a few decades) and any non-medicinal consumption was prohibited during the 1920s. Later, cocaine was relegated to exclusively medicinal purposes. Exhaustive controls over manufacturers and producers were added to the regulatory tasks of several governments and the League of Nations. Production limits and forced government crop control produced a State monopoly. With US production control first, followed by the League of Nations, it was postulated that abuse and consumption by non-authorized individuals would be avoided and recreational use drastically limited.

The Substitution of Cocaine by Amphetamines and Coca-Cola

The disappearance of coca and cocaine from businesses, laboratories and health centers occurred parallel to the nearly global spread of Coca-Cola[34] (which did have the other alkaloids of coca and caffeine) and amphetamines, which were discovered in Germany in the 1930s and widely distributed during the Second World War. While the Axis powers used amphetamines as an important stimulant, the Allies — mainly the US Army — had Coca-Cola. Both substances had taken on a mythical character[35].

The highly stimulating nature of amphetamines and their legal status meant that use of the highly toxic, easily addictive synthetic drug spread and gained in popularity. The fact that millions of pills were manufactured (production for US domestic use in 1966 was 8,000 million pills, or 35 per person, per year, including children), meant that other stimulants like cocaine were not necessary[36]. Only in the mid-1970s, when amphetamines were no longer legal or easily obtainable, were they substituted by cocaine from an emerging black market.

The Cocaine Boom

During the 1960s and 1970s, the drug culture of the Beat generation spread to the larger Hippie movement and to the younger generation more or less as a whole. Drug use extended its popular base and participation in the market. As cocaine began substituting amphetamines, many individuals became involved in the trade, distributing small quantities among people they knew. The principal channels of distribution still in use today were formed during that time[37]. Drug policy leaders were slow to respond, busy as they were

---

34. Bottling popularized and democratized Coca-Cola. In 1898, when it still contained cocaine, it had spread throughout nearly the entire country and was sold in Mexico, Cuba and Hawaii. In 1930, it was distributed throughout Europe and Hong Kong, and in 1940 it went to Peru, Bolivia, Chile, Switzerland and Austria. In addition to the medicinal virtues of the tonic since it contained the coca extract, the business and diplomatic skill of its second president and promoter of Coca-Cola worldwide allowed the company to circumvent the Geneva Convention (1931) controls, which demanded that coca leaf could only be imported for medicinal purposes and impeded re-exportation. Though a factory was built in Peru to remove cocaine from the leaves before they were sent to the US or anywhere else, it was never used. Through subtle negotiations and a hefty contribution to anti-drug organizations, the company was able to revoke such prohibitions. Pendergrast, op. cit., 1993.

35. The suicidal courage of Japanese kamikazes came from meta-amphetamines; Escohotado, op. cit., 1990. Today young Spanish kamikazes who bet millions of *pesetas* to race the wrong way down highways, consume meta-amphetamines and alcohol. During the Second World War, Coca-Cola was much more than a soft-drink: it symbolized the US spirit and was the greatest identifying factor of the soldiers overseas. During the war 64 Coca-Cola factories were established on different continents. In a "strictly reserved accord," the US Army named Coca-Cola representatives as "technical observers" who enjoyed pseudo-military status. Every member of the company had a military rank according to his position in the company and could have direct access to the lines of fire. Pendergrast, op. cit., 1993.

36. Escohotado op. cit., Vol. II, p. 387, 1989. In the 1970s, it was common for Spanish youth to get high on a mix of amphetamines, barbiturates, alcohol and Coca-Cola: rum & coke with Optalidon.

37. Sabbag, Robert, *Ciego de nieve. Traficando con cocaine*, 1976 (Edición Española,Compactos Anagrama, 1990).

pursuing the "drugs of protest" — marijuana and LSD, but the new drug preferences and the advent of Cuban managers and professionals on the international economic scene meant that tons of top-quality cocaine into the US.

This coincided with a series of attitude changes at the highest levels of society. After the pacifism and reflection of the movements of the 1960s, the economic crisis of the 1970s and the very recent technological revolution, a kind of "work fever" emerged which valued competition, speed and productivity over solidarity, tradition and family. Thus were created the ideal conditions for a growing market for cocaine. The Cuban exile groups (aided by US politicians, in an effort to support the Cuban counter-revolutionary effort[38]) organized a cocaine-smuggling ring based in Miami. Backed by excellent government contacts with the armed forces and authorities of various Latin American countries[39], cocaine in all its forms was supplied by the Cubans. In the early 1980s, cocaine use was surrounded by a halo of prestige and exclusivity throughout the Western world, which made it invulnerable and free of any social stigma for users.

As cocaine use and control policies increased, the black market adapted. The 1980s witnessed the cocaine boom. According to *The Economist*, of the 150 billion dollars Americans spent annually on drugs, $60 to $70 billion went to buying cocaine on the retail market. In the 1990s, this went down to $30 billion (UN, 1998). Occasional drug users went from 232 million in 1985 to 14.5 million in 1988 and 12.9 million in 1990[40]. Anti-drug policies were very effective in

---

38. Cuban mafia involvement dates from pre-Prohibition. From the 1930s — 40s to the Revolution, Batista's Cuba protected business from the Italo-US mafia, with US secret services. Cuba was already cocaine's last stop before the US market. Enriques Cirules, op. cit., 1993. After the Revolution, anti-Castro exiles kept their roles as intermediaries because of their magnificent relations with the Bolivian military, which ensured funding for counter-revolutionary activities. Bagley, Bruce Michael. "Colombia and the War on Drugs" in *Foreign Affairs*, Vol. 67, #1, p. 74, 1988. Grinspoon and Bakalar, op. cit., p. 80, 1982, accused the exiles of establishing a network from Miami, citing the following declarations of a DEA agent: "...The Cuban brigades requesting political asylum in Miami...the majority sell drugs. I am not saying a few or some, but the majority." CF. *New York Times*, August 25, 1973, op. cit. p. 80.

39. Roncken Theo, "Bolivia: la impunidad y el control de la corrupción en la lucha anti-drogas," en *Guerra antidrogas, democracia, derechos humanos y militarización en América Latina*, editado por TNI, CEDIB, Inforpress Centroamericana, Guatemala, 1977.

controlling consumption in the large US middle class and among occasional users, while in the suburbs and in African American and Latino ghettos, what government officials had begun to call *the crack epidemic* spread.

3.   PASTE COCAINE AND CRACK

In 1985, the Drug Commission's internationally valid decision to block the trade and distribution of solvents for processing coca leaf into cocaine led inadvertently to the production of paste cocaine and crack.

Turning coca leaf into cocaine is quite simple with chemical products that are readily available in industrialized countries (sodium carbonate, hydrochloric acid, acetone, benzene and petroleum ether), but these were restricted in the Andean area since 1985. The result of the restriction was the exportation of increasingly large quantities of paste cocaine, the product of the precipitation of the alkaloids with sulfuric acid after the leaves are mashed with kerosene. The fact that paste cocaine was easy to make, along with its higher aggregate value, led many peasants to participate in transforming and distributing it. The scant scientific research on this substance, its considerably cheaper price, and the rapid growth of the black market have made paste cocaine and crack (its immediate derivative) into common drugs of the African-American and Chicano ghetto. They are increasingly available to youth and children in large Latin American cities in the form of cigarettes mixing paste cocaine with tobacco.

Crack is paste cocaine mixed with sodium bicarbonate. Its many impurities make it impossible to inject or inhale, so it is consumed by heating the chips in pipes and smoking them. It numbs the mouth and throat, and stimulates the user, like high doses of cocaine, though its effects last for a much shorter time. Thus, the frustrated user is led to prepare more and more pipes, anxiously trying to repeat the effects.

---

40. US Government, *National Drug Control Strategy* (NDCS), 1989 and 1991.

Crack is very destructive and, while it has not been proven to be physically addictive, it is an understatement to say that it is hard to put down once one starts.

The combination of the effects of the black market and the legal limitations on its predecessors generated a new health problem. There was no case of a fatal overdose from crack in 1976 in the US, but by the end of the 1980s several thousand people had died from crack overdoses. In the 1990s, the term *crack epidemic* was already in use, which served as an official and social prompt to repudiate coca and cocaine.

Marginal and Youth Consumption

While anti-drug campaigns were successful for the middle class or occasional users, they had no effect on chronic users or teens. Between 1985 and 1988, the number of weekly cocaine users in the US not only doubled, but campaigns for the reduction of demand had the least effect among adolescents[41]. Results of home surveys were questioned by experts, governmental and non-governmental agencies, yet they were the information source that prevention policies were based on[42]. In 1987, first-time consumers users around the world were younger, going from teen to pre-teen or even younger. The fact that user age was slowly decreasing was reported with alarm by both the International Narcotics Control Board (INCB, 1997) and the UN (UNDCP, 1998). This phenomenon was not limited to the developed countries: many developing countries reported similar trends in the increasing numbers of youth abusing cannabis, heroin, stimulants, hallucinogens and solvents (glue sniffing, etc.).

---

41. NDCS, op. cit., pp. 23 — 24, 1991.

42. NDCS, *ONU UNDCP 1998*, 1989 — 1991; and Smith, Peter, "The Political Economy of Drugs" in Smith, P.H., ed., *Drug Policy in the Americas*, University of California, San Diego, Westview Press, pp. 1 — 23, 1992. The family survey of the National Institute on Drug Abuse was its fundamental statistical data: large marginal urban sectors of the Black and Latino population were not included, because it was carried out in stable homes and the marginalized users refused to collaborate. Thus, the reduction campaigns have been effective above all in the White, middle class population.

This traces the dramatic process of drug consumption from the 19th century to date: the habitual user went from the middle-aged, liberal professional or doctor (posing no social conflict) of the end of the 19th century, to the young user at the end of the 20th century whom "undue drug use has led to dysfunction or individual and social behavioral disorders, crimes, accidents, health problems (AIDS and hepatitis B) and even death," according to the UN's *Drug Bulletin* (1987).

Consumption In Europe

At this time Europe was one of the main markets for cocaine, and it was growing by 20% a year[43]. According to the UN (UNDCP, 1998), the majority of cocaine use was still concentrated in Western Europe (35% of the total population). During the 1980s and 1990s, user numbers increased in almost every country and, just as in the US, the number of heroin addicts decreased because cocaine abuse was more prevalent than heroin abuse (UNDCP, 1998). Those between 20–35 years of age were the main users, due to cocaine's less noxious reputation.

Another tendency born in the 1980s out of international legislation over mind-altering drugs derived from natural crops, making it difficult to obtain them, was the manufacture of new "designer drugs" in domestic laboratories. This explains the similarities between amphetamines and cocaine, and the difficulty in manufacturing cocaine as well as its high cost compared to the ease and economy of the -amines. It was easy to predict that they would displace the cocaine alkaloid.

These artificial cocaines are made with stimulants like *catina* (an alkaloid of *kat*). On the market, they bear names such as *coco snow*, *crystal caine* and *synth coke*. They were already the object of US

---

43. IRELA, *América latina y Europa frente al problema de la droga. ¿Nuevas formas de cooperación?*, dossier number 32, 64 pages, Madrid, May 1991.

legislation in the form of The Designer Drugs Act, prohibiting and penalizing in advance anything unauthorized[44].

Cocaine Use Or Abuse?

Consumption statistics should be considered with a certain amount of caution. It is also necessary to understand the concept of "drug abuse," which officially computes as annual consumption (use at least once in the last year) because it is not as concrete as monthly or weekly use. In this regard, much to the dismay of official opinion, the conclusions of the World Health Organization (WHO) study on cocaine (1995) may come close to reality:

There is no typical cocaine consumer; the demographics and patterns of use vary widely, both in quantity and frequency, the duration and intensity of use, and the existence of any problem associated with cocaine use.

Sniffing is the most popular way of ingesting cocaine, especially among the ordinary population; smoking free-base or crack, or shooting up, are less frequent forms of ingestion and happen in marginalized social sectors.

Given the important conclusions of this study, official censure and the US rejection of the World Health Organization at the 48th Assembly, it is necessary to comment on this report in greater detail, which we will do later when we analyze the world of legal coca.

Use In Latin America

Drug use modeled on Western patterns of consumption is increasing in Latin America. As in other areas of the planet, the implementation of anti-drug policies has led the traditional consumer to change in favor of a more Western style of consumption. This has not been limited to opium and heroin in Pakistan and Indonesia; the

---

44. Escohotado, *op. cit.*, volume III, pp. 232 — 263, 1989, and Escohotado, *op.cit.*, 1990.

current phenomenon of narco-trafficking has also spread cocaine and crack use in Latin America, to the detriment of the coca leaf consumer.

According to the *Drug Bulletin* (1987), the main drug problem in the Americas is cocaine abuse, whether it is injected or sniffed as cocaine hydrochloride, or smoked as crack (*pitillos* in Bolivia, *pastel* in Peru and *bazuco* in Colombia) in the form of cigarettes mixing tobacco and crack. Every gram of crack contains 700 milligrams of chemicals (kerosene, sulfuric acid and ether) "which may cause more damage to the brain than cocaine"[45]. In 1985, there were 11,000 crack smokers in Bolivia, with estimates of up to 40,000 crack cigarette smokers, mainly 15–20-year-old males from the inner city. A similar process has taken place in Peru. In Colombia, consumers are between 12 and 14 years old. Ecuador reported to the Drug Commission that 18–20-year-olds were using crack and paste cocaine. The UN (UNDCP, 1998) considers that South American levels of abuse at 1.2% are clearly higher than the global average of .23%. Historically, the Western model of drug consumption was introduced in Peru and Bolivia at the end of the 1960s by middle and upper class youth who mainly consumed marijuana[46].

In 1976, crack cocaine began to substitute marijuana because it was easy to get and highly potent. It spread like wildfire to become the "national drug." The current use and abuse of drugs in Latin America is the result of the city turning into a megalopolis, with large pockets of poverty resulting from the transition. This large scale urbanization process was spectacular from the 1960s onward, and in the 1980s was accompanied by the spread of narco-trafficking. The changes in the different phases of the business — production and trafficking — have taken the consumption of cocaine and crack to most Latin American cities.

---

45. CICAD, *Aprovechando e lmomento. Informe de la Comisión Interamericana sobre Política contra el Narcotráfico*, Instituto de las Américas y Centro de Estudios Ibéricos y Latinoamericanos, Universidad de California, San Diego, 49 pages, p. 25, 1991.

46. Beristain, A., and De la Cuesta, J.L., *Ladroga en la sociedad actual. Nuevos horizontes en criminología*, Vitoria, Caja de Ahorros de Guipúzcoa, page. 173, 1986; and Medina-Mora, M.E: and Mariño, M.C., "Drug Abuse in Latin America," in Smith, Peter H. *op. cit.* page 52, 1992.

New methods of use imply serious health risks and not surprisingly, hospitalizations have increased. Yet the paradox is that most Latin American countries have slashed their public health budgets while they commit to providing health assistance to addicts at international conventions. For example, the *Estatuto Nacional de Estupefacientes de Colombia* and other national laws have established the control of the use and the prohibition of production, among other mechanisms, by prioritizing assistance to and rehabilitation for the addict. The same has taken place in Peru, which has created an inter-departmental agency called *Contradrogas* to attend to consumption and the repression of illegal trafficking. In spite of this, all countries have been forced by the IMF to reduce spending on social concerns, among them public health expenditures[47]. Cocaine and crack use in Latin America is accompanied by other no less toxic drugs, such as inhalants.

The most worrisome problem today in the Andean countries as well as in other South American countries is the saturation of the US and European markets and the sustained crisis of the price of coca leaf (which is reduced by the market saturation while the cost is driven up by continuous attacks on the Colombian transport planes). Due to excess production, the economics of the industry, which is informal but economically significant, are in turmoil in Latin America as a whole. This is coupled with skyrocketing use of crack and cocaine[48].

4. LEGAL COCA

Some hundred years ago, an economic sector dependent on legal coca for the manufacture of a broad range of products developed in Peru and Bolivia. The majority of the products are for domestic consumption (except Coca-Cola, which is distributed worldwide,

---

47. Personal interview with the Peruvian Minister of Health, Mr. Costa Bauer, published in the *Boletín de la Comisión Andina de Juristas*, Number 131, Lima, Peru. January, 1998.

48. Rementería Ibán de, *La elección de las drogas. Examen de las políticas de control*, Editorial Fundación Frtiederich Ebert, Lima, 1995; and personal interviews with Hugo Cabieses (Agency of German Cooperation in Peru) and Juan Gil (AntiDrug Director), January 1998.

and cocaine hydrochloride). In both cases, state companies such as ENACO and DIRECO are in charge of developing the economic sector, though in the past few years small laboratories and cooperatives have emerged which manufacture an attractive variety of products.

Coca producing peasants in Bolivia are united in the *Federación del Trópico* and look favorably upon the possibility of turning coca leaf into a national industry to make syrups, honey, teas, lotions for arthritis, tonics and liqueurs, and a long line of products. In the last few years a powerful coca leaf derivative industry has developed in Peru and Bolivia. Coca has begun to be recognized for its important therapeutic value as a natural and homeopathic medicine by prestigious doctors and the growing middle class. In addition to its medicinal value, coca contains many nutrients, vitamins and minerals, which explains why it was used as a food substitute for so long (see Table 1)

There are at least 55 natural products derived from coca, among which are cures for cancer, Parkinson's Disease, senile dementia, alcoholism, depression, kidney and liver deficiencies. Popular culture and the intellectual classes defend coca as a natural resource, while the official structures turn their backs on it.

In the early 1990s, Bolivia and Peru coordinated their policies to defend the coca leaf, vindicate its values and demand a legislative change in international treaties to allow for the exportation of coca derivatives[49]. The negotiations in this budding coca diplomacy were cut short by the US veto, which banned the consideration of coca leaf as a raw material for any legal use.

In an exercise of international sleight of hand, defenders of the Andean resource, with former president of Bolivia Jaime Paz Zamora in the lead, were accused of narco-trafficking. In the 1992 World Exposition in Sevilla, Bolivia intended to use its pavilion to display the

---

49. Cabieses, Hugo, *Notas sobre la revalorización y despenalización de la hoja de coca. Propuestas con protesta*, Consejo Permanente en Defensa de los Productores de Hoja de Coca en los Países Andinos, 1995.

possibilities of the coca derivative industry; but it was forced to hide all its samples. In Bolivia, any public figure who supported coca was and is considered a subversive and a delinquent for joining the claims of coca-producing peasants. Those peasants themselves have been linked unsuccessfully to the Tupac Amaru and Shining Path guerrillas, in an effort to discredit and "disarm" them. So much for defending a resource which — though not harmful — is illegal.

Table 1: NUTRIENTS OF THE COCA LEAF COMPARED TO OTHER FOODS
(amount per 100 grams)

	Coca Leaf		Edible Plants		Condensed Milk		Meats (Average)	
	Fresh, uncooked	Estimated, Dry	Fresh, uncooked	Estimated, Dry	Molina*	Estimated, Dry	Molina*	Estimated, Dry
COMPONENTS								
Calories	305.0	333.3	279.0	465.0	322.0	442.3	115.0	714.3
Protein	18.8	20.5	11.4	19.0	7.9	10.9	19.4	120.5
Moisture	8.5	0.0	40.0	0.0	27.2	0.0	73.9	0.0
Fat	3.3	3.6	9.9	16.5	9.2	12.6	3.6	22.4
Carbohydrates	44.3	48.4	37.1	61.8	53.7	73.8	0.0	0.0
Fiber	13.3	14.5	3.2	5.3	0.0	0.0	0.0	0.0
Ash	6.3	6.9	2.0	3.3	2.3	2.7	1.2	7.5
MINERALS								
Calcium	1789	1955	99	165	276	379	8	50
Phosphorous	637	696	270	450	107	147	186	1155
Iron	26.8	29.3	3.6	6.0	0.1	0.1	3.1	19.3
VITAMINS								
Vitamin A	10.0	10.9	0.1	0.2	0.0	0.0	0.0	0.0
Vitamin B1	0.6	0.6	0.4	0.6	0.0	0.0	0.2	1.2
Vitamin B2	1.7	1.9	0.2	0.3	0.5	0.7	0.2	1.2
Vitamin B6	3.7	4.0	2.2	3.7	0.3	0.4	0.0	0.0
Vitamin C	1.4	1.5	13.0	21.7	0.0	0.0	0.0	0.0

Sources: Based on data from the Nutrition Institute and publications from Harvard University and the La Molina National Agrarian University, Perú.
Compiled by: Hugo Cabieses, Consejo Andino, January 1995.
*Information from the La Molina National Agrarian University.

Intellectuals and union leaders, such as María Lohmann and her husband, directors of the major research center on narco-trafficking in Cochamamba, had to leave the country and seek the support of international human rights organizations and universities to vouch for their honesty and political independence. "They even accused my husband of belonging to the Shining Path, because we went on TV to refute the triumphant stories of the Ministry of Governance on the fight against drugs." In the shadows of his office, Mauricio Mamani, author of *La coca en Bolivia* (the coca expert's Bible) admits, "I was the gringos' good little boy. They all consulted me for everything, and with a great deal of respect because I had gone to US schools and was first a disciple and then later a colleague of Carter, an American." Later, he had to resign from his government position for defending the coca leaf, and was effectively pushed from politics. Thus some governments which depended on international aid and US cooperation abandoned their halting official initiatives before the Drug Commission between 1990 and 1995, leaving only NGOs, with scant resources, to defend a plant that symbolizes the identity of these peoples.

The basic argument, in addition to an overwhelming amount of literature in favor of the coca leaf[50], is that its condemnation is based on the 1950 UN study, which was seriously prejudiced and used a poor methodology. Faced with such an irregular situation, in 1990 the World Health Organization decided to write an exhaustive report on coca and cocaine based on data from nineteen countries. The conclusions presented before the 48th Assembly of the WHO in May 1995 scandalized the US delegation, which felt a WHO study could not conclude that there were therapeutic uses for coca leaf — in teas or pills — for the treatment of cocaine addiction, as it would justify the spread and use of coca leaf to other countries. According to attendant Bolivian deputy Gregorio Lanza and the WHO project director, Peruvian doctor Mario Argandoña, the US threatened to pull any funds destined for the WHO, demanded the report be destroyed and a counter-study prepared, to prove the contrary.

---

50. For an extensive coca bibliography see Cabieses, Fernando, *Coca, ¿dilema trágico?*. Ed. by ENACO, Lima, Peru. It has a complete annexed bibliography on coca and cocaine. See also Castro de la Mata, Ramiro, and Noya T., Nils D., *Coca: Erythrozylum coca, Erythroxilum novogranatense, bibliografía comentada*, Seamos, Drogas: Investigación para el Debate, number 11, La Paz, 1995; Centro de Investigaciones y Estudios Internacionales sobre Droga (CIDNE), *Guía bibliográfica sobre drogas*, Ministerio de Justicia y del Derecho y Dirección Nacional de Estupefacientes, Santa Fe de Bogotá, 1996.

Since the Reagan era, Washington has insisted on removing coca leaf from the face of the earth — but only after the attempt to cultivate it in Costa Rica failed. This is according to Mauricio Mamani (Director of the Museo Tihuanaco, Bolivia), who indicated that the attempt was part of a secret US mission with two goals: first, to test a coca virus, and second, to see if they could adapt the coca bush to the Caribbean[51] climate.

In the early 1980s, Coca-Cola also tried to expand its coca-based product line[52]. When Roberto Goizueta was the technical director of the multinational, Coca-Cola wanted to back an international conference in Ecuador on the beneficial uses of coca, in an effort to legitimize a new product: coca-based medicinal gum invented by Doctor Weil. The pressures of Reagan's conservative revolution and the competition posed by Pepsi forced them to abandon the gum. They even took the coca extract out of Coca-Cola, re-making the formula with the flavor closer to Pepsi, which was progressively gaining in market share. However, the poor response of the market to

---

51. Personal interview with Mauricio Mamani. The anthropologist tells how he was hired by the "gringos," with a blank check, to test an herbicide on the coca plant with a Peruvian agronomy engineer after the US Drugs Act was passed in 1986. First they would plant it in Costa Rica and then they would work on a natural herbicide. The attempt failed because the coca could not be grown outside of its natural ecosystem. With respect to the attempts to grow coca in various ecosystems outside of the Andes, Mamani continues: "We, Carter and I, were able to grow coca in Carter's yard, I went to harvest it, Carter knew how to germinate the coca, the seed; it is a secret, the peasants still don't know how. When I went to Washington to harvest the coca, knowing well the thing about the Yungas, it had grown as long, tall, thin, pale and raw as the gringos, and when I harvested it it had no smell or flavor. It needs air, environment, the earth. It was difficult to do it there. The day the gringos can plant coca on their own land, coca will be free and good for our health. The gringo attempt to plant coca in Costa Rica was probably double-sided — to test the virus and to see if they could adapt the coca to the Caribbean."

52. Pendergast, Mark, op. cit., 1993. According to Mamani, in 1978 in the La Paz headquarters of PRODES, there was a dual meeting of scientists in the University of Florida. In the same place, separated by a folding screen, there were agronomy engineers and anthropologists from the US university with Bolivian and Peruvian colleagues. The engineers had the clear goal to research the herbicide that would eradicate the coca; and the anthropologists had the opposite goal: to seek the medicinal values of the Andean leaf, which was obtained with the dietary analysis of the coca leaf in laboratories in Madison, Wisconsin. Because of this investigation, there was a delegation of Coca-Cola management worried about the study's results which sided with the engineers who were going to do away with the coca. The delegation left satisfied with the conclusions of the anthropologists and the dietician's studies. This coincides with the dates of Coca-Cola's attempts to distribute gum with the coca extract. Personal interview with Mauricio Mamani, 1998.

the new formula and the overwhelming popular response in favor of the traditional formula forced the company to reconsider and bring the original formula back, calling it Classic Coca-Cola. It is still the iconic world product, "the only indisputable mass market," according to an analyst of *The Economist.*

Given the energizing characteristics of coca and its 17 alkaloids as a remedy for altitude sickness, Coca-Coca without cocaine is still useful, as are coca leaf infusions. In Bolivia, especially in La Paz, the highest capital in the world at 3,625 meters above sea level, Coca-Cola is even more omnipresent than Illimani Peak.

According to all historical indicators, besides having enjoyed a pseudo-military and exclusive status during the Second World War, Coca-Cola has not stayed out of the current condemnation and marginalization of the coca leaf. In the postwar period, Coca-Cola representatives became the best ambassadors of their country: in 1974 President Carter bragged of the Coca-Cola company's connections, saying, "they give me reports on a certain country in advance, what its problems are, who its leaders are and when I should go there, in addition to introducing me to the leaders of those nations."

A "tasty agent" based on the coca leaf, without cocaine but with all the other "very beneficial" alkaloids, was allowed to go into free circulation in 1961, when the company was able to get the Drug Convention itself to authorize it. The innocent *mate de coca* is in the same product line as the universal drink, but while it can be obtained in any Andean store, it cannot be exported. Interpol feels there is enough cocaine in a bag of *mate de coca* to abuse it or to extract the alkaloid. Yet it contains less than .1% of the alkaloid, which is in fact permitted by international legislation; you would need about 500,000 teabags of *mate* at about $15,000 to process 1 kg of cocaine. You can buy it directly from the producer for $1,200. According to economist and director of the German cooperation program in Peru, Hugo Cabieses, it is much easier and cheaper to go to the black market.

Of the fifty-four industrial products derived from coca, only Coca-Cola is distributed worldwide. The rest of the products are restricted to Andean countries, except for coca-derived herbicides and fertilizers, distributed by Germany, and the pharmaceutical products from cocaine chlorohydrate, controlled by some multinational laboratories and subjected to a heavy international tax[53].

Given the economic and political power of the multinational corporation and all the historical evidence, and despite the company's secrecy, you could say that Coca-Cola has a monopoly on coca. Stepan Chemical in New Jersey has exclusive DEA permits to import coca leaf and supplies Coca-Cola. Stepan is the only company to legally import coca leaf and extract cocaine from it in the US.[54] (Although the original Coca-cola did have a trace of cocaine, it should be noted that by 1929 the amount was reduced from something under 1/400 of a grain (per ounce of syrup) to just a memory. Caffeine is used, now, to supply the "buzz."

Even so, the coca-leaf monopoly confers a power on the multinational which can resolve such uncomfortable problems as doping among elite athletes in international competition. In the 1994 World Cup in Atlanta, Georgia (Coca-cola's headquarters), one Bolivian and one Brazilian soccer player were seriously sanctioned and expelled from the FIFA for testing positive for cocaine. Both had drunk a *mate de coca* hours before the game. All of Bolivia came out to protest and defend the innocence of the player who had drunk a *roadrunner*, a mixed tea of coca, anise and chamomile. All their efforts were in vain. Only the intervention of Goizueta, then Coca-Cola's president, convinced the FIFA to lift the sanctions. Coca-Cola was the official sponsor of the games, and it would have been inconsistent for a drink originally based on coca leaf and kola nuts to be advertised heavily while a player was punished for drinking *mate de coca*[55].

Cocaine is an excuse for the US to continue the war on drugs in Latin America, even though it makes up only 17% of the illegal drug

---

53. Cabieses, 1995, *op. cit.*
54. 'El país de los negocios,' *El País*, Michael W. Miller, December 11, 1994.
55. Cabieses, 1995, *op. cit.*

market. Meanwhile, Coca-Cola reigns with supreme majesty while the coca leaf begs for a little corner in the homes of the Andean world. As long as there is no real evaluation of drug policies and as long as Europeans continue to allow an international drug policy that ignores the evidence of its own failure, this will only serve to promote US hegemony.

Chapter III. Illegal Drug Trafficking

Illegal drug trafficking[56] is an economic and social process that includes the consumption of narcotics, stimulants and hallucinogens and the supply of such products through a growing and diversified production and distribution chain. It has two branches. The difficulties and risks imposed by illegality have made it the most lucrative business on earth, which has in turn triggered enormous incentives for developing production — from the fields to retail sales — thereby inviting broad sectors of the population to participate in the production and marketing of drugs. The industry moves $500,000 *million* annually, according to the United Nations. High demand coupled with prohibition create conditions for an imperfect market which shelters all kinds of abuses, violence and corruption.

The market also adapts perfectly to the socio-economic and political environments of Latin America. In the midst of a grave recession in the 1980s, Latin America did not stop the spread of coca and poppy crops, the acquisition of cocaine chlorohydrate or its trafficking, or the laundering of narco-dollars. These factors pushed production from the most favorable enclaves into other points, creating an international division of

---

56. This concept is more apt than "narco-trafficking," which, like "terrorism," "narco-terrorism" or "narco-guerrilla," has many ideological connotations and does not allow a deeper analysis of the phenomenon.

work that was flexible and astonishingly vibrant and dynamic. Since the macroeconomic and political circumstances were so favorable, coke processing spread throughout the continent. The many repressive actions against cocaine and coca leaf during the 1980s, thanks to US initiatives as the world's main drug market, only drove up the price and stimulated the market.

The spread of illegal drug trafficking, its economic importance and the incorporation of many sectors of the population have meant sweeping economic and political changes and have led to an increase in violent crime, further complicating attempts to rein in the runaway horse. Weak State institutions in South America have not been able to mount a serious response.

1.   ECONOMIC SIGNIFICANCE

Coca's advance in South America in the 1980s is surprising. It stabilized and even decreased toward the end of the 1990s, but it never went back to initial position of the 1970s, when crops outside the Andes were practically nonexistent and, if they did exist, they were few and followed the norms of traditional consumption.

Andean Countries: Net Exporters of Capital

The deterioration in the terms of currency exchange and the international debt crisis of the 1980s made the Andean economies even more dependent on revenue from narco-trafficking, and it fostered participation in illegal trafficking by other countries in the region as well. The crisis drove away capital that could have been invested in legal enterprises, and it stymied growth policies and investment that would have upgraded antiquated industries. Adjustment policies supported by the least-favored sectors and the decline in prices for exportable materials provoked poverty in the countryside and unemployment or underemployment in the cities. The endemic deficit in the balance of payments and the dire need for currency cemented the structural conditions that guaranteed the "cocalization" of national economies.

They needed coca dollars to pay the debt that, oddly enough, was created with narco-trafficking currency because of extra-official acceptance by national organizations and international organizations. There was no objection whatsoever to where the money came from, which was openly contradictory to the international policy of the fight against drugs.[57] This situation, a constant in Andean countries, became ever more difficult because of restrictive international legislation that was always a few steps behind the widespread money laundering. Though the proportion of profits returned to the producing countries (0.63%) is insignificant compared to the amount remaining on the US and European markets (88.22%), coca still is significant in overall exports. At the end of the 1980s, paste cocaine and cocaine were Bolivia's main export, according to some reports; in Peru, they were equal to legal exports and in Colombia they were greater than one-third of all legal exports.[58]

Coca/Cocaine: The Boom in the Production Cycle

Currently there are hemp crops (marijuana) in most of Central America and the Caribbean, and poppy crops (heroin) in several Latin American countries (Mexico, Guatemala and Colombia), but the main activity in the sphere of drug production is the cultivation and transformation of coca leaf into cocaine. Coca/cocaine has become another production cycle, very similar to other highly profitable historical crops. It provides constant economic activity, employs a large labor force, creates new activities parallel to or derived from it, and at the same time provokes undesired economic processes and negative consequences for long-term development. As with cash crops

57. Campodónico, Humberto, "La política del avestruz," pp. 226 — 258, in García Sayán, op. cit. in Chapter 2, p. 251, 1989.

58. In Bolivia, paste cocaine and cocaine make up 36% of legal exports; in Colombia, 38% and in Peru, 51%. Ibán de Rementería, *La elección de las drogas. Examen de las políticas de control,* Fundación Friederich Ebert, Lima, 1995.

tried in the past, the majority of the benefits remain overseas. Many industries are created or expanded to supply and support narco-trafficking — some of them legal, such as telecommunications, raw chemical products, banks, financial and service institutions; of course, the sale of guns also increases.

The economic cycle of coca and the profits associated with the opportunity to participate in the first phases of turning coca into cocaine make it the most productive plant, well over and above any other agricultural product. The decline in prices due to overproduction, inefficiency or prohibition have meant greater participation in turning coca into paste in Peru and Bolivia. Before that, it was an operation exclusive to the Colombians.

A New Chapter in Criminal Economy

What makes this whole process so distinctive is that it is illegal — it is another process in the criminal economy which has made history in the region since colonial times. In the Spanish Americas, colonial fortunes were made in spite of, and to spite, the Empire; while in the British colonies to the north, fortunes were made through cooperation and collaboration with the Empire. The monopolistic Spanish mercantile system was incapable of providing for the needs of its own colonies, and the strict colonial regulation, centralism and bureaucracy therefore became the immediate catalysts driving the proliferation of many unofficial or illicit economic activities that were needed to fill in what was missing. This could take the form of dealing in contraband, piracy, or the establishment of oligarchical control over political and economic processes based on favoritism, nepotism and arbitrary rule.[59] This continues to this day and is aggravated by narco-trafficking. Since it is illegal and therefore kept hidden, it is hard to get good information on the related movements of capital and the economic activity as a whole.[60] The economic importance of the

---

59. Kaplan, Marcos, *Aspectos sociopolíticos del narcotráfico*, Instituto Nacional de Ciencias Penales, México D.F., pp. 9 — 13, 1990.

cocaine business is assessed on the basis of partial data and profits and returns between one phase and the next, from production to retail in US and European cities.

The participation of most Latin American countries in illegal drug trafficking ironically has led to the economic union of Latin America, which had been a goal for so long; it is "the only powerful and broad Latin American multinational [industry] with economic, socio-cultural and political success."[61]

The countries in the Caribbean basin participate in the circuit as important centers for laundering narco-dollars and were the main transport route in the 1970s–1980s; today Mexico plays that role. There is also evidence of small coca plantations in other countries like Brazil, Guyana and Venezuela. In Venezuela, after the decline of petroleum prices, some 150,000 people began to participate directly or indirectly in activities related to narco-trafficking. Ecuador, which eradicated consumption and plantations by order of Felipe II in the 16th century, by raising the prices of other products and stimulating more profits for them, is now a small producer and transit country, as well as a growing consumer in its own right.[62] In the Southern Cone, Argentina and Uruguay have joined in as money-laundering centers and raw material producers. And finally, Central America has become an important transit route, money-laundering center and producer of both marijuana and the poppy (in Guatemala). Some authors also point to Myanmar, Tanzania, Pakistan, Java and India as coca producers, and to the US for its experimental crops.[63]

---

60. Nadelmann, Ethan A., "Latinoamérica: economía política del comercio de cocaine," in *Texto y contexto,* number 9, p. 27, Universidad de los Andes, Bogotá, Colombia, September — December 1986.

61. Kaplan, Marcos, op. cit.

62. UN, UNDCP, 1998; and Bonilla, Adrián, "Ecuador: actor internacional en la Guerra de las drogas," in Bagley, B. and others, ed., *La economía política del narcotráfico. El caso ecuatoriano,* FLACSO, Ecuador, North-South Center of the University of Miami, p. 11, 1991

63. According to Mauricio Mamani in a personal interview, La Paz, 1998 (see Chapter II).

2.   CROPS

Traditionally, Bolivia and Peru have dedicated large parts of their ecosystems and agricultural production to coca. In the last twenty years, economies that were self-sufficient with coca as just one part of a varied complex of crops have become "cocalized," so that coca is the main or only crop.

Monocrops of the Coca Bush

Throughout the entire Andes region, the amount of cultivated land dedicated to coca has increased continually. In most cases, the data of Andean governments and the US differ.[64] UN data indicates that currently 179,000 hectares (over 540,000 acres) are dedicated to coca leaf. Production surface and volume have changed the order of the main producers, because Colombia and Bolivia enjoy higher productivity than Peru, and that leaves Colombia as the main intermediary and the main producer.[65]

The increase in cultivation has been continuous since the end of the 1970s. The most favorable regions have seen the addition of many immigrants in processes that began with the respective agrarian reforms of Bolivia in 1953 and Peru in 1959. Two kinds of agricultural workers participate in growing coca: the settlers themselves — or Quechua and Aymara immigrant farmers, from the sierra, who have organized as autonomous producers; and the floating, marginal, proletariat sector, the rural and urban workers who join in the coca

---

64. According to the independent calculations of Ibán de Rementería, it went from 138,500 hectares in 1985 to 211,700 in 1992. Coca leaf production has gone from 137,730 metric tonnes harvested in 1985 to 246,785 Tm in 1992; 767 Tm of which were used to extract the cocaine alkaloid, an increase of 117% in seven years. In 1990 Bolivia produced 64,400 Tm of coca leaf. Peru is still the main producer with 138,300 Tm of coca leaf and, at that time, Colombia produced 32,100 Tm.

65. According to economist and cocologist Hugo Cabieses, the maximum productivity of illegal coca in Peru is from 600 — 650 kg/hectare, while in the Bolivian Chapare it is at 2,600 kg/hectare and in Colombia, 1,500 kg/hectare. Bolivia has the highest productivity with the least amount of surface of the three countries (35,000 hectares). Colombia went from almost no production at the end of the 1970s (at 35,000 — 40,000 hectares in the 1980s and most of the 1990s) to 81,000 hectares in 1997. Personal interview, January 1998.

cycle as opportunity allows, just as in years past workers joined any other highly profitable cycle. The members of this group are not landowners and so they have no right to credits or technical or governmental assistance. They just need a job. It is they who are the targets of the many eradication campaigns.

Table 2: Total surface for coca production 1988-1997.

	1988*	1997**
PERU	200,000 h.	60/70,000 h.
BOLIVIA	49,500 h.	50/54,000 h.
COLOMBIA	27,230 h.	80,000 h.

*Data from the US State Department, cited by García Sayán, 1989.
**Data from the US State Department, USAID, Lima, 1997.

The Fallacy of Environmental Degradation

Coca has become a single crop which has led to the rotation of new low-quality agricultural land or forestal lands. Some feel this is the main reason for the environmental degradation of the Amazon region, while others believe that the deforestation and erosion in the Amazon area has nothing to do with coca.[66]

Currently, the "biological" war on drugs, based on eradication by means of plant plagues that do not distinguish between legal and illegal crops, has generated strong rejection from Colombian peasants and generalized protests in Bolivian agriculture (see Chapter VI). What does constitute degradation or a loss in biodiversity is the establishment of coca as a single crop and the contamination of the

66. The US embassy is determined to show that coca cultivation is bad for the environment, and it funds studies which in many cases show results that ironically and inconveniently support coca. Roger Rumrill, environmental journalist, and Antonio Chávez, National Agrarian University professor, personal interviews, January 1998. "It is already a fashion statement to denounce narco-trafficking as detrimental to the environment in the Andean-Amazon. But illegal crops in the region make up only 0.2% of the total agricultural area — 97,798,000 hectares. If we consider the entire area used for agriculture, illegal crops represent only 0.05% of these 387,847,000 hectares." Rementería, op. cit., p 77. FAO, *Year Book*, Rome, 1990.

basin with industrial chemicals. This is due to anti-drug policies and the coca/cocaine complex as an intensive crop.

Thus, many are the setbacks and destructive elements in this illegal economy. It is true that any agricultural project implies a big difference between the producer and the seller, but in illegal coca activity the contradiction is constant. Its tensions are not resolved in courts of law but through violence and abuse by the stronger party, which explains the dominance of narco-traffickers, guerrillas and paramilitaries which establish an order that runs parallel to the State.

Coca in Peru

The Cuzco area has traditionally produced coca leaf. The nationalization and monopoly of coca by the State were organized through the company ENACO, and it controls 10,000 hectares of legal coca. The exploitation, promotion and commercialization of products derived from the coca leaf are part of the legal coca economy, and constitute a serious alternative to the current international drug policy banning the export of products containing coca leaf.

The illegal coca-cocaine circuit is much larger and includes extended areas of recent settlers: Alto Huallaga, San Martín, the Apurímac Valley and Aguaytía. The success of coca in these areas is parallel to the failure of agrarian reform. The demographic growth in the sierra, the disposition of the lands and state promises for reform pushed many colonists to this edge of the forest and promoted family-labor, hard work and not very profitable. Independent producers looking for higher product profitability in a region with a deficient infrastructure predominated, and they generated a poorly structured and scattered system of agricultural commercialization. These negative tendencies began to disappear as coca gained ground in what had been diversified production. Its profitability and the growing demand for it allowed the producer to absorb constant losses from other crops. Speaking of the coca boom in Aucayacu and Huallaga, Roger Rumill comments:

At that time, anyone not in the drug market starved to death because it was impossible to survive in a dollarized and inflated economy. As a result, very few resisted the temptation of drugs.

Hence the area under coca cultivation in Huallaga went from 3,000 hectares in 1975 to 70,000 hectares at the end of the 1980s: 3% of the population lived directly or indirectly off coca.[67] This bonanza attracted a large underclass population to Huallaga and in 1970 the annual growth rate of 4.2% was much higher than the national rate of 2.6%. Most settlers had arrived in the last fifteen years and 40% of them had lived on the coast before emigrating to the jungle. This floating population owned nothing. They settled in marginal lands and held no right to credits or technical or governmental aid. Since they operated outside the rule of law, they easily fell prey to the networks of narco-trafficking and subversion.

The Huallaga coca variety was more bitter and higher in cocaine content, so it also attracted Colombian narco-traffickers in their day. Until then, they had been supplied by Cuzco and Bolivia. Along the banks of the river, Colombians found the ideal climate for coca production; it was hard to access yet relatively close to the Colombian border, which facilitated aerial transportation.

In the early 1990s when presidential candidate Eduardo Galán was assassinated, Colombians declared all-out war on narco-trafficking. This was the beginning of the end of the Huallaga bonanza. The Medellín cartel challenge, led by Pablo Escobar, had the entire country at war and stopped the flights of cargo planes to Huallaga. According to Rumrill, "in the days that followed there was not one single Colombian plane and coca leaf prices fell along with sales, sparking a crisis that persists today." Hugo Cabieses agrees: "This is a crisis of market efficiency. A 50% decrease in price is not because of the success of alternative development programs or a

---

67. *Comisión Especial del Senado sobre las causas de la violencia y alternatives de pacificiación en Perú.*, 1989, cited by García Sayán, 1989. Some 600,000 people, APEP, *Cocaína: problemas y soluciones andinos.*, Asociación Peruana de Estudios e Investigaciones para la Paz, pp. 232 — 233, Lima. 1990.

decline in the US demand for cocaine, or even of prohibition, but because of the position of the Peruvian product on the illegal market and its substitution by coca leaf from Bolivia or Colombia, where greater productivity allows for lower costs." Thus, according to the economist, "the organization of production in Peru was in the hands of narco-trafficking rings which could not harvest large amounts; they had to harvest in parts. So during the squeeze it was cheaper and safer for Colombians to obtain raw and paste cocaine in Colombia instead of trying to import it on planes from Apurímac or Huallaga."

Along with the coca crisis there was an economic shake up in Peru, where Fujimori sought to introduce liberalizing policies. Rumrill underscores that "economic adjustments from 1990 — opening trade with no restrictions or regulations and the demolition of the State apparatus — threatened to collapse the legal productive structure in the country, particularly in the Amazon, facilitating the process of massive cocalization throughout the Amazon region. The 'corrections' to the liberalizing structural adjustment measures, which were supposed to be microeconomic alternative development policies pacted with the US in 1991, were useless. They were not viable."

Thus, the economic problems and crisis brought on by misguided liberalization policies fattened the highest levels of society but still did not help for the poorest sectors (which were suffering from the low prices of the past decade); rather, it encouraged greater participation of peasants in the processing of paste cocaine. As a result, there was greater involvement in the illegal coca/cocaine cycle as a subordinate to the Colombians and, now, to the Mexicans.

Coca in Bolivia

Between 1960 and 1988, the percentage of Bolivia's surface area dedicated to coca leaf was doubled. At the end of the 1980s, it was at 49,500 hectares and of those, 12,852 in the Yungas zone were legal while the rest, in the tropical zone of Cochabamba in Chapare, were illegal.

During the 1990s, there was constant pressure from the US and there was funding for to encourage alternative development (the building of infrastructure and the introduction of new crops), and forces were provided to fight drugs. According to the local authorities and the US Embassy, Bolivia held the record in surface area eradicated, but that achievement was overshadowed every year by new plantations found in marginal territories.[68]

Global production in 1996 reached 50,000 hectares, employing more than 70,000 peasant families in farming and processing paste cocaine. Though the number of Bolivians living directly or indirectly off coca has reached 350,000 (they have organized, now, both in unions and politically), it is the only viable resource for them. It has high, stable prices and a market, while price liberalization and importing of agricultural products drowned all other segments of peasant agriculture.[69]

Since Bolivian production is unique in that it is highly unionized (657 unions and 5 federations in 1988), the peasants have been able to channel their demands and defend their positions before the government and international organizations. Demonstrations to defend coca cultivation have placed peasants in violent confrontation with the police and the army, with states of siege being declared on several occasions in Chapare, the region with the highest growth.

During the 1980s, Chapare welcomed the most migrants from the high plateaus and the valleys. The migrations began in the mid-1960s. Between 1977 and 1981, the annual growth rate of coca producers was at more than 20%. Just like its Peruvian counterpart, Huallaga, Quechua and Aymara peasants resettled spontaneously in family-

---

68. In 1997 the *Fuerza Especial de Lucha Contra el Narcotráfico* (Special Forces Against Narcotrafficking) boasted 7,512 hectares eradicated. The detection of 7,200 hectares of new plantations by a US satellite leaves a balance of 312 hectares eradicated, which was criticized by NGOs for development and human rights, because eradication has come at the cost of the peasants who suffer multiple human rights violations. Personal interview with María Lohmann, CEDIB, Cochabamba, January 1998.

69. According to Rolando Vargas from the Federación de Productores del Chapare and Silvia Lasarte from the Federación de Mujeres de Chapare. Interviews in Shinaota and Villa Tunari, Cochabamba, Bolivia, January 1998.

oriented clusters, creating small farms. Though the organization of crops in new farms continued to be diversified as a way to gain access to the market (coca, plantain, yucca, rice and oranges), in 1980 coca crops expanded and neared single crop status. The coca plantations in Chapare are harvested four times per year and, except for the initial preparation of the land and planting, they demand little labor.

The work is distributed into the different functions required by narco-trafficking: from the coca leaf-presser, or *pisador*, to the *hormiga*, the ant — the one who carries the coca — and the *mula*, or transporter between one boss and another. Illegal demand and high profits have fixed a rather high wage-per-day, with the resulting repercussions in other agricultural sectors, consumption habits and the customs of the producing peasants. The growth in production and the fall in prices has led some producers, as in Peru, to process paste cocaine, increasing profits five-fold.

Despite the continuous police and military controls in Chapare, coca is still grown and sold. When it is impossible to obtain the industrial chemical products which are now limited by law, the peasants find a way to process paste cocaine by substituting natural products. Curiously, in Potosí, La Paz and Cochabamba, there are periods when it is impossible to find onions. Onions and decayed urine are used in coca zones to turn coca leaf into paste. (On the way from Cuzco and Quillabamba, Peru's legal coca zone, hundreds of peasants board the train to supply the onions that do not make it to the city).

If the US DEA follows its current policies, then the day will come when onions in the Andes will be confiscated because they are part of the coca/cocaine complex.

Coca in Colombia

Coca leaf production is something new in Colombia; it was practically nonexistent in the 1970s. There are sixteen production areas in the Amazons, including Guaviare, Putumayo and Caquetá, though production has also begun in the departments of Cauca,

Chocó and Nariño. In 1988, the planted surface reached 27,230 hectares according to the US State Department. Ten years later, total surface planted was 80,000 hectares according to the US, but independent experts estimate between 120,000 and 160,000 hectares.[70]

The first coca zones were colonized after the 1948 period known as *La Violencia*, when governmental persecution forced peasants to organize self-defense groups and flee to new lands inside the Amazon zone. The new zones of colonization became the bastion of the Communist Party, which fully participated in the organization of united communities, and later became the refuge of the armed insurgency and places of historic legitimacy for the FARC. Though at first these settlers cultivated a range of crops, coca slowly took over as it was more profitable, and it was in demand by the incipient illegal industry; and the guerrillas supported it.

As narco-trafficking spread and the economic power of the narco-landowners increased, an obvious contradiction came to the fore. The peasant sector's most profitable crop is coca, which was protected by the (Marxist) guerrillas; and the landowning, industrial sector with its vested interests in the illegal industry of narco-trafficking, was ideologically conservative and was backed by the establishment's paramilitaries. This provoked a worrisome "agrarian reform" that is changing the peasant crops into huge, difficult-to-access commercial plantations designed to supply coca or poppy for processing and distribution.[71]

Given the high productivity of the "business" agriculture of commercial plantations, today Colombia is the main producer and transformer of the coca leaf, though, as we shall see, Mexico is replacing it with respect to distribution. Both countries are also huge producers of the poppy. The combined surface of Colombia and

---

70. According to Sergio Uribe, in the 1994 — 1996 electoral term, mentioned by Hugo Cabieses in a personal interview in 1998.

71. Vargas Meza, Ricardo, "Las FARC, la Guerra y la crisis del Estado" *NACLA Report*, Volume XXXI, number 5, March — April, 1998. *Informe de la mission de parlamentarios europeos a la region andina*, March 1998.

Mexico dedicated to poppy cultivation is 12,000 hectares (UN, UNDCP 1998).

3.   PROCESSING AND DISTRIBUTION

The Colombians have promoted illegal trafficking, and have found ideal conditions for intensively and extensively growing coca leaf, first in Bolivia and then in Peru. They organized traditional producers and began demanding coca leaf in large quantities to process into paste cocaine in jungle laboratories.

The Colombians have historical experience in contraband, but they also have prior training in production and illegal drug trafficking. The secret export of marijuana from La Guajira in the 1970s made them one of the main suppliers to the US market. Later, the concentration of profits, its light weight and ease in transportation (as well as the anti-marijuana campaigns in La Guajira) piqued interest in cocaine as an alternative to marijuana, and this attracted the entrepreneurial attention of the capital, Antioquia, which was in recession.

Interest in narco-trafficking can be explained by a speculative economic culture. The magnificent narco-trafficking business multiplied initial value by 33. The $50,000 generated by one hectare of coca meant one million dollars on Miami streets.

Table 3: Coca/cocaine circuit. Value-added by country, In millions of US dollars. 1990.

Country Type	Producer	Transit	Consumer
	469 0.63%	8,241 11.15%	65,210 88.22%
Source: Rementería, 1995.			

For the manufacture of one kilogram of pure cocaine, 500 kilograms of dry coca leaf and various chemical products are needed. Processing coca into paste cocaine does not require anything sophisticated. It can be done by the farmers themselves in simple laboratories or jungle "kitchens" near the coca plantations, and then they sell the paste, or drums of dry coca leaves, to Colombian and Mexican intermediaries who make the final product. From there, the transportation and sales infrastructures ferry the product to distribution points in the US and Europe. The incorporation of different countries with separate goals and the seemingly automatic substitution of some groups or cartels by others proves that this is more than a systematic criminal organization. It spontaneously incorporates increasingly broad sectors of the population into the criminal labors of narco-trafficking.

In the late 1970s, Colombian narco-traffickers substituted the Miami-based Cuban pioneers in distribution. Now the Colombians are being replaced by the Mexicans. Colombians have appropriated 65–70% of the retail income (which includes production and transportation costs, between 10 and 15%).

The minority market earns the highest profits (between 80 and 90% of the final value) because it is limited by Americans, and now Europeans, to consuming areas. Thus we can distinguish among producer, distributor and consumer countries such that producer countries in the Andean area earn only 0.63% of the profits, while 88.22% of the value added stays in consumer countries and 11.15% in transit countries.

Table 4: Coca/Cocaine Complex: Accumulated Value Added, By Participant, in US$ Millions. 1990.

Peasants	Companies	Cartels	Confiscations	Distributors	Dealers
305	128	9,530	(2,405)	19,735	41,817
0.41%	0.17%	12.9%	(3.25%)	26.70%	56.57%

Source: Rementeria, 1995

The illegal nature of this industry along with its astronomical profits have made it a highly competitive sector that exercises a vicious control over all stages of production and marketing using extra-economic, illegal and violent means. Competition has meant the development of many narco "wars."[72]

Big bands of traffickers organized the circuit from the Peruvian and Bolivian coca plantations to the street, the local points of sale in the US and Europe. The Colombians had a cultural tradition of prolonged violence and historical experience in contraband. The region of Antioquia and its businesses, which declined in the 1970s, offered ideal conditions for the development of the business because of pre-existing feudal landowner/peasant relationships and the entrepreneurial culture which traditionally turned toward contraband. The modern industrial development of Colombia, based on monopolies and State protection, stimulated the speculative economy and, with it, a "facilist way of thinking, daring when maintaining the profits of speculation, but cowardly with respect to innovation and social imagination, feudal in the management of people and conflicts and oligarchic in the management of the State."[73]

The cartels which have succeeded each other since the early 1980s put into relief a sophisticated and implacable multinational conglomerate which is highly adaptable to adversity — via corruption or alliances with other criminal mafias — and the diversification of supply sources, routes and contacts with new corruptible governments, all the while strengthening relations and international bases throughout Latin America. Despite efforts to portray the cartels as being distanced from the exercise of power and isolated, vulnerable to removal, experience shows that they are endogenously and not exogenously developed. They are closely linked to the power structures. "They are not completely autonomous individuals nor are they stronger than the political power that has created, cultivated,

---

72. Note the debunking of the Cubans between 1979 and 1981 by the Colombians, with many murders in Miami, disputes between the cartels of Medellín and Cali for control of the New York and Los Angeles markets in the 1980s, wars between rival bands in Peru's Alto Huallaga in Peru, the all-out war begun by President Barco in 1989 in Colombia which included the fight between the Medellín and Cali cartels and their violent methods, the eruption of the Mexican narco-traffickers substituting the Cali cartel with the Guadalajara cartel, Trial 8,000 against former Colombian president Samper; and the successive political scandals in Mexico with overwhelming corruption, demonstrating the competition among the Mexican cartels of the Gulf and those of Juárez, Tijuana and Sonora.

73. Petro, Gustavo, "La economía de la mentira," in *Papeles de cuestiones internacionales*, number 62, CIP, Madrid, 1997.

grown, protected and tolerated them, used them for their own purposes and thrown them away or subdued them without any major problem when the time came."[74]

The current replacement of the Cali cartel by Mexican cartels[75] as well as the eruption of Russian mafias on the world scene point to a globalization of illegal trafficking, which has taken advantage of the opportunities in a world with fewer restraints on the circulation of capital and goods. Furthermore, the Free Trade Zone created in North America has stimulated and facilitated the exchange and traffic of drugs and capital between South and Central America.

All these modifications and adaptations, along with the level of incorporation of different social sectors into the producing process, indicate an open organization where one can decide to participate with varying degrees of responsibility.[76] Many people participate in it, from the kingpins to the low level workers, the leaf-pressers on the plantations. The process of transformation and distribution, and money-laundering and the resulting investments, require many skills and specializations. The range of directly of tasks indirectly provides occupation for a large part of the population of the producing countries (who may be implicated either through their actions or consumption or investment). In addition to peasants, chemists, transporters, operators (*traqueteros* — buyers, usually young, of coca leaves, paste cocaine or cocaine in coca growing areas), security forces (bodyguards, hit men), lawyers, public relations experts, accountants,

---

74. Fazio, Carlos, in VVAA, *Crimen uniformado*, CEDIB Bolivia, 1997.

75. Eddy, Paul. *"Cocaine Wars."* WW. Norton &Company, 1988. Pablo Escobar, Rodríguez Gacha and Carlos Lehder's Medellín cartel was replaced by the Rodríguez Orejuela Cali cartel. This was replaced in Colombia by the Norte del Valle cartel (José Nelson Urrego) and the Mexican cartel of the Gulf (García Agrego), Juárez (Amado Carrillo) and Tijuana (the Arellan Félix brothers). An important development is the "non-aggression pact" signed by the Juárez, Tijuana and Sonora cartels made them into a "Federation." *El País*, February 20, 1998.

76. In 1977 one of the first DEA reports on the cocaine business refers to the "Medellín Union of Traffickers" as a "vertically organized transnational corporation." Bagley, Bruce Michael, "Colombia and the War on Drugs" in *Foreign Affairs*, volume 67, number 1, p. 75, Fall 1988. This vision was later accepted by US leaders and, as a result, by the press. The 1989 and 1991 references to the cartel by the Drug Control Strategies is significant in this regard.

politicians, all have roles to play. In total, 3% of the active population in Colombia in 1990 worked directly in narco-trafficking.[77]

A cartel is the confluence of several families organized and specialized in the many tasks related to trafficking. The information disseminated daily by the media refers to an implacable hierarchical organization. It is open to anyone who has nothing to lose and everything to gain. It is an organization that has not yet attained maturity and cannot control market prices or many other economic variables.[78] Since it is not a closed organization, it is impossible to dismantle it. It reproduces automatically,[79] giving the impression that there is no effective recourse and that measures against it only irritate small-time traffickers without changing the power at the top.

With respect to processing and trade, Peruvian mafias have used less violent methods than the Colombians. They have opted for corruption and buying influence; but they still manage to weaken any institutional apparatus: the police, political parties, judges and most of all, members of the military who, in the past few years, charged a "toll" for drug trafficking as payment for services rendered when they eliminated the subversive guerrilla The Shining Path.[80]

Bolivia's role in processing and distribution has been even greater than Peru's. Its greater distance from Colombia implies higher transportation costs and this has forced it to invest and include value-added perks. Its exports are now in the form of purified paste cocaine.

---

77. APEP, op. cit. page 138, 1990.

78. Nadelmann (bibliography p. 36) 1986, believes in the macroeconomic "inexperience" of these organizations, which was true then. However, the eruption of the insatiable Russian mafias and the plundering the former Communist country has been subjected to, along with the alleged alliance among the Italo-US, Russian and Colombian mafias in 1993 to operate and distribute on the European and US markets, grant perspective on their growing economic power, and, of course, their capacity for power. Sterling, Claire. *"Thieves' World. The Threat of the New Global Network of Organized Crime.* NY: Simon & Schuster, 1994. Notes refer to Spanish version.

79. Bustamante, Fernando, "La política de EEUU contra el narcotráfico y su impacto en América latina," in *Estudios internacionales,* number 62, CIP, Madrid, 1997.

80. Soberón, Ricardo (expert from the Comisión Andina de Juristas), interviews in January 1998, Lima; Soberón, Ricardo and others, *Crimen uniformado, entre la corrupción y la impunidad,* CEDIB, Cochabamba, Bolivia, 1997; and Soberón, Ricardo, "Entre cuarteles, caletas y fronteras: fuerzas armadas y lucha antidrogas" in VVAA, *Guerra antridrogas, democracia, derechos humanos y militarización en América latina,* ed. TNI, CEDIB, Inforpress Centroamericana, Guatemala, 1997.

Union and political organizations more or less peacefully shepherd the business. Military participation in cocaine trafficking began in the between-war period and culminated during the García Meza dictatorship (1980–1982), which gained international fame as the "cocaine government."[81]

Currently, several groups of Bolivian narco-traffickers refine cocaine and have access to autonomous export and distribution networks. They still maintain contracts with Colombians, Brazilians and (increasingly) the Mexicans, as well. The development of the business and government sponsorship have led to a level of corruption comparable to Peru's, implicating magistrates, politicians, police officers, journalists and members of the military.

Other countries in the region benefit as points of transit and sites for money-laundering. The entire Caribbean basin has become a path for cocaine heading toward the US, and the enormous Mexican and Central American territories are now truck routes to the north.[82] A 1996 European Union expert report underscores that in large areas of storage and the free ports in Central America (such as Colón in Panama, and in Costa Rica, Nicaragua, El Salvador or Guatemala), there are no established controls over large containers. Trafficking develops on its own, with stopovers on countless Caribbean isles before landing at Miami and other nearby ports of entry, a fundamental point for later distribution.

4.   FINANCIAL CONVERSION

The Latin American debt crisis and narco-trafficking have become two parallel and inter-related phenomena. During the 1980s, in the three countries we have analyzed, the IMF encouraged certain types of free trade which were not questioned by any world financial institution, even if they were tied to narco-trafficking. The annual

---

81. Roncken, Theo, in VVAA, *Guerra antidrogas...*, see previous citation, 1997.
82. VVAA, *Centroamérica: gobernabilidad y narcotráfico*, Transnational Institute and Heinrich Boll Foundation, Guatemala, 1997.

injection of $25,000 million into the US retail market, divided among Colombians (50%) and Peruvians and Bolivians (50%), was enough to revive economies in crisis or those in the process of structural changes. Narco-trafficking and the many jobs it created, its acceleration of consumerism and the way it spurred investments (mainly in real estate) provided these economies with a great outlet, which explains the ambivalent attitude of the authorities. Wary of violence and nervous about the precarious situation created by the power of narco-traffickers, they nevertheless cannot afford to forego the money. This leads to the creation of two-faced policies.

Given that financial and economic systems happily receive contributions, and international commitments to fight drugs require results, spectacular operations are developed while in fact, on the ground, everything stays the same. After the official rhetoric of the war on drugs and the war on money-laundering, there are scant initiatives coordinating Latin American policies. According to the 1996 EU *Report on Drugs in Latin America*, there is not even any coordination between commercial and central banks to combat money-laundering, nor are central banks under supervision with respect to commercial banks and their laundering activities.[83]

Colombia

Since 1983, the profits in Colombia have been so high ($4,000 million annually) that the excess was invested in international capital markets, depositing $18,000 million in the US and $1,500 million in Colombia every year. Free trade policies allowing such absorption began in 1974 after the agreement with the IMF.

This determined and constant policy has allowed Colombia to escape the crisis in spite of its foreign debt. Colombians were, therefore, pioneers in nurturing coca-capitalism, since the national bank built a bridge between the underground and formal

---

83. Most banks plead banking privacy when police authorities request information. In some countries there is a legal framework to discourage laundering but it is inoperable. The European Union *Report on Drugs in Latin America*. Mission of Experts, September–October 1996.

economies.[84] As a whole, the entire economic system was able to absorb such sums through real estate investments and in the industry and commercial sectors, even with the current limitations on foreign currency, since they neither accept nor have accounts in foreign currency.[85]

Bolivia

Though Bolivia was the second-largest producer throughout the 1980s, the structure of its productive system and lack of development did not allow it to take advantage of narco-dollars. Of the $5,372 million corresponding to Bolivia, only 15% was absorbed by the Bolivian economy. Freedom of exchange during the military dictatorships (1971–1982) generated hyper-inflation. This was exacerbated by the production crisis, and the rise of parallel black markets as well as increasing reliance on the dollar to the detriment of the local currency, aggravated by crises in the tin and gas industries. Meanwhile, the country found it was unable to obtain foreign credit when it could not take on foreign debt. Estenssoro[86] New Economic Policy for Peace entailed the legalization of narco-dollars in 1985, which allowed for the stability of the economy and pulled back inflation, thus earning the praise of the US government and the IMF.

---

84. Campodónico, op. cit., pp. 247–250, 1989. Money-laundering mechanisms were many: direct deposit of cash, the well-known "evil window"; the use of pre-existing banks through buying; placing banking agencies overseas and wherever there is business; fiscal amnesty every four years; non-refundable exchange licenses allowing the purchase of capital goods overseas and payable with narco-dollars; foreign credits for domestic activities; issuing transferable bonds for the public foreign debt to the bearer; travelers checks and money orders; buying gold overseas and selling it to the *Banco de la República* for *pesos*; and the authorization of income by inexplicable dollars to finance agro-industrial companies in the central zone of Colombia (80% controlled by the Medellín cartel).

85. According to Rafael Andrade, Colombia's Ambassador to Peru, in the round table *Narco-Trafficking: the Current Situation and Perspectives for Action*, Peruvian Center for International Studies (CEPEI), 1995.

86. Estenssoro, head of the populist Movimiento Nacionalista Revolucionario (MNR), was brought to power in 1952.

Peru

The path to free trade has been more difficult in Peru, but it has finally arrived at complete dependence on narco-dollars. The liberalization of the economy began in the late 1970s, and ended the previous control of trade. The issuance of negotiable securities and the ability to open foreign accounts allowed for the creation of a legal market parallel to the single exchange market. With this exchange policy, the Peruvian commercial banks expanded their offices until there was a greater supply of dollars, i.e., zones where an incipient coca (and its derivatives) trade meant a greater circulation of currency.

The crisis began during the Belaúnde Terry administration — president of Peru (1963–68, 1980–85), and peaked with Alan García (president from 1985 to 1990), who at first tried to apply heterodox economic measures, the main component of which was private investment. Thus was established a fixed exchange rate, without completely discarding the dollars of the parallel market. When the policies failed, the country turned to IMF recommendations. Faced with serious recession, they finally decided to use the dollars of the parallel market. At the end of the 1980s, the Ocoña narco-trafficking market fixed the exchange rate of 70% of the imports and most public institutions bought their dollars directly in Ocoña.

Confronted with the difficulty the national economies had in absorbing these overwhelming amounts of cash, they decided to incorporate narco-dollars into the legal economy by passing them through so-called "financial havens."

Financial Havens

It is estimated that by 1985 these international finance centers were managing some $300,000 million, and half a billion in 1987. Currently about $125 to $150 million are laundered annually in industrialized countries, or the Group of Seven.[87] At first, the Colombians established relations with international investment centers from the unfortunate Panama through Costa Rica and the Cayman Islands, Bermuda and the Netherlands Antilles.

The US role is also important in financial conversion. The Caribbean basin, including Florida and most of the Caribbean islands, is where most narco-trafficking money-laundering operations are focused. These places are famous tax havens characterized by frantic financial activity related to large scale drug dealing. These off-shore banks are refuges, free of the legal regulation that might be expected in New York or Paris, for instance, and they are paradigmatic examples of the free market system. They are the main problem posed by narco-trafficking because all illegal money is channeled through them and they are growing rapidly.

Among the many examples of small island-refuges, the power of Anguilla, or Snake Island, is curious. It went from 3 banks in 1980 to 96 financial institutions in 1983. Legal operations are mixed in these havens with illegal funds in a recycling process such that the money can once again form part of the legal economy.

Before the US tightened up its control mechanisms and began to discourage massive or too-obvious money-laundering operations in Miami, Los Angeles or New York in 1985, the Colombians decided to seek new markets for laundering in Europe, targeting the new, secretive and computerized stock system in Great Britain and Switzerland. The Southern Cone (mainly Argentina, Paraguay and Uruguay), after the first convulsions of hyperinflation, has also become an ideal place for financial conversion.[88] But Russia is now laundering staggering sums of money, too, as are its former economic satellites. The process of laundering/plundering is still gaining speed to this day. The privatization of State goods, the absence of any economic oversight, and the power of the mafias have allowed the former socialist power to become a money-laundering center for

---

87. According to the Financial Action Group, GAFI, in Garzón, Baltazar and Mejías, E., op. cit. 1997.

88. Lejtman, Román. *Narcogate. El dinero de la droga*, Editorial Apóstrofe: Barcelona, 1994; Soberón y otros, *Crimen uniformado...*, Bibliography, 1997; and VVAA, *Guerra antidrogas...*, Bibliography, 1997.

illegal drug trafficking and any other non-declared or criminal business.[89]

Panama is a prime example of a financial haven. More than any other country it symbolizes the complex ambiguities of US international policy, the traditional symbiosis of military and economic strategies and the polyvalence of the war on drugs. The historic peculiarity of Panama's creation as a US protectorate conditioned its subsequent development. The first 1904 Constitution and the successive Constitutions of 1941, 1946 and 1972 explicitly designate the nonexistence of a national currency; the country is exclusively dependent on the dollar and, as such, on the US Federal Reserve. This distinction marked the Panamanian nation as an ideal candidate for an international financial center. The 1972 Banking Act and the Offshore Companies Act offered the best economic conditions within confidentiality and freedom of movement, which meant a rapid rise in and the establishment of banks, depositors and intermediary companies of all kinds. US support for the creation of an international financial center[90] and the dependence on the dollar were determining factors when it was decided to establish the US's largest military base, the Southern Command — headquarters of President Reagan's anti-communist crusade in Central American — in Panama.

This crusade used drug trafficking to generate resources for low-intensity wars. The conjuncture of the continent's most important maritime route (overtly controlled by the US until 1999), the CIA's secret services, the financial center and the Southern Command in

---

89. From the beginning of the 1990s, international delinquents associated to Russian delinquents or corrupt politicians opened bank accounts and obtained export licenses, bought rubles with black market dollars at a huge discount and could acquire raw export materials and pay with these rubles. Thus not only were enormous amounts of money laundered, but enormous fortunes were also made, as Claire Sterling recounts, op. cit., p. 30. This unprecedented plundering has led to a chaotic situation for the Russian economy and contributed to aggravating and extending the financial crisis from Japan and the emerging Asian economies to a large part of the developing world in 1998.

90. Steinsleger, José. "Los paraísos financieros. El caso de Panamá" in García Sayá, Diego, op. cit., 1989. In US military circles it was a well-known secret that the creation of the financial center was a condition that the US government imposed in exchange for accepting and supporting a new treaty on the Canal.

Panama, all worked in favor of the use of this enclave for the political and strategic ends of the great power. One of the major players was General Manuel Noriega, who had been collaborating with the CIA from 1959 until the mid-1980s, when he began to be seen as cooperating with Nicaragua and Cuba. Having lost Washington's trust, he was indicted in Miami for his role in laundering Medellín and Cali cartel dollars. These events were used as a pretext for staging an economic boycott of Panama as a financial center, and for invading Panama with the US marines in 1989.

After Noriega's imprisonment and renewed negotiations over the scheduled handover of the Panama Canal, which the US had been controlling, the Southern Command's war on drugs intensified and the international financial center was restored to its former functions. This renewed its financial vocation as the only Latin American location whose official currency is the dollar and does not have to complete exchange transactions. In addition to the Columbus *zona franca*, banks and financial companies, money laundering happens in legal businesses like the real estate sector, large nightclubs, luxurious art galleries and even agricultural and livestock activities. A rule of silence rules the country, and everyone participates by exercising the most immediate responsibility of not asking too much or looking too far. Panama is "a paradise for narco-launderers and narco-traffickers. In this country they own luxury hotels, have direct access to the big banks, freedom of movement and, to a certain point, protection. They can establish businesses with relative ease and build high-cost infrastructures, whether it is for shopping centers or luxurious housing. They have the means to blackmail, bribe and buy, at any level and whenever they feel necessary, in public administration or legal institutions. This norm is applied to private companies, lawyers and professionals as well. In short, beach, breezes, the sea... and dollars from narco-trafficking."[91]

---

91. Reyes, Herasto, "Panamá: de paraíso de lavado a sede del Centro Multilateral Anti-drogas," in VVAA, *Centroamérica*, op. cit., 1997.

The Role of the US

Though today drug trafficking and consumption has spread to most nations on the globe and more and more countries have joined in production, it is necessary to consider the role of the US as the main consumer and an important link in the production chain. Since drug control policies originated in the US, the US is also where the first mafias controlling illegal alcohol and, later, opiates and cocaine, began. Even popular books and movies illustrate this. US prohibitionist policies, its economic and social potential and the role of the secret services have strongly encouraged illegal trafficking.

The US is the world's largest consumer — of drugs, as of almost everything else. America is also a drug producer and distributor, and an investor of its profits. More than 80% of narco-trafficking profits remain in the US. In the distribution process, from final processing to consumption, cocaine's value increases sevenfold ($17,000 dollars/kilogram on the streets). This, along with growing consumption and the proliferation of criminal groups, denotes a great consuming power but also, and increasingly so, power as a producer, distributor and financer. Not only has there been a rise in natural and synthetic drugs, but the manufacture of chemical products needed for processing have also increased, as confirmed in the financial system necessary for its conversion.

With regard to marijuana, the US produces one third of what it consumes. Given the increase in domestic production, the country has given up on eradicating crops (even those in national parks). The growing acceptance of marijuana consumption and wider participation in its production has led the country to consider marijuana's commercial value, and substantial legislative changes are ushering in progressive legislation for hemp derivatives.[92] The US has also become a marijuana exporter and a re-exporter of cocaine to Canada, Western Europe and Japan.

---

92. Grinspoon. L., and Bakalar, J., *Marijuana, the Forbidden Medicine.* Yale UP, 1993.

With respect to synthetic drugs, the US government admits that "almost all methamphetamines, LSD and PCP are illegally manufactured using chemicals from US suppliers." Most of the chemical products needed to process coca leaf into cocaine are from the US, too.

Many US groups live off narco-trafficking, and the millions of dollars in profits stay in the US. Retail cocaine is the most useful in the entire process because it stays in the US financial system and becomes part of the flow in international banking. An estimated $8,000 million in cocaine dollars were passed through US banks every year in the 1980s. Florida's banks then had more cash than all the other states together. The Miami banking system was "the vital link between financier, seller, market and the tax "refuge" off the continent."[93] Today, Miami's role is important as an international money-laundering center and in some respects it serves as the "capital of the Americas." Such economic sleight of hand has achieved levels of corruption similar to that in the Andean countries.

This entire economic and financial framework, as well as the double standard that prevails in the US, has led to the radicalization of the Latin Americans. It is they who suffer the consequences of the war on drugs, and it is on their land that the war is fought. They have a completely different view of the problem. Their demands, at anti-drug summits and other events, that money-laundering be treated as a crime, have contributed to increasing financial surveillance in the US. Banks are now required to report any cash transactions greater than $10,000. Furthermore, anyone who manages large amounts of cash is suspect, yet financial engineering and the use of tax havens still facilitate the laundering of enormous fortunes.

---

93. Garasino, Alberto M., "Droga y política," in *Revista argentina de estudios estratégicos*, Year 6, number.
11, p. 20, Buenos Aires, 1989.

5. THE TRANSFORMATION OF ANDEAN SOCIETIES

Economic and social transformations caused by the coca/cocaine complex are two-fold. On the one hand, there are changes proper to a primitive economy experiencing a boom in one of its products; and, on the other hand, there are changes that take place in the same society when one of the basic patterns of its culture is constantly threatened. One of the most serious problems has been the gradual food dependence of the coca zones because of the tendency to grow the coca bush alone. The increased reliance on buying food has caused a hike in food prices and has put an end to the people's self-sufficiency. The family pantry now needs cash, which is often obtained via salaried work on coca plantations. The coca economic pattern has driven an increase in working days for all other agricultural activities, provoking inflation. The rural society has been affected by all of these processes as well as the eruption of the consumerist mentality, which is linked to sudden wealth and which ignores factors that make up the Andean culture. The closer you get to the cocaine production centers, the more socio-cultural and socio-economic changes can be seen.

With respect to urban zones, the biggest problems lie in the political and business spheres. The business philosophy has been infected. Now, high-profit or speculative activities are the only stimulus for investment. Investments in fixed capital, finance or human preparation seem less worthwhile, although in fact they are required for long-term stability and growth.

The coca/cocaine cycle and financial conversion have generated a large underground economy which does not contribute taxes to support the general welfare, and it implies unstable and unequal services and activities (besides the criminal). Few legal companies are established with coca dollars. Narco-traffickers prefer to invest in legal companies of long standing, that is, companies in developed countries, once the narco-dollars have been recycled. Thus, currency flow from the black market prevents the development of a rational economic policy.

All of this influences politics and politicians in countries with weak democracies, fragile state apparatuses, inadequate State judicial systems and a history of human rights violations. The coca/cocaine process and the fight against drugs are both undermining what little progress had been made for democratization in the past decade.

Through social and economic interdependence, narco-traffickers use broad sectors of the nation, including the lower levels (which benefits from their good deeds, partly because they benefit from the massive employment as security forces), the middle class (the myriads of commercial and service companies, the generalized economic and employment activation), and the high society, which has maintained an ambivalent attitude toward the *nouveaux riches* ranging from complete rejection (in the traditional organizations/institutions and most firmly demonstrated in the extradition treaty signed between the Colombian and US governments), to collusion in mutual businesses and national financial systems.

In Colombia, violence in narco-trafficking has resulted from a society and culture of violence that are the product of a weak State. Narco-trafficking is not a hierarchical and monopolistic organization. It is a lifestyle offering different ways to participate. The economic power of the traffickers grew quickly, which meant they could make hefty investments in the country and that created a growing social labor market seeking recognition and respectability. This fed the drug barons' desire to invest in land. In the past few years, 3,000,000 hectares have passed into the hands of narco-owners.[94]

The need for protection and to join the system led to the conquest of the entire society and the political power, which was accomplished through direct control (blackmail, intimidation, buying the media, political pressure) and indirect control (submission or abstention).

---

94. Vargas, Ricardo, "Colombia: la herejía de los maniqueos," in VVAA, *Guerra antidrogas*, see bibliography.

A large part of the political class is affected by the "law of the two metals:" silver and lead. Peru and Bolivia do not have large criminal organizations, but are administrators of local offices for Colombian and Mexican cartels. The penetration into political spheres there is slow, and is manifested largely through buying favors and governmental collusion. They are both distanced from the violent systems of Colombia.

In both Peru and Bolivia there has been a considerable increase of corruption in the army and the police, because of the incorporation of the State security forces into the war on drugs, which has given them control over extensive zones (for Peru, to control the Shining Path and for Bolivia, to control coca leaf production in rural zones with a strong union influence). Services rendered are paid generously and corruption has spread overwhelmingly in these sectors. But the paradigm of violence and political complexity, aggravated by the war on drugs and the spread of narco-trafficking, is seen mostly in Colombia, and is not only a problem of the guerrilla forces, but mainly a problem of paramilitaries. Both sectors overlap in narco-trafficking as well as in the war on drugs, and constitute a new chapter in the low-intensity war.

In conclusion, illegal trafficking in drugs took off after US prohibition was implemented in the early 20th century. It is an open process which large social, economic and political sectors of the Andean countries have joined. The coca/cocaine economic cycle, including production and processing, distribution and consumption, as a real, daily problem, and it brings together the two sectors of the production/consumption equation which are paradigmatically centered in the US and Latin America. The need to understand US anti-drug policies and their specific target of Latin America emphasizes their historical relations. They show how the war on drugs gained a prominent position in the era of globalization and interdependence, and how the paradigm of containing narco-trafficking adapted to and substituted the paradigm of containing communism (as a privileged form of relations between the US and the rest of the hemisphere), which demonstrates key issues and points to alternative directions and policies for the future.

CHAPTER IV. US–LATIN AMERICAN RELATIONS

Renewed US attention to Latin America, motivated by drugs, led to colder relations between the two regions. Absent the heavy hand from Washington, which was felt off and on throughout the last century and more, the region enjoyed a period of relative autonomy in the 1970s. The US fight against South American drugs is essentially equated to a fight against communism (personified by the Marxist guerillas). The North/South confrontation paradigm goes back to the rivalry between the empires of England, Spain and Portugal, and after the colonies became independent it continued as a complex set of international relations where the mutual benefits of exchange flows (economic, demographic, environmental) were tempered by the fact that the North, which was stronger, had a goal of obtaining economic and political dominance.

Given the alternating seasons of close relations and distancing, cooperation and rivalry, it is necessary to consider relations between the US and its southern neighbors in a historical context to determine to what degree the war on drugs, and in particular the war on cocaine, is truly intended to limit drug consumption, motivated by a concern for the harms of drug use, or is one in a series of political, economic or military mechanisms designed to effectively gain control of Latin America. The US had enjoyed a certain hegemony in the region, until the 1970s crisis, and could be expected to seek to regain that advantage. The war on drugs would be an effective and very useful doctrine for the continuity of asymmetric relations marked by the domination of the great power and capital.[95]

1.   HISTORICAL RELATIONS

US/Latin America relations are not continuous or homogenous. The perception and importance of Latin America for the US has varied over time, and the US position in foreign relations with the diverse Latin American countries demonstrates the lack of harmony. In addition to lack of continuity, there are unequal perceptions, going from times of interest and rapprochement to others of distance and disdain. Within this instability there were attempts at, and searches for, diplomatic doctrines and strategies favoring relations and defending US interests, its political idiosyncrasies and its particular form of civilization, in an area where it feels it has a special interest and has or should have special rights.[96]

The US "zone of influence" was already pre-figured in the early 19th century with the unilateral Monroe Doctrine declarations.[97] But the US did not actually act upon this assumption of influence until recent decades, when it uses technological advances and "interpenetration" to merge two very different and quite separate geographic and political spaces: North America (which we might consider to extend from Alaska to Panama, including in this context the Caribbean basin, which has traditionally been considered vital to

---

95. US/Latin American relations are based on an asymmetry compensated by hegemonic power. According to a Chilean political scientist, "hegemony in a determined area is characterized by the existence of a combination of power and consensus which varies in its mutual balance, but power never exceeds consensus." Van Klaveren, Alberto, "La crisis de la hegemonía norteamericana" in *Cuadernos semestrales*, number 8, CIDE, p. 108, 1980. This is fundamental when seeking a doctrine guaranteeing hegemony.

96. Drekonja and others, *Teoría y práctica de la política exterior latinoamericana*, CEREC, Bogota, 1983.

97. President Monroe's speech (1823) warned the European powers of the Holy Alliance which, after Napolean's fall and the restoration of absolutism, were not keen on intervening in the new Latin American countries. This unilateral declaration marked the US zone of influence over the entire continent and would be used from 1840 on to justify US territorial expansion.

maintaining US power and hegemony), and South America (from Panama south, an area that has been considered more marginal, a sub-region of Latin America that has enjoyed less attention from the US and less interest, thus less manipulation to gain influence.[98]

Faced with insistence from the US on hemispheric control (of which many Latinos feel the war on drugs is just one more ploy), a close analysis of the history of American relations and US expansionism — which has been characteristic since it declared independence, or before — is needed.

Up to World War II: Expansionism, Imperialism and Hegemonic Power

The traditional US vision of relations with Latin America is based on its own view that the Western hemisphere is the pillar of US foreign policy. The presumption that the entire North and South continents should conform to US desires, even to the detriment of local interests, and that all the Americas should be natural allies of the US, accompanied the expansion of trade relations and the defense of anything that could foster these "natural" relations.

This hemispheric vocation began after the Independence of the thirteen colonies, when their basic foreign policy principles were established. From the first settlements on American soil, an expansionist attitude has been persistent.

The consolidation of the new nation, preservation of its vital space and independence were maintained largely via isolationism throughout the 19th century. The conquest of the West, that is, the territories west of the early colonies, all the way to California, came about through the highly advantageous purchase of Louisiana from the French, and by annexations and war at the expense of the former

---

98. Portales, Carlos, "Sudamérica: seguridad regional y relaciones con EEUU," in *Estudios internacionales*, Santiago de Chile, July — September 1986. Cf. Cline, R.S., *World Power Trends and US Foreign Policy for the 1980s*, 1980; and Maira, Luis, *Los intereses políticos y estratégicos de EEUU en América Latina del Sur*, working papers South American Peace Commission, p. 45, Santiago de Chile, 1988.

Spanish possessions (1845–1848). The US won half of Mexico's territory (including Texas, New Mexico, Arizona, parts of Colorado, and California). This annexation was a determining factor in future relations between the neighbors, and in Mexico's distant and haughty attitude as it attempted to salvage its independence and avoid legitimizing the expansionist Monroe Doctrine.[99] Today, the NAFTA Free Trade Zone has had to overcome many patriotic obstacles, among them the Mexican army's traditionally anti-US position. Narco-trafficking and the war on drugs have proven particularly useful for molding opinion and bringing along the desired cooperation.

In addition to territorial expansion at the expense of the Mexicans, an accelerated industrial, urban and financial development was proposed, with naturally high demographic growth from massive European migrations. US interventionism during this period was mainly centered on Central America and the Caribbean. The US attempted to avoid instability, which would invite European intervention; in effect, this meant the US intervened itself in the domestic affairs of the small Caribbean and Central American states. Thus the United States supplanted Great Britain in its position as hegemonic power in Central America and the Caribbean, as well as inheriting its imperialistic expansionism as illustrated by the Spanish-American War. Theodore Roosevelt's motto, "Speak softly and carry a big stick," was his equivalent to the Monroe Doctrine, and he used that style in establishing the Cuban protectorate and many other interventions in Central America and the Caribbean.

In South America, mainly the southern countries, European influence remained much greater than Washington's and was more "civilized." Those countries saw the US as an annexing power, laying the foundations for subsequent anti-American sentiments, especially after 1898. This was when Washington encouraged Panamericanism (1890–1920) to compensate for British influence on Argentina and the

---

99. Van Klaveren, Alberto, "El lugar de Estados Unidos en la política exterior latinoamericana," 1983. See Drekonja and others.

Southern Cone. The strengthening of hemispheric relations not only alienated the Europeans, it also paved the way for the defense of US interests and the expansion of its markets. US economic influence and investments were increasing throughout the region. It also formed the basis of post-World War I relations and the Wilsonian presumption of exporting US democracy.

The benevolent, good-neighbor attitude of the Franklin Roosevelt administration from the 1930s on was framed in a global vision of US influence as a great power facing pre-war conditions taking shape in Europe. It continued along the lines of hegemonic preeminence drawn by President Woodrow Wilson.

The gestures for peaceful co-existence and the political and economic spirit of compromise demonstrated by the US during the good-neighbor period were complemented by the automatic alignment and economic and strategic support of almost all of Latin America during World War II. Thus was strengthened the whole network of inter-American relations, essential for the future of the hemispheric system, especially since a constant Latin American demand was agreed to in the Montevideo Conference (1933): the declaration of non-intervention as a cornerstone in the inter-American system.[100]

US/Latin American relations up to World War II could be summarized as a long period during which the hegemonic nation settled into its closest zone of influence, to culminate in hemispheric dominance after the war.

---

100. Cuba regained sovereignty through the repeal of the Platt Amendment legitimizing the Protectorate; Panama was completely independent as the US renounced claims to intervene in its domestic affairs; relations with Mexico were strengthened based on tolerance for the nationalization of oil and thanks to the commercial support by law of the mutual trade agreement (1934) and the creation of the Export-Import Bank (1934). Military personnel withdrew from the area. The right to the free political determination of the Latin American people was recognized, allowing the Popular Front in Chile. Kryzanek, Michael J., *Estratégias políticas de EE UU en América Latina*, Gel, Buenos Aires, 1987; and Maira, L., op. cit., Para la consolidación de las relaciones interamericanas, Van Klaveren, op. cit. p. 127, 1983.

From World War II to the Crisis of Hegemony

a)   Stability and Globalism

At the end of the war the monopoly on atomic power and the formation of new international institutions served the hegemonic purposes of the first power. In a short time it assumed world leadership and spread its own particular civilizing vision over the western zone of influence (the "free world"). It also established political, military and socio-economic alliances against its ideological rival, the USSR. Soviet socialism soon achieved greater status as a military rival when it became privy to the nuclear secret. Thus was begun the stage (1945–1960) in which competition was the rule in the ideological, economic and military relations of the two great powers. Latin America would remain linked to the US through the inter-American system (the Organization of American States — OAS — and the Pact of Río, or Inter-American Treaty of Reciprocal Assistance), which served the great power in developing its policies throughout the region. However, differences would soon begin to arise, stemming from demonstrated US disdain for the region. In addition to the nearly clientelist relations, lack of interest in the particular problems of the Southern countries was evident.

The impossibility of an atomic or even a conventional war led the confrontation to the ideological plane, key to the Cold War. In Latin America and the Caribbean this meant a confrontation between two concepts of civilization: communism and democracy. The US "automatic mechanism" of response to attempts of the most autonomous countries, such as Argentina and to a certain degree, Chile and Brazil,[101] speaks to the impossibility of developing partially independent policies because of inflexibility bordering on dogmatism. This "impeded a correct reading of the internal processes in Latin

---

101. Argentina, the South American counterpoint to US's historically hegemonic tendencies, broke relations with the Axis late in the war in 1944, and maintained neutrality almost until the end; Chile also attempted to resist US pressures and Brazil, before courageously supporting the US, pragmatically used pre-war rivalries. Drekonja, op. cit., p. 6, 1983; and Van Klaveren, op. cit., 1983.

America in light of its own internal specificity."[102] It also speaks to the homogenous relations characterized by stability. Latin America was considered a monolithic bloc and its international support was considered natural and guaranteed. In light of subsequent revolutionary events, we can interpret this as a period of incontestable US hegemony when political, economic and social relations demonstrated the traditionalism of the Latin American society. Most countries were governed by oligarchies, the epitome of domination which, by maintaining order and developing limitless private enterprise, guaranteed the stability needed for the capitalist system and US companies.

b) The Cuban Revolution and the Search for Policies on Latin America

The eruption of the Cuban Revolution and the series of events seeking autonomy from the US, which spread across the entire region, highlight the tensions inherent in the unfettered capitalist economic model applied to a region with little democratic progress or social conquests. After the Cuban Revolution, the US not only tried to lay siege to the Castro regime, it also attempted to prevent other countries from emulating his example; it intensified its attention to the region. From then until now, the US had been debating its design of a reasonable and useful policy on Latin America. It is trying to find the basis of lasting and harmonious policies that will guarantee US security and access to resources and markets. Of course, to this effect the US wants principles of the free market and, in some ways, democratic processes, to be adopted by Latin America.[103]

Immediately after the Second World War, the US implemented a global focus; but after the Cuban challenge, a regional rapprochement

---

102. Rojas and solís, *¿Súbditos o aliados? La política exterior de EEUU y Centroamérica*, FLACSO, Costa Rica, p. 23, 1988; and Lowenthal, Abraham, *Partners in Conflict. The United States and Latin America*, John Hopkins University Press, Baltimore and London, 1987.

103. Ianni, Octavio. "Diplomacia e imperialismo en las relaciones interamericanas" in Maira, L., ed. *¿Una nueva hegemonía norteamericana?*, pp. 35 — 66, 1985. Ianni grants fundamental importance to the search for this "doctrine," which harmonizes relations and thus the political and strategic importance of the current policy supporting the "fight against drugs" for the US

was attempted. This was more in accordance with the real long neglected need for economic progress and political reform.

Thus was inaugurated a series of integrated policies within the framework of the Alliance for Progress, an attempt to respond to internal changes in Latin America by reforming and modernizing, and by minimizing the development of leftist or subversive movements. Both tasks implied direct US participation in all types of domestic affairs, which intensified nationalist reactions. In the end, the US was able to reinforce and extend its dominance over Latin America by calling for democracy and development with the Alliance for Progress, in many cases assuring advantages for a wide variety of interests. The Marxist writer Octavio Ianni sees the Alliance for Progress as a counter-revolutionary operation combining reformist language with counter-reform policies, similar to the tough Doctrine for National Security which prolonged World War II to contemporary times by taking the ideological confrontation inside nations. US historian Joseph Tulchin sees the Alliance for Progress as the double dimension (Latin America/US) of hemispheric security, which took up issues of security and economics. However, the failure of that determination and the contradictions between economic reformism and orthodox policies indicate that such approaches under the scheme of ideological confrontation were not ideal for solving the problems.[104] The decadence of the Alliance for Progress came from its contradictory framework and its emphasis on security issues. From the missile crisis and USSR aggression in the Third World, idealism supporting democracy was definitively abandoned and a doctrine of counter-insurgency was shaped as a way of stopping Castro's offensive and preventing communism from taking hold throughout the Third World. Multidimensional rapprochement was attained with help from the CIA, the FBI, police training and US AID.

---

104. Ianni, O., op. cit., p. 38, 1985; and Tulchin, Joseph S., "The United States and Latin America in the 1960s," in *Journal of Interamerican Studies*, p. 30, "1, pp. 1 — 36, Spring, University of Miami, Florida, 1988.

All of this created great confusion in policies on Latin America. In country after country, military counselors defended the "free world" via the doctrine of counter-insurgency, and at the same time, the State Department was busily seeking to implement structural reforms. Both groups clashed and ended up implicating themselves in the intrigues of civil wars,[105] just as in the war on drugs.

During the Johnson Administration (1963–1969), the spirit of the Alliance was completely forgotten. Seeking effectiveness in many issues, it advocated pragmatism and neutralism with respect to non-democratic regimes, and strengthening favorable conditions for US companies through the Mann Doctrine.[106] After the invasion of the Dominican Republic and the failed invasion of Cuba, Latin America wanted nothing to do with US rapprochement, and even less so within the OAS, which was considered a US tool. The Dominican invasion and Latin American rejection frustrated US intentions to create a military force within the inter-American system, further distancing aspirations for harmonious relations between the US and its neighbors.

In 1958, Latin America returned to its position of low priority on the US agenda. Events in Asia, the Korean and Vietnam Wars captured the attention of the US. By comparison, Latin America was insignificant for US strategy. This was a period when Latin America began to concentrate on independence in international relations and economic development, which could be pursued best when the US lost influence and its hegemony was weakened — and which, if

---

105. US intervention in Guatemala (1954) was organized by the CIA without the State Department; the latter was more inclined to a multilateral solution with other OAS countries. Kurth, James R., "The Rise and Decline of the Inter-American System: a US View," in Bloomfield, R.J., ed., *Alternative to Intervention; A New US — Latin American Security relationship*, p. 19, World Peace Foundation Study, Lynne Rienner Publishers, 1990.

106. The so-called "Mann Doctrine" (1964), named for Assistant Secretary of State Thomas Mann, called for a US approach to Latin America including:

1) promotion of economic development with absolute neutrality on questions of social reform; 2) protection of US private investments; 3) display of no preference, through aid or other means, for representative democratic institutions; 4) opposition to communism. Within two weeks, the US-backed coup took place in Brazil. University of Oregon website, at *http://dark-wing.uoregon.edu/~caguirre/483_11a.html* (March 2004).

successful, would further weaken US influence and control in the region.

The invalidity of regional schemes: globalism and third worldism

After the failure of the Alliance for Progress, uncertainty led the great power to share its economic and political preeminence with other nations, going from a bipolar system to a more multipolar approach, where the watchword was détente. The post-war lack of balance on the global scene signaled the end of the post-war order. Japanese and European reconstruction and the de-colonization of the Third World complicated the international scene and curtailed some of the former hegemonic power's perceived opportunities. The process of de-colonization introduced new actors with diverse nationalist claims in international relations. Added to this was the increasingly defiant attitude of most Latin American countries. The insecurity generated by the US in its Latin American neighbors and its concentration on the Asian southeast led most countries in the region to diversify their foreign policies and call on national pride, often marked by anti-Americanism. Hence they obtained autonomy from the US. The Cuban Revolution was the intellectual basis for the future, the impetus for effective attempts at regional autonomy, with results on the national and international scene and on the international system and its organizations.[107]

When confronted with problems posed by the nationalism of developing countries, the US bet on "globalism" as its tool for maintaining the upper hand. It classified Latin America as a homogenous space where it must gain (or regain) territory that had come to sympathize with the Soviet Union. US policy toward the Third World was an extension of the Truman Doctrine to contain communism by use of overwhelming force[108] and test cases like Chile were planned to serve as examples.

The entropy of Third World nationalism and the transition from the bipolar to the more open system whereby the US shared its power opened a space for talking about the hegemonic crisis. Over time, this devolved into nothing more than the great power getting used to the new international reality, characterized by the search for political and diplomatic doctrines to deal with international problems posed by an aggressively anti-American Third World. As a result, all the policies of those years — Low Profile, Most Favored Nation Status, Middle Status Powers — were US attempts to implement a broad restructuring of international activity so as to retain as much advantage as it could over as much of the globe as possible.

Surgical operations (a combination of negotiations and harsh actions like those undertaken in Chile) and alliances with relatively moderate governments were used in the hemispheric rhetoric of inter-American institutions. Despite all the indications in the 1960s that seemed to grant Latin America autonomy were clouded over by the US recovery of hegemony. The apparent steps forward in Latin America of the 1960s and 1970s were made possible only by the lack of interest from the US, because it was occupied with the Vietnam War. After the oil crisis in the 1970s, US priorities shifted again.

---

107. Jamaica (M. Manley: center-left government with control over US mining companies); nationalist military governments in Bolivia, Peru (diversifying their weapons sources), Ecuador (maritime sovereignty) and Venezuela (nationalization of oil); Uruguay, left (Frente Amplio); Chile, 1970: Unidad Popular (transition to socialism and the nationalization of copper). The Brazilian military maintained political autonomy in foreign relations (nuclear energy exchange with Germany) and independent relations with African countries.

Intellectual forums on Latin American autonomy were founded: The Colegio de México (1959) and the journal *Foro internacional* (1960); in Brazil, the ISEB (Instituto Superior de Estudios Brasileños) and international relations were extended by Itamaraty; in Chile, the Instituto de Estudios Internacionales (1967) and *Estudios internacionales*, inaugurating with Gabriel Valdés a second generation of Latin American foreign policy that would follow the steps begun by the first Economic Commission for Latin America (CEPAL) school of Raúl Prebisch.

Organizations: Venezuela encouraged the creation of OPEP; Argentina, Peronist Gaullism; Chile and Venezuela tried to associate the negotiating capacity of the Latin American States with the inter-American system; the creation of CECLA, or the Special Commission for the Coordination of Latin America in the UNCTAD; put by the Chileans at the service of foreign policy to manage the Consensus of Viña del Mar (a collective memo of aggressions to Nixon) in 1969, and the Buenos Aires Letter to Europe which proposed a special relationship; the Andean Group developed extensive activity encouraging foreign policy with common economic accords; Mexico (1968), the international activity of Echeverría: Carta de los Deberes y Derechos Económicos de los Estados; the UN General Assembly (1974); and Panama, the re-thinking of the Canal Treaties (1977).

108. And without concern for the means, using all legal and illegal processes, including financing and arming counter-revolutionary groups in the Dirty War, arms trafficking and, of course, drug trafficking, all coordinated by the secret services or the CIA.

Preaching globalism to the Third World and scant concern for developments in Latin America gave way to an increasing engagement. This concern remained superficial, in word, but during the Carter administration it changed when human rights rhetoric began to be relevant to the North/South confrontation. Then it became evident what real processes were driving important US initiatives in US/Latin American relations. The anti-communist dictatorships (bureaucratic/authoritarian systems), which in the 1970s came to power in countries that were active in what has come to be called economic nationalism, resulted from the policy of control and security which the US supported. The Alliance for Progress emphasized control of subversion in spite of its contradictory reformist attempts. Thus, even with the region's attempts at autonomy in the 1960s, it is obvious that by ripple effect the political consequences of the Alliance for Progress and the doctrine of National Security for Latin America could be seen in the strengthening of the military and repressive sectors and the implementation of authoritarian systems.

Likewise, progressive and fragile democratization culminating in the 1980s was the result of the distancing, and of Carter's human rights policies of withholding military programs in countries with human rights violations. It could be said that the drugs issue also became a crucial political issue in the region precisely when the US government made it so, since it was an important part of the conservative recipe before the crisis of the 1970s. This decision, again by ripple effect, resulted in the explosion of police corruption (which became so common since Prohibition in the US) when dealing with drugs issues, extending throughout Latin America. Structural conditions all favored the spread and globalization of corruption alongside the updating of the Doctrine of National Security for the fight against drugs.

2.   THE CRISIS OF THE 1970S

The capitalism crisis at the end of the 1960s affected the US in a special way. Thanks to widespread national support begun by Roosevelt, the country had become the first indisputable world power, which allowed Americans to enjoy increasing progress and well-being. Then, the prolonged post-war prosperity and the historical New Deal began to show signs of exhaustion. The US, which had allowed and encouraged the economic reconstruction of its rivals, now carried the weight of a large share of the capitalist bloc though it was no longer the only indisputable economic or political power. The political construction of the imperial presidency, so efficient in those years, showed its limits when faced with new challenges. In the same way, the political system created in the 18th century based on checks and balances, intended to retrain abuses of power, was now obsolete, given technological progress and the strength of the executive.

The crisis at the end of the 1960s highlighted the system's ability to renew itself, adapt to new circumstances and continue to function efficiently. The Chilean historian Luis Maira believes the Kennedy political project of the New Frontier and the Alliance for Progress would have proven to be big problems, but US historians Lowenthal and Tulchin believe they were serious but contradictory attempts that would have had less effect: given the brevity of the Kennedy administration and the obstacles which arose during the Johnson administration, the latter and the subsequent Nixon, Ford and Carter administrations were mere administrators of the crisis. Some historians see that crisis as structural, while for others it was global, affecting the US because of the relative modification of its international position[109] (interpreted by Secretary of State Kissinger as a relative loss of hegemony since it would never again attain the

---

109. Structural Crisis: Maira, Luis and Borón, Atilio in Maira, Luis, ed., *EEUU. Una visión latinoamericana*, 524 pages, Fondo de Cultura Económica, Mexico, 1984. Global crisis: Rico, Carlos and Bitar, Sergio, in Maira, Luis, ed., *¿Una nueva era de hegemonía norteamericana?*, Rial, Gel, Buenos Aires, 1985; y Lowenthal, Abraham, op. cit., 1987.

margins of absolute power it had enjoyed in the years immediately following the war).

Whatever the case may be, many complications completed the picture. A new national project was needed in order to solve the problem. The neo-conservative proposal was a reaction to a critical moment.

The political crisis raised questions about institutional legitimacy and demonstrated a lack of confidence in the nation's democratic institutions, starting with the indirect presidential elections (which negate the very essence of democracy, in part because of the extremely high rate of abstention — the president can win with 27% of the 50% who have voted) and the lobbying system, which included more than 13,000 regulated lobbies representing different (fundamentally economic) pressure groups. The fact that the parties themselves cannot express social concerns and have become merely coordination offices to develop publicity campaigns simplifies political discussion to a crude, primary level, and distances it from university research and specialized media.

The problems of political structure coincided with or were reflected in the watershed events of the 1970s: university student rebellions, anti-Vietnam War protests, radical ethnic minorities and the Watergate affair, which epitomized the government's functional problems and, in the end, became an issue of legitimacy.

An economic crisis was superimposed on the political crisis, aggravating the nation's social situation. In addition to the 1971 monetary crisis there was the deep and long recession that lasted the entire decade. Economic policy-makers were unable to solve the problem with theoretical recipes: the fiscal deficit grew substantially, unemployment sky-rocketed, American products lacked drive before the foreign competition — even in domestic markets, and the vulnerability of energy and monetary policies became evident.

To top it off, the loss of international hegemony aggravated the generalized crisis. Failure in Vietnam was a historic trauma that brought with it substantial loss in global credibility. The great power could not control the situation and had to solve problems as they appeared. Political bipolarity turned to multi-polarity and the military confrontation between the United States and the Soviet Union remained. Many problems arose in the early 1960s with the "challenge" of the developing countries, begun by Cuba's emblematic revolution. Furthermore, de-colonization in Africa and Asia allowed many developing countries to unify, in groups such as the Non-Allied Movement and the Group of 77, which made up a stable majority in the UN and became critical obstacles to Western and specifically US-led action.

For Secretary of State Henry Kissinger, the decrease in US economic and military power margins was just one manifestation of a certain decline in imperial abilities, which he felt good political manipulation could delay or guide in less damaging directions. Presidents Ford and Carter were but administrators; their decisions in international politics no longer reflected initiatives, but responses or reactions to the tensions encountered as events unfolded, from defeat in southeast Asia and socialist experiments in former Portuguese colonies to the revolutionary movements loosed in important strategic zones; from the Sandinista revolution in Washington's own backyard (which was ironically initially supported by the US) to the defeat of the Shah of Iran and the shameful embassy crisis there, and even the strengthening of Palestine radicalism with respect to the West.

Though the crisis had many shades and was transitory (global power structures remained untouched), a bitter aftertaste remained. There was a tremendous lack of confidence domestically and credibility internationally, and the country had undergone repeated humiliation — the most fertile breeding ground for new patriotism.

This boosted the neo-conservative ideology and the Republican Party. Among other changes, the Republicans again took up the rhetoric of morality and began the crusade against drugs as a symbol of the conservative revolution. President George H. W. Bush demonstrated the minimal political and geo-strategic worth of this crusade which, like other political doctrines applied to Latin American relations, turned out to include concepts of security and economics and which was designed so as to enable the great power to recover hegemony in the area.

3. SECURITY AND DEVELOPMENT IN INTER-AMERICAN RELATIONS

The inter-American system structuring US/Latin American relations was based primarily on security and economic development, and a series of components which would become part of the "hemispheric rhetoric." The inter-American system (the Organization of American States and many military pacts) established after World War II illustrates the power schemes of that time and conditioned the perceptions of security on both sides.

For Americans, "security" means certain protection from a domestic or foreign attack, protection of the main means of communication, protection and security of raw materials supply and protection from attack by an American country allied with a non-American force. "Security" in Latin America, besides the classic notions of continuity and territorial defense, means political security: independence in its political and socio-economic development and internal affairs with no foreign interference.

The problem is that the US has automatically linked leftist reformism to a security threat (i.e., the external, hostile socialist alliance). For the US, joint projects (security and economic or political reforms) have been based on the need to accompany and complete military rapprochement with a socio-economic component to make it more palatable; when the geo-political threat disappeared, the socio-economic programs were also cut.[110]

Latin Americans consider the ideas on which the inter-American security system are based as myth, because the whole system is a big part of the rhetorical relations between the US and its southern neighbors. Using the myth of a "hemispheric community," the US has defended its own vision of the inter-American system by delimitating a zone of influence allowing the intervention in and protection of its interests in the rest of the continent. The completely different Latin American concept of the system leads to a sort of schizophrenia.

Latin Americans see the inter-American system as a way of defending themselves and avoiding the more dangerous effects of the Monroe Doctrine[111] by invoking the principle of non-intervention, for them fundamental to the system and, for the US, not very important since it has constantly violated it.

Security in US terms is based on excluding any European power as upsetting the balance of domination over the southern area, and supposing a potential threat to transport and communications via the Caribbean. Latin American rationale is different. They view the European counterweight as essential in balancing the North American weight.

Thus hemispheric rhetoric, reverting to the community of interests, lifestyle and value systems, has remained to this day, but with a clear imbalance since the US subrogated leadership. There is no equality among partners: the power is clearly unequal. Security for the US has been translated into incontestable hegemony over the entire region and interventionism in any countries that manifest serious reformist movements (Guatemala, 1954; Santo Domingo, 1965; Chile, 1973; Granada, 1981; Nicaragua, 1979). The US has been unwavering in every case; social and political movements attempting to remove legitimate government structures generally come from outside.

---

110. Alliance for Progress (1961); Caribbean Basin Initiative (1982); Kissinger Proposal for Central America (1984). Muñoz, Heraldo, *Agenda de seguridad en las políticas externas sudamericans*, doc. Number 5, Comisón Sudamericana de Paz, Santiago de Chile, 1988. These programs were more fleeting when defeating a certain government by force (for example, in Nicaragua after the 1990 victory in Chamorro, the US had no political program or any policy designed for the country after the elections where it did everything possible to defeat the Marxist Sandinista regime).

111. In 1823, President James Monroe presented to Congress a statement crystallizing the position (first proposed by his Vice President John Quincy Adams) that the United States would not interfere in European wars or internal affairs, and expected Europe to stay out of American affairs. In effect, this was an assertion of a certain degree of control in the region.

The continuity of the Cuban-Soviet connection served to automatically label any serious reformist movement as part of the international communist movement, thereby provoking international activism, and political and economic mobilization. US public opinion also participated by stopping or sabotaging these attempts or interfering directly. Thus was developed the phenomenon of self-fulfilling prophecies because Americans liked nothing more than political stability, the status quo and formal democracy, but for Latin Americans democracy structural reform would have to come first.

Security and development, hemispheric rhetoric and equality among unequal partners. Constants in the inter-American system, these values were weakened over time by the US, which uses them for the purposes of hegemony, and by Latin American martyr-syndromes. They considered the OAS as a US tool which, just when Latin American seemed to have regained some independence, was not valued by the US. The US saw it as the forum for bitter protests by the Latin Americans.[112]

Currently the war on drugs, and in particular the war on cocaine, has been so useful and effective for the great power because it has used the inter-American system. Thus the inter-American system is still a mechanism for the transmission and application of US political and military initiatives, just as it was in the 1950s and 1960s.

In the 1950s, Latin American nations conformed to the conditions set by its "big brother" to the north on the ideological, political, military-strategic, economic and social planes, and the inter-American system was located in a rigid politico-military apparatus established to limit the expansion of communism. In the 1960s, the Cuban Revolution forced a rapprochement in expectations and did away with prior security set-ups. The Alliance for Progress, a shock from the revolutionary movements, included important economic rapprochement, though in the end it too turned out to be a tool for intervention in Latin American internal affairs.

---

112. Van Klaveren, Alberto, "The United States and the Inter-American Poltiical System," in Wesson, R. and Muñoz, H., eds., *Latin American Views of US Policy*, Stanford University, 1986.

It is very important to know the role Latin American armies played in the first Doctrine of National Security (containing domestic communism and subversion) and the current one (containing narco-trafficking and narco-terrorism), and how military accords which had "considerable importance on the external orientation of the armies and their policy and strategic concept" came to be signed.[113] Indeed, how was the inter-American military system developed?

"The period was characterized by a substantial increase in hemispheric military cooperation when the traditional system, originally designed to repel a foreign attack, was restructured to show opposition to the domestic processes of the guerrilla ,and to participate in development projects that prevented the rise of revolutionary forces."[114] The inter-American system began to support many institutions, which strengthened armies by complementing bilateral pacts for mutual aid in the 1950s. It systematized counter-revolutionary training, encouraged the elaboration of the Doctrine for National Security, established the Central American Defense Council with periodic meetings, and set up close relations and communications between US and Latin American armies, which shared maneuvers and exercises. The accords and institutions redefined "the role of armies in Latin American policies, which had a substantial influence on the development of Doctrines of National Security adopted by the new authoritarian regimes in the mid-1960s." Thus the Alliance for Progress effectively contributed to making the Latin American military corps into anti-democratic institutions, and to forming the first regional anti-Communist army, which debuted by invading the Dominican Republic (1965).

While the US was occupied with Vietnam, Latin American countries enjoyed a period of peripheral autonomy with more autarchic national policies, some reforms to the inter-American system and greater military independence. They diversified arms

---

113. Van Klaveren. See bibliography page 128, 1983.
114. Van Klaveren. See bibliography page 26, 1986.

supply, developed national war industries, decreased technological dependence on the US and developed new strategic concepts.

According to Lowenthal, "the US government level of activity in the Western hemisphere fell dramatically in the mid-1960s when it reached its peak. Foreign aid and diplomatic personnel were sharply reduced in the 1970s. Economic assistance in bilateral aid to Latin America went from 77% in 1970 to 30% in 1980. The majority of assistance in 1980 was concentrated on the Caribbean basin. The number of military advisors in Latin America fell from more than 800 in 1968 to little more than 100 in 1980. Renewed military aid from 1980 was strictly limited to the Caribbean basin."[115] The diminishing US influence on the military, economic and political plane was due to the deliberate low profile policy, the nationalist reformism of some governments and the changes in rightwing dictatorial regimes. This came about because several countries refused military aid (Guatemala & Brazil–1977) and military cooperation programs (Chile and Uruguay–1976; Argentina, Nicaragua & El Salvador–1978).

The Nixon administration delegated the economic issue to the private sector, disconnecting it from security issues. The appropriate framework for US investments was created with no thought or scruples about the political regime. Together with the ideological monolithic view and the Doctrine of National Security, this led to the creation of bureaucratic-authoritarian regimes which systematized repression.

When ideal conditions for private capital were created, massive investments flowed, but outside political considerations of security and diplomacy, and serious problems like the debt issue, were

---

115. Narco-trafficking and the war on drugs have substantially changed US presence in the hemisphere, and especially in South America. Until 1980 the influence of Soviets, Germans, Japanese, French and Spanish in South America increased to the point that though they could not cast doubt on US primacy, they could "substantially weaken the overwhelming presence of Washington in the past." Lowenthal, op. cit., p. 35, 1987. Thus, somehow the war on drugs and the unilateral US vision of the problem has not only allowed the annulment of a great presence of other countries outside the hemisphere, but it has also again extended US dominance and influence, which is why the US, which was without a doubt the biggest external actor, has become an interior force, an actor in full action.

generated. With Carter, the inter-American system was still useful in transmitting the rhetoric of human rights. This compensated for the bad image of the OAS, for a time, among intellectuals and dissidents.

In the 1980s, the lack of the inter-American system was highlighted because it ignored serious issues (debt, the Central American crisis).[116] Both the conflict in Nicaragua and the Falklands Islands demonstrate the uselessness of the OAS. They also show how US security frameworks were imposed and indicate that Latin America had to defend itself against the US and its renewed interventionism. The renewed continuation of the Nicaraguan conflict via the Contras' "deferred intervention" reversed the crisis and complicated other Central American countries. Thence the tasks of *Contadora* and *Esquipulas* with respect to maintaining their concepts of security, attempting to avoid militarization and the spread of the conflict because of Reagan's anti-communist obsession. The Nicaraguan case demonstrates US pragmatism and the rhetoric on the drugs issue. The US used narco-trafficking as a double weapon in Central America to generate resources and to pay the armies.[117]

The inter-American system is now in crisis. The OAS lost legitimacy due to its unilateral use by the US. As far as the rest, there was a certain vigor and independence in judging the different critical moments of the continent, such as in the invasion of Panama (1989) and the coups in Haiti and Peru (1992). The fact that the system failed to address the most serious issues, the fact of the lack of US interest in

---

116. The serious debt problem remains outside the ineffective inter-American system, since the creation of the ad-hoc mechanism in the Cartagena Group. The Central American crisis, provoked by the revitalization of the Cold War framework through the Reagan doctrine, remained outside the OAS because of the independence demonstrated on other occasions (Nicaragua, the Falklands). The US invasion of Granada was legitimized through another Anglo-Caribbean institution, the Organization of Eastern Caribbean States (OECS), while the OAS condemned the intervention and requested the withdrawal of troops.

117. Narco-trafficking was carried out in Honduras with complete freedom from its armed forces because of the participation and support it gave since it was the rearguard in the US war against the Sandinistas. Along with Costa Rica, Nicaragua and Panama, Honduras sheltered 40,000 men from the Contras. Mejía, Thelma, "Honduras: militares y drogas, una relación inconclusa," in Soberón, R., and others, *Crimen uniformado, entre la corrupción y la impunidad*, edited by CEDIB, Cochabamba, Bolivia, 1997, and Zirnite, Peter, "CIA Admits Knowing about Contra Drug Trafficking," *Inter-Press Service*, March 18, 1998, Washington.

active participation, and the position adopted by the Inter-American Commission on the Narco-Trafficking Policy (CICAD, 1991; this was dependent on the OAS and tempered but also revitalized the US interpretation of the narco-trafficking issue[118]) all show that the OAS is inefficient and, in fact, downright useless. They also show that it covers up a much more complex and controversial reality, like the problem of the war on drugs and US/Latin American relations and the US hegemonic re-implantation.

One could say that the new hemispheric security framework has overcome the East/West dichotomy and is now based on a much more subtle perception of security. As Lowenthal notes, "US military security will not be seriously threatened by any direct attack from the Western hemisphere. However, US security in its broadest sense — the ability to protect the individual and collective well-being of its citizens — could be critically influenced by events in Latin America and the Caribbean."

It is within this context of neighboring countries and interdependence that the new security framework is established, corresponding to a North/South counter-position with respect to the differences between the developed and developing countries. Economic crisis and underdevelopment in Latin America are both threats to US security, as are the problems derived from this situation (massive migration, contraband, narco-trafficking, environmental degradation, nuclear and weapons proliferation and fundamentalism, etc.). The inter-American system which was based on three principles (non intervention/collective security, ideological orthodoxy and economic clause) has become unilateral or multilateral/direct or deferred intervention, neo-liberal ideological orthodoxy and the North/South confrontation (development/underdevelopment, westernism/

---

118. This is the agency which has defended the position of "shared responsibility." It really works as a hand of the US: never did it contemplate the possibility of defending the coca leaf or of a critical interpretation of the problem; on the contrary, in 1995 it began to work on the document called *Estrategia para combatir el narcotráfico para el siglo XXI* as an initiative of the US State Department.

nationalism, modernization/radicalization, drug consumption/narco-trafficking, the war on drugs/submission or extradition).

The economic clause again becomes part of the security system within this framework, just enough to validate the other two components but not enough to solve the problems. As long as there is a progressively larger counterpart of economic aid, a certain amount of US intervention is going to be allowed (though with initial protests) by the Latin countries. In the zone of influence (the Caribbean basin, Central America), the drug problem could be solved in critical situations by rapid military operations (such as the unilateral invasion of Panama and covert operations on the Colombian coast and throughout the Caribbean) and by the creation of combined forces backed by the OAS. That could serve as a sort of inter-American Peace Corps; this was foreseen for Panama through the transformation of the Southern Command into a complex web of US military facilities and functions in the region. Then the security threat from the South would be countered by an inspired army led by the US, with the participation of the army of the Americas, a new multilateral force with a concrete task and strategic breadth allowing for the development of low intensity wars.[119]

In South America operations are implemented with the mediation of one of the partners (Bolivia, Peru, Brazil.). The US offers training and logistical, intelligence and arms support to local forces (military or police) to fight drugs, making the principle of non-

---

119. After the return of the Canal and the Military Base to the Panamanians in 2000, the US has attempted to prolong its stay in Panama. The Multilateral Anti Narcotics Center has been harshly criticized by the population and the political class. In light of this controversy, the US has opted to created Operative Centers (FOL) throughout the entire subcontinent, with new military bases in Ecuador, Aruba, Curacao and El Salvador. Puerto Rico has replaced Panama for forward basing headquarters in the region for the Army, Navy and the Special Forces, while SouthCom headquarters itself is located in Miami. John Lindsay-Poland, "US Military Bases in Latin America and the Caribbean," *Foreign Policy in Focus*, Vol. 6, no. 35, October 2001: http://www.fpif.org/briefs/vol6/v6n35milbase_body.html.

intervention the veritable practice of "deferred intervention"[120] —
always with the necessary appearance of the economic clause.

This all forms part of the US war on cocaine waged in the
hemisphere. It is a process of turning the paradigm of containing
communism into the paradigm of the war on drugs, begun during the
Republican administrations of Reagan and Bush as a response to the
hegemonic crisis.

---

120. The difference between the two zones and whether the army would intervene directly
in South America is clearly established in WOLA (Washington Office on Latin America), *"Clear
and present dangers: the US military and the war on drugs in the Andes,"* 1993.

CHAPTER V. THE CONSERVATIVE REVOLUTION

Though the organizations and structures that support illegal drug trafficking had their roots in the Prohibition of the turn of the century, today's narco-trafficking is more a result of the political and military initiative which replaced the defunct fight against communism with the fight against drugs. The Reagan Conservatives proposed the rhetoric of the fight against drugs as a symbol of US moral and political recovery. This was their solution to the 1970s malaise.[121]

1. THE NEO-CONSERVATIVE PROGRAM

Reagan's arrival at the White House ushered in a reactionary program that some tried to call revolutionary. The idea was to re-establish traditional values, including trust in the power of the individual and a recovery of the US reputation for greatness in the world. This ideology was a defensive ideology — a weak response to structural crisis and the exhaustion of the plan which had made the US the most powerful country on the planet. It could only be based on appeals to the

---

121. Maira, Luis, ed. *¿Una nueva era de hegemonía norteamericana?*, 360 pages, Rial Gel, Buenos Aires, 1985.

deepest national symbols — religion, nation and family — in an effort to paper over a real loss of position.

Religion was important. There was a perceived failure of the contemporary culture to provide a strong set of values to shore up the principles that religion once provided. "The Protestant ethic and the Puritan spirit have been corrupted to their very core by abundance and the generalized prosperity caused by the power of US capitalism; in their stead a hedonistic materialism and a rabidly acquisitive value system have installed themselves," proclaimed the Conservative ideologues.[122] This was said to have resulted from the victory (and not the defeat) of the capitalist system, although there is some doubt. Criticism of the political and economic system came to be tarred as irresponsible and unreal. The conservative backlash sought to re-install a protestant ethic that it applied to all social manifestations. Confronted with the moral decadence brought on by abundance, they went on to drug consumption as an expression of boredom.

In fact, it affected economic productivity, as workers were more and more likely to dabble in marijuana or cocaine during business hours. The business-friendly solution encouraged a return to moralism and the "protestant work ethic," the secular form of which boils down to keeping busy with community, sports and family; and a constant flow of rhetoric denouncing drugs. The Republican Party included important theologians and preachers with large national followings. The US decline in prosperity was associated with the reversal of the nation's international influence due to moral decadence, and the abandonment tradition. Religious leaders and parents were united in a movement to give the nation back its confidence in traditional values. The corporations whose advertising pays for most television and radio broadcasting supported the campaign.

---

122. Borón, Atilio A., "La crisis norteamericana y la racionalidad neoconservadora" in Maira, Luis, ed., *EEUUUna visión latinoamericana.* pp. 90 — 123, Fondo de Cultura Económica, México, 1984.

Nation. There is a dramatic diagnosis of the US and the Western or Capitalist world's situation, which mistakes the symptoms of the crisis for the crisis itself. By this reasoning, the solution would be more of the same: strengthen the framework of the established powers, and appeal to patriotism to recover ground lost with the disproportionate growth of competition against a State that was approaching socialism. (In fact, outside of "security" issues, the US tends to paint any public expenditure as near-socialism which is seen as an attack on individuality.) It was confirmed: there was a profound political crisis, loss of legitimacy for democratic regimes and the governing classes, instability and conflict threatening to destroy the legacy of the liberal civilization. And the causes for this concern were sought, but the crisis could not be attributed to serious problems in the US productive structure. The source of the unease could not be in the economy or politics, because that would imply the need for corrective measures, or even a re-thinking of the system. Thus, the problem was determined to be in the culture of universities and state bureaucracy.

The values of the counterculture were disdained and denied, and any nonstandard artistic manifestation was viscerally rejected. "The long-term consequences of the US presence and the disgraceful defeat in Vietnam were not considered in the neo-conservative analyses, nor was the bitter aftertaste of the 1960s social movements or the economic and political legitimacy problems. The only plausible explanation was interpreting the hegemonic crisis as a product of an "enemy" socialist country. The adversary was eminently subversive and contrary to all conventions and routines of the Bourgeois society," Borón explains. The need for national unity, loyalty and discipline was emphasized, to confront responsibilities arising from a world increasingly hostile to US values and interests. This goes perfectly well with the division of the world into two great culture blocs in confrontation. It would favor the recovery of hegemony and Occidentalism and the replacement of the North/South dichotomy as opposed to the East/West of the previous administration.

Family. The fact that the State was overwhelmed with its fatherly duties was the source of its inability to solve its problems. A "counter-revolution of decreasing expectations" was proposed, to lessen the expectations of the population. The system was overburdened and on the brink of collapse, welfare payments had created a subclass "with their infinite housing, employment, poverty, delinquency and social inability to adapt problems," in which "not working" was more attractive than "working."[123] Traditional religious and family values had to be reaffirmed because they were the best instrument devised to date for promoting pious and stoic justifications that would convince the less prosperous to meekly cross that "vale of tears." By restoring confidence in the ethical content of traditional institutions as well as its pragmatism and usefulness in setting up social programs for wellness and charity, they could allow the welfare State to fade into the background. The family and the church took back the task of organizing and administering charity. From then on, many religious institutions took over the establishment of social programs for detoxification and rehabilitation for addicts, as well as caring for HIV/AIDS victims, among other charity missions.

2. THE CRUSADE AGAINST DRUGS

Early in Ronald Reagan's first term as US president, prohibitionist measures were adopted and the war on drugs took shape. This resulted from an environment forged over a long period of time. Then the war on drugs was one more open front of the Cold War, and as such, it was subordinate to it. It was only with the second Reagan administration and the worrisome changes in the socialist world that a veritable political corps for the "war on drugs" was established. This was not only an expression of a deep-rooted traditionalism, but also a highly valuable strategic political option.

---

123. Borón, see bibliography. This subclass was the main consumer of cocaine and crack and the one that Conservative administrations completely marginalized when they drastically cut social spending.

From the time the "crusade" was formed in the early 1980s and following the neo-conservative political framework up to the 1990s when the fight against drugs replaced the Cold War as the major effort to stem the spread of Communism, there were four phases: 1. the proliferation of war rhetoric, 2. formulating the Crusade as a diplomatic and strategic doctrine, 3. replacing the Cold War with the crusade against drugs, and 4. the globalization of the war.

1. Rhetoric (1980– 1984): Symbol of the Conservative Revolution

The rhetoric coincided with Reagan's first administration and it corresponded to the neo-conservative ideology when the concepts of the crusade were established. The conservatives gained power with a strong will for national reconstruction and the recovery of international hegemony. The importance of traditional values in Reagan's proposal was reflected in the beginning of his administration when he was backed by teams with greater ideological weight. In the 1970s, the US prioritized bilateral relations with Latin America, removing various issues from its agenda. The Carter and Reagan administrations denied that there was or should be any special relation between the US and Latin America, or that the latter had any relevant unity in world politics. As the conservatives suggested, countries would have to align themselves according to the two great cultures or life-styles — capitalism or socialism. The East/West confrontation was the basis of US recovery and this was why putting down Central American revolutionary movements and political instability was given top priority over any other foreign policy consideration. Everything was subordinated to the highest priority: fighting communism. This was when narco-trafficking was used — even favored — as another method of intelligence during the Cold War. Cuban exiles who set up the first Miami cocaine networks were now used, supporting the anti-communist guerrilla Golden Triangle, supporting the Nicaraguan Contras by buying cocaine from the Medellín cartel and selling arms via Noriega in Panama and other less well-known cases.[124] All of these operations demonstrate the subordinate position of the anti-drug policy with respect to foreign policy.[125] The focus on drugs was clearly a ruse behind which other struggles were being conducted, and it was a successful ploy not only because of its moralizing nature but also because there were no laws or even firm measures against it. Meanwhile, cocaine use sky-rocketed.[126]

The main public target of renewed morality was the spread of drug use to large sectors of the population and the rebellion and freedom implied by the popular culture. The propaganda apparatus developed an extensive anti-drug offensive.[127] In some ways, this type of moral battle is as dangerous as religious war, and very similar to it. For many Americans, opposition to dangerous substances gradually came to seem normal, rather than "just fun"; it was not only a logical but an ethical issue. Every form of subtle persuasion was used to impose a specific type of morality and pharmacological culture with the States. This led people like the Los Angeles Chief of Police to comment that "occasional users should be executed because the US declared war on drugs and users would be committing the crime of treason. Execution is the punishment for traitors in times of war."[128]

124. According to Michael Levine, an undercover DEA agent who operated in Buenos Aires, the US CIA sponsored García Meza's coup in Bolivia in 1980 to prevent leftist control by someone like Siles Zuazo. "La narco-DEA y la narco-CIA," *Cambio 16*, February 8, 1993; and Blixen, Samuel, "El doble papel del narcotráfico en el terrorismo de Estado y en la democracia militarizada," in VVAA, *Guerra antidrogas...*, op.cit., 1997.

125. Smith, H., ed., *Drug Policy in the Americas*, University of California, Westview Press, San Diego, 1992; Gónzalez, Guadalupe, *El narcotráfico como un problema de seguridad nacional*, Comisión Sudamericana de Paz, Santiago de Chile, 1989; and all authors consulted: Bagley, Grinspoon and Bakalar, Escohotado, Kaplan, Garasino, Musto. Likewise, the Government accused Sandinistas, Cubans and Eastern countries of narco-trafficking and intelligence services attempted unsuccessfully to prove these implications: Benítez, Raúl, "Narcotráfico y terrorismo en las relaciones interamericanas," *Polémica*, #5, Second Epoch, pp. 2 — 21, FLACSO, San José de Costa Rica, 1988. This was when the spotlight was on the circumstantial connections between narco-traffickers and guerrilleros, thereby creating the "narco-guerrilla" concept.

126. US Government, *National Strategy for Drug Control*, 1989 and 1991.

127. In addition to freedom in drug use, the beat culture supported peace among nations and free love. It was all contrary to the Conservative revolution, enraged at the world of the hippies. Reagan's inflexibility with drugs was demonstrated in his first nominations: Chief of Staff of the Alcohol, Drug Abuse and Mental Health Administration was a pediatrician activist in the Father's Movement. He would become the administration's loudest voice on the drugs issue. Musto, David, op. cit., p. 305, 1993.

128. *Los Angeles Times*, 6 — 7 September 1991, in Smith, see bibliography, p. 12, 1992.

But it was also a rhetorical war. Effectiveness was not the goal: Reagan opposed appointing one figure to unite the many drug policies, and very controversial measures were implemented, causing great sensation but resolving no problems.[129] This lack of decisiveness and the growing public concern spurred harsh criticism of the Reagan approach and led to pressure to modify the goals for national and international efforts to control narcotics.

2. The Formation of the Crusade (1984–1988)

Washington's denial of structural problems and the costs of running a welfare state led to the "externalization" of the problem. Deciding to seek the cause of the epidemic elsewhere, they pinned it on the Latin American countries who were providing drugs (and they targeted cocaine, this time, not marijuana). This led to the declaration of a "Latin Conspiracy."

According to Youngers and Walsh, "externalizing the threat saved politicians the thorny problem of correcting the horrendous social and economic conditions prevalent in the US inner-city, the source of the desperate poverty which made crack quite tempting either as an escape or a business."[130] The way to solve the drug problem, then, was to attack the source, eliminate the supply and the production.

But the issue was quite complicated. If the simple act of production had become a criminal act, for Washington, what about the views of everyone else? The different precepts and ethical considerations about what was criminal and what was legitimate were highlighted particularly clearly in the drugs issue. In the US, cocaine and organized crime have been linked, so the US public "tended to feel the growing drug addiction was mostly a result of the

---

129. At the end of 1986 Reagan requested Government employees to undergo random urine analyses. This was the beginning of opposition by special interest groups and the Civil Liberties Union and generated intense debate. Since then anyone hired by the administration or for a government job must undergo this testing.

130. Youngers, Coletta and Walsh, John. "La guerra contra las drogas en los Andes: una política mal encaminada," in García Sayán, Diego, ed., pp. 346 — 360, see bibliography, 1989.

secret conspiracy of criminal elements vying to destroy the society from within."[131]

This level of rhetoric has been used by every US government means, much as the rhetoric of the Cold War was used. Given the existence of circumstantial connections between narco-traffickers and Latin American guerrillas, and faced with the need to present a common front uniting the nation in the collective task of national reconstruction, the "crusade against drugs" was formed as an amalgam of very different concepts (national security, criminal Latin invasion, international Communist movement, the recovery of morals, etc.). The drug problem was presented as an external evil that had to be uprooted, instead of being a problem of social imbalance and economic inequities. (Only later, when the lack of results was clear, and loud resistance from Latin American was high, was drug use considered; but the retaliatory efforts always concentrated on production and trafficking).

The fight to cut off supply, along with the will to recover world hegemony and a sense of power, meant adopting a series of warlike concepts and vocabulary straight out of military manuals. The occasional coming together of guerrilla groups and narco-traffickers was exaggerated in propaganda and rhetoric. There was not only the drug threat, but also — and mostly — the threat of "Latin drug conspiracies, which were dramatically more successful in subversion in the US than any conspiracy out of Moscow."[132] The fight against drugs — or against cocaine — was set up as an ideological fight.

The frameworks of the Cold War, the East/West confrontation and its lack of applicability to the Latin American reality instigated the crusade by simplifying the Latin American problematic to a zero-sum game. The development of the concept of "narco-terrorism" as a

---

131. Bustamante, Fernando. "La política de EE UU contra el narcotráfico y su impacto en América Latina," in *Estudios Internacionales*, number 90, pp. 240 — 276, Universidad de Chile, April — June 1990.

132. Declarations of former director of the Southern Command in Panama before the Senate Subcommittee on Narcotics, Terrorism and International Operations, cited by Youngers and Walsh, op. cit. p. 343, 1989. The name of the subcommittee is quite expressive of how narco-trafficking, subversion and intervention relate.

subversive movement linked to drug production and trafficking melded the ideas of international communism and drug trafficking, inventing a threat that sounded very real to US society obsessed by hygiene and health.

By this means, the deep structural imbalances in Latin America (poverty, injustice, agrarianism, banditry and clientelism) all became threats to US national security. As a result, according to Fernando Bustamante, in the US response and policy formulation "subversion, disease and anthropological otherness were united in a powerful symbolic cluster catalyzing a vigorous defensive reaction. The search for policies on Latin America included points on crime fighting, counter-subversive measures, culture and epidemiology, and made its agents into a multi-hat-wearers combining the policeman, the soldier, the educating missionary and the medical doctor."

According to a former US Chief of Advisors to El Salvador, "the alliance between some narco-traffickers and some insurgents created an "ideal opportunity" for the US government to recover a "moral base" on which to support military intervention to fight insurgency."[133] The war against drugs was established by supporting and training Latin American armies; and "narco-trafficking" was the transmission belt that ideologically linked US and Latin American military apparatuses.[134]

The Doctrine of National Security

Already in 1982, with the first anti-drug propaganda campaigns, the National Defense Authorization Act was passed, allowing the US federal army to participate in the fight against drugs.[135] The joint declaration of the Secretary of State, the Secretary of Defense and the Attorney General about the "serious threat" posed by drugs was the first public declaration allowing military participation in anti-drug

---

133. Youngers and Walsh, see bibliography page 343, 1989.

134. First, "narco-terrorism" was synonymous with "narco-guerrilla"; since the military and urban offensive of the narco-traffickers from the Medellín cartel at the end of the 1980s, this word designates this activity separating it from the guerrilla.

operations. However, the army would be limited by the scant budget that was allotted for this purpose. The increasing use of cocaine,[136] the direct accusations of lack of commitment on the part of Reagan and intense social concern translated into the consensus of both parties to encourage the war on drugs.

The consensus between Congress and the President's Office (starting with Reagan's second administration), more specifically for the passing of the 1986 law on the repressive anti-supply strategy, was based on the "realist" analyses of the international system and the US role.[137] A series of military and police operations based on the new law were developed. Operations were inaugurated by the April 1986 National Security Decision Directive, which declared drug trafficking a "lethal" threat to US national security. Geopolitical concepts based on the "realist" paradigm fully updated the doctrine of national security, or the doctrine of counterinsurgency, which had elaborated joint actions among American armies since Kennedy's administration.

The "realist" reasoning completely inverted the entire national drug problem, which went from a public health problem (as simple as "our society is going wrong somewhere") to a problem of national survival. The reminders of the widening social imbalance in the US, which was reflected by the high levels of drug use, no longer made sense. Any such claims sounded absurd, since the nation was not suffering from pathology or a problem of distorted markets, but rather

135. Authorized for advising, equipping, logistics and intelligence as support for civilian corps, which implied a modification to the 1878 law expressly prohibiting the army from intervening in civilian affairs. This was obtained by both parties led by Democratic Senator Nunn; the Posse Comitatus Act (1878) was amended. Reuter, Peter, "Can the Borders be Sealed?," in *The Public Interest*, #92, pp. 51–65, Washington, summer 1988; and Bagley, Bruce M., "Myths of Militarization: Enlisting Armed Forces in the War on Drugs," in Smith, op. cit., 1992.

136. Between 1985 and 1988 the number of weekly users doubled (National Drug Control Strategy -NDCS, pp. 23–24, 1991), to stabilize only at the end of the Reagan era.

137. The "realist" paradigm proposed the following international system: 1) Nation-states are the fundamental actors in international politics; 2) State elites design and develop strategies for foreign policy to defend and promote vital national interests; 3) interest in national security is greater than the agendas of foreign policies and in the hierarchy of priorities; 4) threats to national security from the international system justify the call on the full capacity of national resources for power (including the use of force) to obtain the desired results from hostile or non-cooperative Nation-states: "self-help" or political self-sufficiency is as much a right as a last resort of every sovereign nation in defense of its national interests and security.

from an attack by dangerous, poisonous substances sent in by foreigners.

The circumstantial guerrilla-narco-trafficker link substantially alters all Latin American political views on the doctrine of national security. The "realist" doctrine caused Reagan's anti-drug policy to fail, because it meant applying a political philosophy that was disconnected from reality. It did not consider the complex inter-relation among countries or the multiple factors of interdependence. The "realist" doctrine implemented an offensive, repressive policy which, with Congressional approval,[138] included training, logistical support for anti-drug police forces, and political, economic and diplomatic pressure (in addition to the threat of force). Every attempt was made to redirect the complex process of narcotics production and use without taking into account any other factor that aided in the development of narco-trafficking — such concerns as economic crisis, rural pauperization, institutional weakness, territorial disintegration, and spreading violence would be far too difficult to tackle. Instead, progressive militarization meant many new military-police operations,[139] in which the military component was not as important as the type of strategy developed. Until 1988, production repression was primary, with 70% of the budget targeting policies to reduce supply, or production.[140]

In 1989, the Department of Defense was not convinced of the value of having the armed forces intervene in the war on drugs, and stated that any new aid from the army for anti-drug programs would require a legislative re-thinking of its role, "modifications in the

---

138. The 1986 Drugs Act: In March, Congress evaluates the anti-drug efforts of countries receiving economic aid. No certification means no economic aid and a US veto in international financial institutions.

139. Both allow for the expansion of the army's role in the war on drugs on the borders and overseas from mid-1986 and in the future, with the following conditions: 1) the armed forces had to be invited by a foreign government; 2) the armed forces had to be commanded and coordinated by civilian heads of US agencies; and 3) its role would be limited to support tasks. In practice its labors were completely mixed. Marine ships captained by soldiers with civilian functions on board, who carried out the confiscations and detentions. This happened with the Air Force as well. Bagley, page 131, 1992.

priorities of the armed forces," or additional funds provided by Congress.

The army's reluctance to participate in the war on drugs[141] gave the impression that it was the Legislative branch, namely Congress, that was leading the initiative to take a greater role in foreign policy, which according to the Constitution belonged to the President. Yet Congress desired a much greater involvement of the armed forces.[142] It was only with the dissolution of the USSR at the end of the 1980s that the army would accept its new role as global guardian of order, health and morality.

From 1989, with Plan Bennett, the Andean Counter Narcotics Initiative,[143] the war escalated. Army presence along the borders and on the sea was stepped up and the US increased pressure on other governments in the hemisphere to assign a greater role to their armies in fighting narco-trafficking.

The new task was accepted not only because of bureaucratic interests and to maintain a large US military sector, but also because war intelligence is a powerful technological instigator for innovations that could later be adapted to civilian needs and would endorse US technological competitiveness.[144] In other words, military investment

---

140. 1982-1986 US drug control budgets:

> 1982: reduction in supply 78% – $1,100 million
> reduction in demand: 21% – $305.1 million
> 1986: reduction in supply 82% – $1,900 million
> reduction in demand: 17% – $391.8 million
> 1982–1986:reduction in demand budget grew 14.8%
> 1982–1986:reduction in supply budget grew 55.4%

Source: GAO, *Controlling Drug Abuse. A Status Report.* 1988. DC: GAO/GGD 88-39, March (Washington D.C.).

141. They alleged: 1) Intervention would not work. The only effective way to reduce the drug flow would be to reduce demand. Increasing prohibition would increase the risks of the narco-traffickers but it would not completely or permanently change the entrance of drugs; 2) It would distract the armed forces from their main task of defending the US from possible nuclear or conventional attacks and serving as support for US interests throughout the world. In order for this involvement in the war on drugs not to affect such vital functions, they could only implement it with a large budget increase; 3) It would affect civil rights and liberties very seriously. Furthermore the Armed Forces did not feel prepared for the task; 4) It would expose the military to corruption (as in many Latin American armies), seriously altering discipline and effectiveness. Similar arguments were used by Latin American armies to distance themselves from the commitment to the fight on drugs starting in 1990. WOLA, op. cit., 1993.

can be good for the economy. After the aborted Star Wars Program and the disappearance of the Soviet Empire, the Pentagon and the US scientific and engineering communities needed a new and powerful stimulus to guarantee the continued funding of the weapons industry and surveillance, aerospace and other technologies. In addition to the bureaucratic and economic interests of the army, the war on drugs was intensified and justified when in 1988, in the midst of an electoral campaign, the General Accounting Office published its report on the drug situation for the decade. The report indicated:

> All kinds of illicit drugs, more readily available and cheaper in 1989 than in 1981; a general increase in drug use in the 1980s; a US drug market: the most lucrative in the world; crimes and violence related to drugs plague cities; crack epidemic; US national health system inefficiency; the saturation of police services and the lack of funds and corruption; the saturation of the justice system and prisons; serious threats to political systems and the state organization of some Latin American countries: consequently, vital interests to US security in the hemisphere were at risk.[145]

The failure of policies undertaken up to that point, which ignored users and turned to the persecution of production and trafficking, forced the government to re-think strategies. It began to dedicate 50% of the drug control budget to reducing use by repression; only 30% was designated to education/prevention and

---

142. In this case, the decree for the army to seal the borders in 1986 is important. (Bagley, page 1973, 1991; Garasino, p. 28, 1990; and Reuter, 1988). It was a mission impossible, underestimated by the Senate but which demonstrated how Congress wanted a much greater participation of the armed forces. Also in 1986, with the 99/570 law against drug abuse, US civil servants were allowed to train and support foreign police and military forces in prohibition-related tasks, nullifying the express prohibition of the 1961 law of foreign aid, and of Congress in 1974, to avoid US security forces involvement in cases of human rights violations. Perl, Raphael Francis, "Narcopolitica: la ley norteamericana contra el abuso de drogas y las relaciones EEUU — México," in *Cuadernos Semestrales*, number 20, 2nd semester, México, 1986.

143. "Drug Czar" William Bennett named a panel of experts to issue recommendations to the National Security Council on counterdrug programs in the Andes region.

144. Many conferences on the low-intensity war and the war on drugs were sponsored by the Technical Marketing Society of America. WOLA, op. cit., p. 74, 1993.

145. Bagley, op. cit., p. 171, 1991. Cf. US General Accounting Office (GAO), *Controlling Drug Abuse. A Status Report*, 1988 D.C.: GAO/GGD 88 — 39, March (Washington D.C.).

treatment programs. They were attempting to control demand by strengthening the law enforcement, which fit perfectly with the repressive nature of the anti-drug policy from 1988–1989.

For Bruce Bagley, professor of International Studies at the University of Miami, the failure of Reagan's anti-drug policy was mainly due to the adoption of "realism" to confront a problem that was much more complex, because Nation-States not only exist but they also move. Furthermore, some subnational and transnational figures (drug traffickers, multinational corporations in the chemical industry, private, commercial and multinational banks, manufacturers of weapons, electronic devices and airplanes) were operating against national authorities. On the other hand, it was necessary to accept the fact that many Latin American states were not consolidated and could not even control their own territory, so it was unrealistic to think they could implement a particular policy. According to Bagley, in spite of all its resources the US was unable to eliminate the Italian *Cosa Nostra*, on its own soil; how, then, could the institutionally weak Latin American states eliminate their own mafias or effectively exercise the law over the terrorists? Weak Latin American states cannot possibly comply with anti-drug laws without US technical and financial assistance. Penalizing them through the certification system,[146] therefore, does more harm than good.

The intensification of the war and the complete incorporation of the army into the war was obtained in 1989 with the National Defense Authorization Act, which designated the Department of Defense as the "only" US agency authorized to direct detection tasks and monitor air and sea trafficking of illegal drugs into the US. It was the

---

146. The Inter-American Drug Abuse Control Commission was established in 1998 in Washington to develop a multilateral system for evaluation of national efforts in the war on drugs. The idea was endorsed at the summit of the Americas in Santiago, Chile. The Latin American and Caribbean countries hoped the development of a comprehensive evaluation mechanism for the drug war would bring an end to the unilateral process of certification by the United States. The US congress established the certification process during the Reagan administration; it requires the president to certify annually whether drug-producing or drug-transit countries are fully cooperating with the United States to combat drugs. Countries not certified were denied US economic and military assistance.

responsibility of this department to integrate communications and technical intelligence into a federal network. The Drug Enforcement Administration (DEA) also joined enthusiastically with an almost paramilitary role and the CIA, which created the Anti-Narcotics Unit in 1984, designated 25% of its resources to Latin America for the "new priority" war on drugs.[147]

The beginning of the Bush administration meant renewed interventionism, from the Panama invasion to the deployment of the US fleet over Colombian waters and the interception of Mexican planes by US satellites, which increased distrust and aversion to the US.

After the Panama invasion and Noriega's arrest, Latin American distrust was so high that the Bush administration had to work to convince its neighbors of the need to step up the war on the continent. The Cartagena Accord began a series of anti-drug summits, which would incorporate Latin American armies into the war and would assuage resentment by providing hefty economic aid for the war on drugs and the establishment of alternative crops, all under the control of Washington. When once again *security* and *development* were juxtaposed, and the US regained a degree of hegemony. Consensus works as well or better than domination.

3) THE CRUSADE REPLACED THE COLD WAR (1988-1990)

After the bipartisan consensus in Congress and the internationalization of the war on drugs, a whole series of international conventions was dedicated to the fight. This phase began in 1988 with two key elements: Law 100-690, specifying the international role of the US Congress, and the 1988 Vienna Convention. Both are fundamental to understanding the fight against drugs now and for analyzing the series of international military,

---

147. Youngers and Walsh, op. cit., pp. 353-358, 1989; and WOLA, see bibliography, p. 66, 1993. Cf. *New York Times*, March 25, 1990.

police, educational, economic and political compromises for and from the war on drugs.

In Reagan's era, based on the Kennan doctrine of containing communism, the doctrine of national security was updated to support the anti-supply strategy. Subsequent military involvement, political development, legislative production and international relations indicated continuity and the adaptation of containing narco-trafficking to the logic of containing communism, through bipartisan consensus. Consensus between the two parties with respect to a unified foreign policy, established in 1946 and supporting post-war hegemony, was broken in the early 1970s as a result of the Vietnam War. Consensus was regained with anti-drug policies, which neither Carter's human rights policies nor Reagan's intervention in Central America had achieved.

The vigor with which the US presented its war on drugs on the international scene corresponded to the vigor and the consensus that same policy enjoyed with the US domestic audience. It took up one of the main motives of social and public concern; therefore, it was easy for Congress to show concern and dynamism, paving the way for bipartisan consensus. It also fostered consensus between the Legislative and Executive powers, based on the 1986 anti-drug abuse law. This considerably expanded Legislative and Executive power over foreign policy, responding to the concern that had been generated among the electorate; "it was becoming a very important political issue with important electoral effects."[148] Thus bipartisan consensus became the foundation of an ideological/moral bloc encompassing all of Congress, defending a "concrete fight" against drugs and denying any other type of approach to the problem. Their task took on a "defensive" and almost corporate feel.[149]

---

148. The electoral importance of the drug issue began in the 1988 campaign and not before. In 1984 the only mention of the drug issue in both conventions was the Conservative condemnation of the Sandinistas for illegal trafficking in the US USIA *Convention Chronology, 1984 Conventions.* The concern increased in 1988. Democrats and Republicans sold the idea of containing drugs in the party line because it was a threat to national security. USIA. *1988 Democratic Platform and 1988 Republican Platform.*

Congress' "imperial" command. The war on drugs allowed Congress to considerably extend its influence in foreign policy leadership. It imposed restrictions on the broad power of the President to concede or suspend aid to producing or trafficking countries through "certification." In prior legislation, the President determined sanctions, and now Congress certified and the government implemented what Congress stipulated — or, at least, had to present and transmit exceptions to certification to Congress. In the prolonged fight between Congress and the President, Congress prevailed.

The creation of the Drug Czar (Director of the White House Office of National Drug Control Policy) to bring together the many anti-drug policies demonstrates Congress' power. He was not a symbolic figure but a Legislative prop in the Executive branch which was facing Congress' expanding powers. Since the war on drugs was the war on cocaine, and cocaine was produced entirely in Latin America, its influence on foreign policy and, in particular, on the hemisphere, increased.

The "internationalization" of the war on drugs. The extension of the "realist" paradigm to the Clinton administration led to a further emphasis on enrolling other countries in the US-led war. In essence, the anti-supply policy continued, though with signs of interdependence which contributed to the diffusion of some values, the extension of some policies and consensus on some strategies. This went hand in hand with economic rapprochement, more evident in Latin America than any place else. Internationalization was obtained through the initial financing of the war as it spread the anti-supply strategy to drug use by means of repression.

Federal, state and local agents proliferated (111,520 at the end of the 1980s[150]) and all of them had bureaucratic interests in obtaining

---

149. Francis Perl, US Congress drug expert, demonstrated in the 1989 Lima conference on narco-trafficking how it was impossible for any member of Congress to vote for legalization. S/ he would not be re-elected. They could not even contemplate the debate because the public would interpret it as support for legalization. García Sayán, Diego, ed., *Narcotráfico: realidades y alternativas*, Conferencia Internacional, Lima Feb. 5–7, 1990, Comisión Andina de Juristas, Lima, p. 144, 1990.

150. According to political scientist Scott Palmer in García Sayán, op. cit., p. 172, 1989.

funding — which meant perpetuating the problem, in order to justify their existence. The legislative and international process was similar to what had happened a century before with the prohibition of opium. Two US laws (1986 and 1988) developed the domestic and international aspects of the war on drugs, but the 1988 Vienna Convention gave the final shove to the globalization of the war.

The Vienna Convention, or The Cocaine Convention (1988)

The UN Convention on Illicit Traffic in Narcotic Drugs and Psychotropic Substances, approved in Vienna in 1988, could also be called the "Cocaine Convention," as it revolved around cocaine.

The rhetorical backing and the need for an international convention arose after the 1984 Quito Declaration designated narco-trafficking a "crime against humanity." That, in turn, came about after the assassination of Colombian Minister of Justice Lara Bonilla. The true push behind the Vienna Convention and the strategy of international involvement came from the US, which, besides looking for a multinational anti-drug force and world court in which to try suspects, also proposed the international conference to fight illegal production. The Convention was approved after four years of UN negotiations on issues of confiscation and extradition, with no participation by Latin America. The main goal of the Convention was economic, along with the repression of supply and trafficking. Though the preamble justified the Convention as a protection of the health and well-being of humanity, there were not even fourteen lines about issues related to consumption or prevention.[151] Most authors consulted thought the Convention was an extension of US policy. There were some exceptions, such as US diplomats or politicians, who felt it was an indispensable international legal mechanism, and in

---

151. For an exhaustive analysis and critique see Del Olmo, Rosa, "La convención de Viena," in García Sayán, Diego, ed., *Narcotráfico: realidades y alternativas*, CAJ, Lima, 1990. Compared to other drug conventions in Soberón, Ricardo, "La ley internacional en materia de lucha contra las drogas y los efectos en el ordenamiento jurídico de los países de la región" in VVAA, *Drogas y control penal en los Andes*, CAJ, Peru, 1994.

their minds any criticism of it raises suspicion about ulterior motives.[152]

The Convention universalized the crusade against drugs, justifying the existence of a police state and the monopolistic regime of narco-trafficking by the corrupt sectors of most State security forces. The Convention was supposed to stop illegal trafficking, yet it authorized the use of shady legal practices[153] to persecute trafficking, allowing and justifying corruption at the highest level; it was criminal legislation.[154] As international cooperation between the police and the judiciary became standard, some countries were able to apply the law of pre-eminence over others. This made international cooperation susceptible to repressive policies, since the most appropriate ("efficient") State was supposed to take charge of fulfilling the Convention objectives (confiscations, trials etc.). That State had a free hand in the extra-territorial application of penal law.

In like manner, consecrated trial guarantees were violated as the burden of proof was inverted. The accused had to explain the illegal origin of his goods before being sentenced. In scientific issues, imprecise terms were still used, like "narcotic" and "mind-altering drugs," and coca leaf and hemp were placed in those categories. Addiction and delinquency were linked (just as heroin had been linked to crime and cocaine was said to have led African Americans to commit rape, in the era of greater intolerance before World War I). The door was also left open to banning substances to be designated in

---

152. Like in the 1920s, European criticism was considered a conspiracy or even participation in contraband. Musto, op. cit. 1993.

153. Observed handing over and provoking agents were two methods inviting participation in the business: what is the limit between justifiably legal and illegal? And who watches over the watcher?

154. Reciprocal judicial aid can be denied if it affects "sovereignty, security, law and order or other fundamental interests." So, when the war on drugs took front stage on the police and repressive scene, as the doubtfully legal extra-judicial mechanisms were dedicated, like "supervised submission, or provoking agent and the inversion of the criminal charge," the millionaire dimension of the narco-trafficking process allowed for crimes with no judicial control since the faculty or reserve was set forth in the Convention (article 7, paragraph 15, section b and paragraph 17).

the future and persecuting anyone associated with them. Given the anti-tobacco campaign, that would be its most likely target.

With respect to the status of legal, traditional coca, events of the 1990s vindicating Peruvian and Bolivian policies with coca diplomacy obtained the recognition of the rights of traditional peoples. However, new contradictions were created with respect to the 1961 Single Convention on Narcotic Drugs which required the absolute elimination of coca fields, even for traditional use, though a door for reform was left open.

4) THE CONSOLIDATION AND GLOBALIZATION OF THE CRUSADE

This coincided with the Bush and Clinton administrations. It implied the complete involvement of the United Nations in the "crusade." The ratification of the Vienna Convention in 1988 and its legislative adoption became the US's main goal along with the development of determined national and international strategies.

The National Strategies of Drug Control show the "realist" frameworks were intact, and the development of anti-supply policies were a key component of the doctrine of national security and the internationalization of the US interpretation. The drugs issue was not considered a domestic problem with domestic means of solution; it was considered a problem external to the US, an invasion by outside forces, and thus a motive for defense:

> The origin of the most dangerous drugs that threaten our nation is mainly international. Few foreign threats are as costly for the US economy. None causes more damage to our national values and institutions or destroys more US lives. While the majority of international threats are potential, the damage and violence caused by drug trafficking are real and infiltrate everywhere. Drugs are a big threat to our national security.

When the process spread geographically, it also affected other nations and their national security:

The demand for drugs is an international problem. A future reduction in the US drug demand will depend in part on the reduction in the amount of drugs which enter this country. If other nations would like to cooperate with the US and among themselves to reduce the drug supply, they will have to understand that drug production, trafficking and consumption are a threat to their domestic well being and for the entire community of nations. The US is trying to convince other nations that participation in any of the segments of the chain of narco-trafficking ends up in the long run in corruption and the use of drugs in the country and that, sooner or later its consumption will affect national security because it destroys the essential elements of society.

To defend against this evil, they not only need the decision of the entire US society, but also international cooperation to end the criminal organizations promoting narco-trafficking. The targets of the fight are not just in the US:

but rather within the countries of origin, since the interception of drugs and traffickers en route to the US is an immensely complex, expensive resource that is less effective for reducing the drug supply in this country.

This was how the US justified the war on drugs outside its own territory, as a threat to its collectivity.

It is a veritable war, and like most wars from which the US has benefited, it is waged on someone else's territory: in this case, in Latin America, the remote Andean countryside and Amazon jungle, or in the streets and cities of Colombia. (Some of the activity does take place inside the US, in marginalized zones.) Therefore, the implied threat for other countries led the US to extensive diplomatic efforts, first to convince them of the severity of the problem and then to increase the "level of international intolerance for illegal drugs," because, "in the past, programs in this area have been blocked by the lack of importance this country grants to the drug issue as a point of interest for international policy."

We can see how far the drug issue went in generating policies, particularly US foreign policy. But they requested, suggested and encouraged that this control would be above all control over cocaine. Through the 1986 and 1988, anti-drug laws the US dominated the Americas. But for the fight against drugs to be truly effective, the goodwill of the European Union, invited to participate as a partner, was needed, as was the "legitimacy" provided by a UN Convention (just as in 1912). This time it led to the 1988 Vienna Convention. Countries were urged to ratify it because it was fundamental for international unifying law and for guiding future policies and instruments. The US adapted its legislation to the Vienna Convention and was able to "make the ratification of other countries in a priority issue for bilateral relations."

For diplomacy, bilateral relations with "consuming nations" were a main focal point, that is, the users in the developed world. In this respect the European role was granted importance, but located on the front lines, as a partner in the war. Latin America was considered the sick subject, or the evil to be extracted; the rest of the Third World was cast as a future sick subject. European participation was all the more important since it legitimated and encouraged US policy; and the Europeans could help cover the costs. Europe had its own concerns, namely that the US should try: "first, to help the European Community develop policies, strategies and programs to energize the reduction of demand; second, to aid the EC in strengthening its own mechanisms to reduce supply, especially programs for the execution and exchange of intelligence information and data; third, to commit EC nations to multilateral efforts with the US to control production, manufacture and trafficking in countries of origin and transit, particularly of cocaine and heroin; and finally, to commit EC support to activities of regional and international organizations involving producing countries and areas, especially those where the US lacked or had very little direct influence."[155]

---

155. All the texts in previous blocks or quotes refer to the 1989 US Government National Strategy for Drug Control.

There was a cosmetic change in the 1991 "Strategy on the formulation of policies on Latin America," in an attempt to calm a region that was anxious seeing the increasing militarization of the fight against drugs. (The invasion of Panama in December 1989 did little to build trust among the locals.) Serious problems of governance were caused by increased terrorism or violence by narco-traffickers and consequently US aid was requested for protection of sectors such as the judiciary.

Economic aid was granted parallel to military aid within this framework. Yet there was no framework for stable cooperation for sustainable economic development or a stimulus for legal exports.

According to the proposals of the 1991 Strategy, US international efforts were aimed at "reinforcing the political commitment of producing and transit nations to strengthen their laws, judicial institutions and programs, to try and punish and, where possible, apply the law of extradition to narco-traffickers and money-launderers."

World Plan of Action. United Nations (1990)

The diplomatic disposition and political, economic and military impetus the US applied to the war on drugs materialized in the complete involvement of the United Nations. The 1990s was declared the UN Decade against Drug Abuse, and the World Plan of Action was made public with the aim of urging the international community to implement it and cooperate.

The UN plan sought to be integral and took up all the facets of the drug problem: prevention, research on causes for consumption, production, manufacture, trafficking, money-laundering, the production of raw chemical materials, weapons and technical apparatuses, judicature, bureaucratic unification and the organization of resources. Of these issues, only two relate to drug consumption, the demand side of the equation. The rest are aimed at strengthening control of production and illegal trafficking.

The Vienna Convention was the judicial mechanism for the US to commit to developing a repressive policy against trafficking. The World Plan of Action made the UN a major player in the crusade, with the drugs issue monopolizing an increasingly greater space in UN concerns and resources. The World Plan inaugurated the phase of "shared responsibility" for producing and consuming countries. Considerable economic efforts and efforts to channel UN resources were directed at support for crop substitution, rural development and infrastructures development in production zones, via the UNFDAC (the United Nations Fund for Drug Abuse Control) though resources remained far below needs. "The special session demonstrated to us the institutionalization of the broad concepts — or issues — of the problem,"[156] which can also be applied to the last UN Special Session in May 1998. Thus the official-officialist position was posed internationally; the latter was formally declared. However, words do not solve problems.

The prohibitionist philosophy were transferred to UN plans, granting universal validity to a false concept of drugs, especially natural drugs. The extension and homogenization of programs for prevention and education, as well as the scientific treatment of the problem, allowed for an "official" consensus on the validity of the fight against drugs. The World Plan allowed for greater and more efficient police cooperation, the strengthening of judicial sectors, the extension of homogenous information, and the delivery of resources to the production zones.

Though the political declaration and the UN program for action were broad, multidisciplinary, and in some respects actually touch on the question of the problem as the increase in demand and consumption, a hearing on the efficiency of the strategy adopted was never proposed. The UN would be the adequate institutional space to reflect on the origin of the strategy, its effectiveness, the results desired (as compared to those obtained), the needs of the countries

---

156. Donelly, Jack, "The United Nations and the Global Drug Control Regime," in Smith, op. cit., pp. 282–305, 1992.

and the difference priorities, current and potential conflicts, cultural questions, etc. However, its "impenetrability" as Nadelmann[157] stated in reference to the 1998 UN Special Session on Drugs, makes reform to the proposals impossible to this day.

The war on drugs is the great parable of the US hegemonic power; it is an oblique reflection of the national myth that America is "supposed to" enjoy global primacy. The current process of the war on drugs takes on all aspects of society. It has not been designed with predetermination, but it is the expression of a certain type of society that is part of the US governing elite. As it is presented to the public, it bears traces of a moralizing political concept and the 19th century positivism in US political tradition; such gambits are used to generate popular support (including tax dollars) that can be turned to this maneuver for national recovery. The war on drugs, nominally focused on cocaine and crack, translates into a battle for hemispheric control because narco-trafficking (cocaine trafficking) has permeated a large part of the economic, political and social spheres of Latin American. The war on cocaine allows for control and the recovery of leadership in a region which had been relatively autonomous in the previous decade. It introduces an era of uncertainty, democratic regression and corruption to the continent of South America.

---

157. US economist who is anti-prohibition and the current director of the Lindesmith Center, the research center of the George Soros Foundation which is backing the debate and the formulation of alternatives to the current international drug policy.

CHAPTER VI. THE COCAINE WAR

Andean countries contribute just 17% of all cocaine to the world market of natural psychoactive drugs; marijuana and hashish make up 35% of world sales while heroin is at 45%.[158] Though the participation of Andean countries is low, widespread propaganda coupled with the war waged to control cocaine indicates the political and strategic intentions of this struggle. Since South America produces 100% of all cocaine, and the illegal trafficking of cocaine extends throughout the hemisphere, the war on drugs is really the *war on cocaine.*

When the Cold War ended, the competition offered by communism was ended; that allowed for intervention through economic and security clauses and unified armies against a common enemy, if one could be identified. The usefulness of the war on drugs can be linked to the extension of the phenomena of corruption and narco-trafficking, by applying war. This double and triple process of feeding into one another has created a system of adaptive behavior,[159] because society's drug consumption is adaptively self-regulated and it is the social, economic and political system itself that forms a second self-regulated subsystem that adapts to the first.

---

158. Iban de REMENTERIA, 1995: *La elección de las drogas. Examen de las Políticas de Control.* p. 84. Editorial Fundación Friederich Ebert, Lima.

159. For the dynamics of systems and processes of self regulation, see Javier ARACIL, 1986, *Introducción a la dinámica de sistemas,* Alianza Editorial.

As Martin Jelsma of the Transnational Institute notes, "there is a much more complex dynamics and intimate mingling between criminal and state structures, where uniformed officials are completely integrated into the operative levels of illegal economy."[160] This criminal dynamics, which is closely related to it, generates concrete pressure on the first circle (poverty, violence, injustice), creating constant imbalance which is the basis for the extension and repetition of the production/consumption process in a continuum. Many of the techniques used by illegal trafficking have been learned and developed in anti-drug strategies, and vice-versa. The progressive militarization puts pressure on the trafficking rings to achieve an ever-greater level of professionalism. Only the strongest structures can survive, and this implies a connection with the highest spheres that is "increasingly frequent; the world's drug trade enjoys institutional protection, and is even controlled by parts of the military, police, or intelligence forces."[161] The consequence is the extension of the entire illegal trafficking phenomenon throughout Latin America, or the "balloon effect,"[162] so that the entire region is ripe for war.

The US has maintained a low profile in Latin America since the 1970s. With the war on cocaine, it achieved what neither Reagan's anti-communist crusade nor the Alliance for Progress had achieved before — hemispheric control via hegemonic principles.

Basically, the war on cocaine is the three-pronged military, economic and social approach which facilitates consensus, which is always equal to or greater than overt domination, for conditions favoring US advantage throughout the hemisphere.

---

160. See VVAA, 1997, *Crimen uniformado...* Op.cit.

161. According to Martin JELSMA, "Daño colateral de la guerra antidrogas — una intro-ducción," in VVAA,

1997, *Guerra antidrogas...* op. Cit.

162. Crop displacement to areas where they had never before existed as a result of an increase in legal measures in currently cultivated zones. The speech of Tom Blickman (TNI) in the Alternative Development Workshop and the UN Special Session on Drugs, in Santa Fe de Bogota, Colombia on May 29, 1998.

1.   THE NEW GEO-POLITICAL DOCTRINE

In the 1980s, the democratizing impetus that accompanied the promotion of human rights allowed for formal democracies to be established in Latin America. Yet, in the United States, the historical exhaustion of communism and its policies left an ideological hole and strategic void and that prompted the need to come up with a new doctrine that would enable the world power to maintain the superficial trappings of democracy while eroding real justice, equality, and development. A shift was underway that gave priority to a form of capitalism devoid of social obligations. In this state, conflict is no longer channeled through political and trade union routes, but through other methods which make compatible free enterprise, increasing wealth for the wealthiest, and social control over the less wealthy. The tensions caused by injustice are plastered over with patriotic jingoism.

The doctrine that currently tames the tensions of unjust societies without endangering the system is one that skirts social revolutionary outbursts in urban zones and the Marxist interpretation of underdevelopment and dependence. It is the war on drugs, and it leads all social demands to narco-trafficking. This doctrine, as well as the imposition of the US's unilateral vision which criminalizes every process and negates its open character, determines the present and the future of Latin America. By making the entire process a crime, structural tensions are swept under the carpet: the problems of growing economic inequality, social uprooting, the lack of opportunity, etc., are removed from the political realm and emptied of content. Meanwhile, the chance to strengthen military sectors is happily accepted, granting a privileged relationship with the US and allowing for opportunities for joint army training, operations development, and a sharing of ideals, objectives, moral precepts.

Many steps were necessary to arrive at the formulation of the war on drugs as a diplomatic and strategic doctrine, including military and police operations, diplomatic pressure, accords and national laws that have shaped the war; these are present in every single Andean country. The Andean Strategy, or Initiative, a pact signed with the Latin American politicians at the 1990 Cartagena Summit, allowed for a military/economic approach to the problem, whereby a definitive geopolitical doctrine was configured. Since it was an integral and regional doctrine, it unilaterally molded US/Latin American relations according to the outlines drawn by the super power.

The economic component was perhaps not the first dimension by which the Southern partners evaluated this pact, yet since Cartagena, the economics of the situation came to convince and soften Southern opposition. The concept of "shared responsibility" among "producer and consumer" countries made possible various new forms of underwriting. The economic chapter is interpreted differently by North Americans and Latin Americans. For the former, economic contribution, both then and now, is seen as a valid means to avoid adverse economic processes that may give rise to indigenous prohibition operations in the fragile, dependent coca leaf economies. For Latin Americans, economic aid must come before the military and police mechanisms, and must be essentially aimed at development and revitalizing institutional sectors, such as the judicial sector. The reality has been neither one nor the other.

Economic contributions have been decisive for the acceptance of the unilateral North American strategy. Until now, economic persuasion has permitted the progressive incorporation of the armed forces of the different countries, and the transformation of mixed economies with a large public sector into more liberal economies.

The War on Drugs, with its two basic components — the military and the economic — seeks to approach the problem from three different fronts: prohibition, eradication or crop substitution, and alternative development. The way these approaches have been implemented, and the depth and complexity of the narco-trafficking issue in America, imply a series of transformations that affect the essence of the democratic system at its core.

2. LOW INTENSITY WAR: THE NARCO-GUERRILLA

The flexible nature of illegal trafficking and its constant camouflage makes it a very poor target for conventional military tactics. Therefore, the insistence on eliminating the flow of cocaine in the places of production means moving the guerrilla war inside the producing zones — as well as processing laboratories.

Designating as criminal the economic activities that relate to cocaine production is a way of standing things on their heads, interpreting the growing demand for cocaine in the US as an invasion of Latino drugs brought in by perverse narco-traffickers who violate territorial sovereignty and endanger national security. In 1989, former director of the Southern Command in Panama General Paul Gorman stated: "our security and that of our children is threatened by Latino drug conspiracies, which are drastically more successful in subversion inside the United States than any of those established in Moscow," by way of justifying the new military objective.[163] The Southern Command and the Special Operations and Low Intensity War Command headquartered in Florida, two sectors of the Department of Defense, embraced the new strategic objectives of the US Armed Forces most enthusiastically. The cocaine war gives both Commands a leading role vis-à-vis other governmental departments; and by calling the War on Drugs a low intensity war, it means they must grant their soldiers combined anti-drug/anti-subversive war training and proper equipment, more often than not directed at the anti-subversive struggle, just like qualified professionals in regular low intensity wars.

The dramatic drug invasion can only be handled through a wide range of tactics based on low intensity warfare, intelligence, the development of covert operations and spy systems with double agents and instigating agents (which were previously "legitimized" by the Vienna Convention), and through an agile system of communications

---

163. Youngers, Coletta and Walsh, John. "La guerra contra las drogas en los Andes: una politica mal encaminda," p 343 in Garcia Sayan, Diego (ed.), op. cit.

linking the jungle spaces with operation centers, embassies, military bases, the Southern Command. Together with them, the various branches of the Department of Defense, the DEA and the CIA carry out covert operations with military personnel and the high technology of the Operational Command System, the Radar Network for the Caribbean Basin and the Aerial Recognizance Program.[164]

Thus at the end of the 1980s and after the fall of the Berlin Wall, the US Southern Command adapted its entire technical, human, and management infrastructure to the Number One priority, containing drugs, and, more specifically, cocaine.

Meanwhile, the economic process of illegal trafficking has adjusted to the political as well as the natural environmental conditions of deep South America, sharing territory with the guerrilla forces in Colombia as well as Peru. In Colombia the prolonged war between Conservatives and Liberals, known as *La Violencia*, which besides prohibiting political expression other than social demands, encouraged the formation of self-defense groups, later guerrilla fighters, which organized peasant emigration from the zones most affected by the oligarchic army to the more remote skirts of the Amazon mountains in Caquetá, Guaviare, Meta and Putumayo. Following the armed colonization was the influence of the FARC in defending the lands of the small farmers from the pressures of *latifundistas* and ranchers. The expansion of the coca crops came along with the progressive demands of the Antioquian narco-traffickers experienced in marijuana trafficking from the Atlantic Guajira.[165]

When the guerrilla and the narco-traffickers met, a power struggle resulted, leaning toward the guerrillas, who knows the territory and have the support of the population. However, the

---

164. Satellites and tactical radars that connect the DEA to Andean anti-drug forces through US embassies in each country, and which in turn are connected to the Southern Command and the CIA in the US (satellites and radars throughout the Caribbean basin: Colombia, Venezuela, Panama, Honduras, The Dominican Republic, Cuba, Puerto Rico and the border with Mexico since 1997). V. WOLA (Office of Latin American Affairs in Washington), 1991, *Clear and Present Dangers. The US Military and the War on Drugs in the Andes.*

165. Bagley, Bruce Michael 1988a, "Colombia and the War on Drugs," op. cit. and Kaplan Marcos, 1990, op. cit.

economic benefits that narco-trafficking offers the guerrilla groups, a new form of financing, and the mutual support of infrastructures, security, and production organization, led to the fruitful collaboration between both groups. The guerrillas act as a government among the peasant farmers, substituting or taking on the functions of an absent State (i.e., the *"gramaje"* coca leaf tax, defending workers' rights by prohibiting salary payment *pasta básica*, providing educational and health programs, and protection against the Army). "Where the guerrillas have control, anyone who has anything worth saving has to pay the guerrillas; where the State has control, similar relations are nurtured with the public bureaucrats. Then traffickers bribe and finance the 'official' security apparatus. In both situations the armed apparatus forms part of the 'local scene' and must be maintained by it. Narco-traffickers are also part of this 'local scene,' and as such they must enter into multiple treaties, understandings and transactions with the local monopolies of fire power, without whose agreement it would not be easy to go about the business of every day life."[166]

The alliance between narco-traffickers and guerrilleros is circumstantial, a "marriage of convenience." It has been so useful to the US propaganda apparatus to elaborate on the concepts of narco-guerrilla and narco-terrorism that the two seem now to be almost indistinguishable to the less alert. Washington uses them to justify superimposing the anti-subversive war onto the war on drugs, as inseparable members of one low intensity war.

Continuing with the past dynamics of de-legitimizing any political movement that radically questions the system, these guerrilla movements have been stigmatized as terrorists.[167] Counter-insurgency slogans and slogans for the fight against drugs seek the collaboration of the American armies[168] and the security organisms which in the past reinforced the oligarchic schemes in alliance with North American economic interests. The alliance between the narco-

---

166. Bustamante, Fernando. 1990, op. cit. p.257.

167. Benitez, Raúl. 1988, op. cit.

168. In the 1987 XVIII Conference of American Armies in Mar de Plata, they stated "there is a close strategic relationship between terrorism and narcotrafficking."

traffickers and the guerrilleros is a golden opportunity for North American strategists who have inherited the counter-insurgency doctrine.

Then US Ambassador to Colombia Lewis Tambs coined the term "narco-guerrilla" and conveniently linked communism to drug trafficking, spurring the early 1980s political and budgetary interests that were directed toward the connection. A US Senate Hearing on Drugs and Terrorism was held in 1984, and Eastern European countries, Cuba, leftist terrorist movements and narco-traffickers were linked. Shortly thereafter, intelligence services attempted to find links to Sandinista Nicaragua (the term is still useful today in rousing public sentiment) in addition to actual links between coca leaf farmers and the guerrilla in zones of Colombia (and previously in Peru). These formed the basis for rumors used to legitimize military intervention in subversive zones. This is demonstrated by continued attempts to generate disquiet with respect to narco-trafficking alliances in Castro's Cuba and the rebel territories of Chiapas, in Mexico.[169] In both cases, the evidence points to a dark pact between military intelligence, the DEA, and a docile sector of narco-trafficking.[170]

The equal strength of narco-traffickers and guerrilleros, though it gave rise to crop extension and illegal production in the 1980s, was broken with the accumulation of political, social, and economic

---

169. In Cuba, the links established by the Medellín cartel were decidedly severed and those responsible were executed. See José MARTI, 1989, *Caso 1/1989 El fin de la conexión cubana*. Editorial José Martí, La Habana, Cuba. Currently and according to *Los Tiempos*, 25-9-97 (Bolivia), referring to the Mexican newspaper *El universal*, Mexican narco-trafficker Amado Carrillo (*El señor de los Cielos*), protected by General Rebollo, high command of the war on drugs, "was able to develop for three years a connection in Cuba, with the support of the political influence of the son of a former ambassador to Mexico in Havana." In Chiapas, there is talk of the functioning of the alleged Southeast Cartel. See BLIXEN, Samuel en VVAA, 1997, *Guerra antidrogas*, op. cit.

170. Amado Carrillo, alias *Señor de los Cielos* because of his domination of air space, died in strange circumstances after plastic surgery. He was protected by General Rebollo who led the fight on drugs in Mexico and made it so Mexico substituted Colombians in the control of international illegal trafficking, and also that narco-trafficking itself would penetrate deeply within the military circles. The initial protection of the DEA granted Rebollo and Carrillo in Bolivia, and the rumors implicating Cubans, as well as the magnificent geopolitical advantages gained by the US when the scandal of the narco-general broke, lead one to believe that there was considerable participation of the DEA and the CIA in the entire process.

power on the part of the narco-traffickers and their transformation into large landowners.

This led to a lateral confrontation with the guerrillas in the form of a dirty war through organized paramilitaries, protected by the Army and by State inhibition. As the narco-traffickers became large landowners, they were not only aligned with the interests of landowners, but also developed systematic repression of peasants who were connected to the guerrillas or who sympathized ideologically. The process is not unlike the way the far left political options were marginalized during Virgilio Barco's administration (Colombia 1979-1990), which undid the beginnings of political negotiations with the guerrillas that had been begun by Belisario Betancur, and opened up a military front against the guerrillas and their political supporters.[171]

This superimposed the military offensive on the paramilitary offensive, which was then in the hands of the narco landowners of the Magdalena Medio region. In a kind of agrarian counter reform, they began expelling small farmers who supported the guerrillas, using military or paramilitary terror[172] to take over up to 7.5 million acres of property. According to sociologist Ricardo Vargas, this implies "a social, political, economic, and violence price of Colombia's narco-trafficking" that is much higher than murdering politicians or judges, since the incorporation of the new social groups from narco-trafficking through "the acquisition of the richest lands, their integration as backers for the counter insurgent dirty war, their potential to accelerate state attempts to privatize power, their ability to continue the phenomenon of impunity, where the scant institutional and state legitimacy in Colombia is debated," amount to a mortgage on the country's future.[173]

---

171. Vargas Meza, Ricardo. "The FARC: War and State Crisis." *NACLA Report*, vol XXXI, N°5 1998.

172. One million displaced from their land for more than three decades of civil war, and thousands killed by the military or paramilitary soldiers, according to Colombian police. *En busca de soluciones* (cooperatives), Informe Misión of European Parliament members, and representatives of NGOs for the Andean Region Colombia, Peru and Bolivia) research the impact of policies to control illegal drug production, March 1998.

Thus a pathetic process has begun to grow: a tumor which impedes social justice and the triumph of democracy and legality. On the one side was the strengthening of the guerrilla groups in the 1980s and 1990s, with solid support from sectors affected by the economic crisis imposed by the war on drugs, and on the other, the increasing power of narco-traffickers, who control 40% of the national territory in Colombia. Since the Army cannot destroy the guerrillas' social support, it has delegated the armed struggle to the paramilitaries in a "privatization of power." The enormous economic and political power of the narco kings is demonstrated by the failure of the negotiations begun by former President Pastrana, who also attempted (and failed) to sign a peace plan with the guerrillas,[174] by the expansion of the military as laid out in Plan Colombia, and by the victory of Alvaro Uribe, who represents the far-right and has the benefits of his family history and support of the emerging narco-trafficking sector.[175] Alvaro Uribe Velez is a tough right-winger known for his commitment to wipe out the rebels who killed his father 20 years ago. He enjoyed a 70% popularity rating in 2003, having won by a landslide in May 2002 with his promise to tackle the Marxist guerrillas who have waged a four decades-long war on the state.

Even though the House of Representatives has repeatedly objected to the use of funds for anti-subversive activities, the different forms of financing the various participating forces, scant or inefficient control of the destination of funds, the priority of some objectives over others, the need to confront the guerrilla in some cases and union

---

173. Ricardo VARGAS, 1997, "Colombia: la herejia de los maniqueos," en VVAA *Guerra anti-drogas*, op. cit.

174. This peace plan was sharply criticized by the US, which thought the attempt at peace interfered with drug eradication programs. *The Guardian*. Canada. 11/16/98.

175. His father, Alberto Uribe Sierra, was a friend of the Ochoa brothers (from the Medellín Cartel), and contributed to the introduction of Pablo Escobar as a deputy in Congress. His brother Jaime participated in narco-trafficking operations with Escobar. In charge of Aeronáu-tica Civil, Alvaro himself gave flight licenses to 350 narco traffickers, created the *Convivir* armed self-defense group (the seed which grew to the current paramilitary group AUC) and, according to accusations in the Colombian press, received money from Pablo Escobar for his political career as mayor and governor, according to Gaspar Fraga in "Colombia: Uribe for President" Revista *Cáñamo* nº 54. June 2002, Barcelona.

demands, in others, have all made the war on drugs into a low intensity war. This has even intensified after the terrorist attacks of September 11, 2001. The all-out war on terrorism renewed the bipartisan consensus in the US Congress, ending the Democrat prejudice against using drug control funds in the counter-insurgency struggle, thereby clearing the way for the complete and thorough application of Plan Colombia. (Washington's Bureau of Western Hemisphere Affairs calls Plan Colombia "an integrated strategy to meet the most pressing challenges confronting Colombia today — promoting the peace process, combating the narcotics industry, reviving the Colombian economy, and strengthening the democratic pillars of Colombian society." Its components include US support for human rights and judicial reform, expansion of counter-narcotics operations into southern Colombia, alternative economic development, increased interdiction and assistance for the Colombian National Police.)

The primary goal of the Andean Initiative is supposed to be to reduce the flow of cocaine to the US; this has been achieved, using local military or police forces. The US is aware of the political wear-and-tear that the direct participation of its own troops in operations of prohibition would have, so it seeks to use Latin American fighting forces to man these operations. Nonetheless, the entire strategy is designed in Washington. In addition to planning and developing operations, the cocaine war is granting the US its long-postponed desire — an Inter-American Army, under its command.

Between 1990 and 1997, the US attempted to expand its strategy to the entire region, which is divided into three sectors for the anti-drug struggle: Sector I encompasses the Andean region, Sector II: Ecuador, Venezuela, Brazil and the Southern Cone, and Sector III: Panama and Central America.

From 1990 to 1998, the incorporation of the armed forces and the unfolding of the War on Drugs by several Latin American governments, were slow. The signing of the Free Trade Treaty with Mexico and its inclusion in the North American economic zone have called for extensive changes in that country in particular, with the Mexican Army dropping much of its "nationalist" bent and its historical anti-Americanism in favor of virtual submission.

3.   THE INCORPORATION OF THE ARMED FORCES

The idea of creating a multilateral military force, a constant in North American diplomacy since the Pan-Americanism of the beginning of the 20th century and especially after the Second World War, in line with the Doctrine of National Security, is once again being attempted. It was formally presented in the 1992 Summit of the Ministers of Defense in San Antonio, when Bush's idea was categorically rejected by governments alleging that the US was planning massive abrogation of their national sovereignty. For the moment, US pressure from several areas, not only "certification" is softening the nationalistic will of Latino countries and their fear of the extension of corruption and the strengthening of the military sector which, in many countries, had recently participated in military dictatorships.

A. The Andean Region

In the case of Bolivia, diplomatic and economic pressures as well as the way the US intelligence service was handling the issue were all major influences, from the beginning. General Garcia Meza's coup was carried out in the early 1980s with the support of the narco-traffickers and with the collaboration and knowledge of the CIA.

Paramilitary forces and the intelligence services of several Central American countries were financed by Bolivian cocaine in the midst of Reagan's anti-Communist crusade.[176] Later the unabashed production and trafficking of cocaine impelled Garcia Meza's fall, even though once the master lines for illegal production and

---

176. Blixen, Samuel. 1997, "The Dual Role of Narco-trafficking in State Terrorism and Militarized Democracy," in VVAA *Guerra antidrogas*, op.cit. 1997.

trafficking were created, business went on with the support of various political and military spheres.

The first pressures for the military to join in the fight on drugs date from 1986 when the anti-drug law establishing certification was newly implemented. The first military operation — *Blast Furnace* — was carried out against trafficking and the suspension of North American military aid was ended. This same carrot and stick policy was useful in firming up the 1987 bilateral pact; domestically, it took the form of the severe Law 1008, passed in 1989, and led to the definitive participation of the Bolivian Armed Forces in the war on drugs from 1991 onward, after the promise of economic and military aid from the US (acquired in the San Antonio Summit).

Paz Zamora's attempt to incorporate himself autonomously in the war and simultaneously to support Andean coca culture was completely broken by Bolivia's economic dependence, its weak diplomacy and the fact that the country's elites were implicated politically and economically in narco-trafficking themselves. The DEA and US Embassy information services have intervened noticeably in this power struggle. In Bolivia it is common to use the drugs issue for political bribery, and this was applicable to Paz Zamora and his independent position with respect to the US.[177] North American success in imposing its military plan in Bolivia has weakened the civilian and police forces, reinforcing dependence on the United States, which finances the entire organization of the war on drugs inside Bolivia.[178]

The model for the fight against drugs, directed primarily toward the eradication of crops, linked US aid to the success of coca eradication, with particular pressure on the peasants during military operations. Their human and political rights were under constant

---

177. The "narco-links" scandal — childhood friendship of President Paz Zamora and well-known narco-traffickers, treated with kid gloves by Bolivian forces of justice, was the excuse in this case to doubt his integrity. In the interim, as in Samper's case later, he was denied a US visa and great diplomatic pressure was exerted so his support of the Coca Leaf and his rejection of the armed forces joining in the struggle would not be taken into account. Roncken, Theo. "Bolivia: la impunidad y el control de la corrupcion en la lucha antidrogas" in VVAA *"Guerra anti-drogas,"* op. cit. 1997.

attack and a permanent state of siege existed in what had been the coca zones. Even so, the strategy was fruitless because of the crops were simply shifted to new zones. While small-scale trafficking was repressed (with extremely severe laws which do not consider any guarantee of trial),[179] impunity was established in the military and police sectors. The game plan permitted US agents freedom of movement and strategies and depended on US financing, all of which favored the professionalization of trafficking, tied it to the highest sectors of the society, led to the manipulation of information, and encouraged the formulation of strategies that suited the DEA even if they were dubious by many standards,[180] as well as resulting in the constant violation of the human, political and union rights of the large Bolivian indigenous sector.[181]

Peruvians have also personalized their focus in the fight on drugs by emphasizing economic over military aspects. The Peruvians negotiated the Framework Accord more skillfully with the US in May 1991, confirming the fight against subversion. They directed more

---

178. The combined US/Bolivian forces work: on the Bolivian side the military unit UMOPAR and the specialized police force FELCN, under the orders of the DEA and US Embassy agents, which finance the current and extra costs. In addition to the payments assigned in each one of the sections of the agencies and the forces, the FELCN, and UMOPAR directors as well as the personnel in the anti-drug fight, student attending anti-narcotics courses and special judges against drugs receive EXTRA SALARIES. The feared taxes imposed by Law 1008 are directly paid by the US, as well as the anti-drugs police. V. WOLA, 1997: *Explorando la guerra contra las drogas*, by Jacqueline Williams. Ed. Washington Office on Latin America, translated by the Asamblea Permanente Derechos Humanos Cochabamba.

179. The trials are truly Kafkaesque: innocent or guilty, those with no money to settle their cases have had to remain in jail for several years, though Law 1008 places three months as the time limit. The lawyers can go to trial though the judge thinks there is not enough evidence. The anti-narcotics police, in addition to the arrests, prepared evidence of guilt for the lawyers. There reports of torture and coercion to obtain confessions. In the majority of the cases the only evidence is the statement or confession itself. In 60% of the cases, it is given under physical or psychological pressure or beatings and kicks and threats of torture. 63% of the cases have no defending lawyer, and 25% with no district attorney. 65% had been cut off from communications before trial for more than two days. (Investigación RED Andina de Informacion, 1995) cit. por Roncken, 1997, Guerra Antidrogas.

180. The 1995 case of the Narco-plane which arrived in Lima with 5 tons of cocaine destined for Mexico, the DEA's knowledge of the cargo and the active collaboration of the Bolivian police FELCN raise many doubts about the support the US intelligence services and the DEA have given so Colombian narco-traffickers would be substituted by Mexican ones, very connected to the military spheres.

funds to civic action than to military labors and the forced eradication in coca producing zones; the risk was that overdoing the repression would build social support for the Shining Path. The military prioritization of the anti-subversive war was compensated by President Fujimori: from his position of power he allowed narco-trafficking in military zones throughout the three years that military participation lasted.[182] Between 1992 and 1997, the US formally punished Fujimori's self-coup and blocked military aid for human rights violations, though there was still explicit support and intense collaboration between the CIA and the Peruvian secret service, the director of which, Vladimiro Montesinos, was directly linked to narco-trafficking and was responsible for murders, tortures and other human rights violations.[183] He was also one of the leading figures in the profoundly corrupt Fujimori state apparatus.

Just as Bolivia prioritizes economic development and overcoming poverty as key steps in the fight on drugs, and Peru emphasizes development and the fight against domestic subversion, so Colombia has priorities that differ from those held by US. Bolivia has attempted to mark distinct perspectives and diplomacies independently of the superpower.

---

181. Peasant repression has strengthened the power of producer unions and their political legitimacy. In the June 2002 presidential elections, the Indian and coca-advocate candidate Evo Morales won second place after a veritable media and legal battle to distance him from the elections, since in 1998 he was the most-voted member of parliament. In the months preceding the 2002 elections, the conventional political powers and the powerful apparatus of the war on drugs attempted to defame him by making him directly responsible for the coca-grower conflicts and their human and material losses. Without parliamentary immunity he was imprisoned and fined, and the press which supported the movement were censured. The pressure against him and his party reached the point the US embassy even threatened to suspend aid if Morales won the presidency.

182. Soberon, Ricardo in *Guerra antidrogas*, op. cit. 1997.

183. He was the great power in the shadows. He was a lawyer for narco-traffickers. He was tried for treason when he passed on information to the CIA. He skillfully handled the country's information and was the head of the secret services SIN). It is suspected that he was protected by the CIA and had all the support of the US Embassy. *Personal interviews* of the vice Ambassador of the US in Peru, Heather Hedges and director of the *Narcotic Asistence Service*, John Crew; and Ricardo Soberón, Comisión Andina de Juristas member of the Congressional Commission on narco-trafficking and corruption, January 1998, Lima and "La cara oculta de Fujimori" in *El País*, 9-8-97. See *El País*, August 5, 2001.

The Colombian government priorities are to end the violence of narco-trafficking, reinforce the judicial system and obtain better commercial treatment of legal exports, while the armed forces concentrate on doing away with the guerrillas. Politically and diplomatically, Colombia has been the most active in defending and prioritizing its own vision of the problem. During the Virgilio Barco administration (1986 to 1990), this meant ending the narco-terrorism bribery associated with the Medellín Cartel (which explains the increased similarity to the repressive US focus). During Gaviria's administration the focus was to reform and strengthen the judicial system by rejecting extradition to the US, which greatly complicated the fight on drugs. The policy of submission and collaboration with justice, and the independence with respect to the North American policy made the already sensitive bilateral relations even more tense, practically reducing them to the drug question.[184] This meant Colombia's de-certification from 1996 until Pastrana was elected (1998-2002) and submitted to the US strategy embodied in Plan Colombia.[185]

President Barco gained an international reputation for his aggressive take on drug trafficking in Colombia and his refusal to negotiate with drug kingpins, but it seems to have created a very messy situation. With respect to the Colombian army, its participation in the war on drugs is very alarming. The Colombian

---

184. During Gaviria's administration, the strengthening of the judicial system underwent the rejection of Extradition considered in the 1991 Constitution, and the confidence in the effectiveness of the judicial system through policies of submission and repentance, to break the cartels and continue prohibition. The war on the Medellin Cartel meant the interested collaboration of sectors very close to the Cali Cartel — Los Pepes or Perseguidos by Pablo Escobar — with the Security Services, which later exploded in the hands of Samper, mortgaging his later policy. The US press has played a very active role in denouncing corruption linked to Samper and the Liberal Party, reinforcing the US focus of the war on drugs and weakening the Colombian position favoring the debate on legalization. Ricardo Vargas, "The Impact of Drugs Control Policies at the National Level in Colombia. Drugs Control Policies in Colombia 1986-95: Prohibition, Institutional Crisis and the Absence of Civil Society," *Release Drugs Edition*, Issue 11, March 1996.

185. It was the first time since 1986 that the US decertified an ally and commercial partner. All economic aid was not paralyzed because of issues of *national security*. Colombian decertification in this period contrasts with the Mexican certification, with serious problems of corruption and narco-trafficking in Mexico, but also very significant US economic interests.

military has always been opposed to the fight, and up until 1995 they supported it indirectly by using anti-drug war materials in counter-insurgency efforts, i.e., by highlighting guerrilla connections with the drug traffickers, thus overcoming some members of the US Congress' doubts concerning human rights violations by the Army.[186] When in 1995 the fundamentally urban police efforts had eliminated part of the power of the organized cartels and their business and processing centers, and the recently-elected Ernesto Samper scandal broke out, prompting the US withdrawal of political support, the Army became completely involved in the fight. It formed the Search Block.

The de-legitimization of the Colombian government by the ongoing de-certification of its anti-drug policy coincided with the army's deep involvement in the war on drugs, notwithstanding repeated human rights violations and its support of the paramilitary dirty war.[187] If there were doubts about US military advisor mobility and independence of action in Colombia in the late 1980s and early 90s, by the end of the 1990s the strengthening of the Colombian military apparatus in the fight on drugs along with the progressive weakening of the civilian sector allowed for action that was completely independent of the North Americans.

Even aerial fumigation was carried out in coca zones.[188] The Colombian case clearly shows the increasing US commitment for advisory purposes and training for special anti-drug troops throughout Latin America, and illustrates the repercussions in other political areas inside Latin America. Faced with the flow of cocaine from the Colombian cartels at the end of the 1980s, and President Virgilio Barco's crackdown on drugs, Bush sent a team from the Defense Intelligence Agency to analyze Colombian intelligence organizations. According to US sources and high officials in

---

186. *GAO* Report, 1991, cit. by Vargas, Ricardo, Herejía de los maniqueos, in *Guerra anti-drogas*, op. cit. 1997.

187. Vargas, Ricardo. "The Impact of Drug Control Policies at the National Level in Colombia. Drug Control Policies in Colombia 1986-95: Prohibition, Institutional Crisis and the Absence of Civil Society." *Release Drugs Edition*, Issue 11, March 1996.

188. Youngers, C. in *Guerra antidrogas*, op. cit. 1997.

Colombia, in 1991 the Colombian government issued Secret Order #200 — 05/91, which expanded on US team recommendations to create an intelligence network. The majority of the intelligence groups, made up of retired officials, were later accused by human rights organizations of organizing the massacre of civilians.[189] As a result of these investigations, and pressured by human rights organizations and Congress, the White House drastically reduced military aid in 1995, limiting training to anti-drug related tasks only. Clinton reduced what was left of military aid between 1996 and 1997 when he decertified Ernesto Samper. Still, according to documents from the Defense Department and declarations of US officials, special operations training continued.

De-certification didn't cut all military aid, because of the "exceptions for national security" clause. The US and Colombia signed an accord in 1997 to guarantee that US military aid would be used exclusively for the fight against drugs and not the guerrilla. As a condition for aid, military units would be examined and those suspected of violating human rights would not qualify. But units being trained for special operations were not subjected to these controls. These special operations increased from 48% in 1995 to 62% in 1998, and they are mainly active in operations in the guerilla zone. This is precisely where military units are frequently accused of human rights violations as they fight either the narco-traffickers' laboratories or guerrilla camps. Thus, US military aid to the Colombian army and its own war against the narco-guerrilla is intensifying the Colombian civil war. The narco-trafficking sectors are getting stronger, by buying land and paramilitary protection, and are spreading a new model for the commercial planting of the coca leaf and the poppy, pushing out small farmers and converting the guerillas' base of support.

The perverse dynamic begun with the militarization of the war on drugs and the forced eradication via fumigations has been strengthened with Plan Colombia. Its $7,500 million budget will take

---

189. Farah, Douglas. "A Tutor to Every Army in Latin America. US Expands Latin American Training Role." *Washington Post*, 13 July 1998.

the conflict to infinity, with no solution for the primary problem of the peace process.[190]

It is worth noting that the slow incorporation of the armies of Andean countries into the war on drugs has evolved parallel to a progressive increase in the US anti-drug military budgets and a progressive intensification of anti-drug rhetoric in successive US elections. In 1996, Congress doubled the budget for international programs for drug control effective in fiscal year 1997. The funding was mainly destined for the Andean region and Mexico, while it reduced budgets for development and international organizations. This US aid slated 66.5% to military and police initiatives and 15.5% to development.[191] The proximity of the 2000 elections led Clinton to propose the largest increase in the Defense budget since the Reagan years, suggesting $100,000 million over the next 6 years, largely destined for the cocaine war.[192] But the most formidable increase in the military strategy began after the events of 9/11, when the US military budget went back to the heights established during the Cold War,[193] and the public discourse regressed to a simplified vision of global reality.

B. The Southern Cone

Just as the countries of the Southern Cone, or *Mercosur*, have historically been the counterpoint to US hegemony, by marking some distance and relative autonomy from the hemisphere's superpower, in the case of drug trafficking interpenetration itself is setting the

---

190. Of this aid, a minimal percentage will be effectively invested in Colombia; a large part of the Plan is destined to the purchase of war material from US manufacturers of helicopters, communications technology or military accessories. The European Union as a whole and the majority of Europe in general have not looked kindly upon Plan Colombia and are financing several planned events in the Peace Process which are part of the social component of Plan Colombia. "Europe and Plan Colombia" *Drugs and Conflict Debate Paper* nº 1, April 2001, Transnational Institute.

191. Youngers, 1997, *Guerra antidrogas*, op. cit.

192. *El País*, 3 January 1999.

193. According to the Stockholm International Peace Research Institute (SIPRI); *Yearbook 2003*.

rhythm of the acceptance of US proposals by the Southern Cone's greatest powers, such as Argentina and Brazil.

While as a continent they may emphatically and institutionally deny greater involvement of their Armed Forces in the drug war, rejecting any proposal for an all-hemisphere army or a multinational force under Washington's command, things are different when viewed bilaterally. In Cartagena, San Antonio and Bariloche, Mercosur categorically rejected this multilateral force as well as the possibility of participating in a center for military anti-drug training on US territory. It seriously objected to greater cooperation on the drug issue and, protective of its sovereignty, demonstrated distrust of US interventionism. The development of joint operations with several countries under the leadership of the US a few months prior[194] contradicted the wishes and fears expressed by the Southern Cone countries in collective meetings, and compromised the autonomy and independence of the middle status powers (as Kissinger would say).

The development of joint operations and the progressive involvement of the Latin American armed forces has limited the relative autonomy acquired by the Southern Cone in the 1970s. The drug issue has been turned into a constant drip that has slowly worn away at governments, societies and the guarantors of national sovereignty — the Armed Forces. Both Brazil and Argentina have demonstrated increasing permeability to US pressures.

In both cases, aligning with Washington's foreign policy and improving bilateral relations has led to greater logistical and intelligence collaboration in the drug war, but the need for a greater international role[195] undermined the principles of regional autonomy demonstrated in Mercosur. Argentina's attempt to become a special US ally by signing a military treaty for cooperation on issues of drugs

---

194. Operation Laser Strike (April — June 1996), to interrupt the aerial narco-trafficking bridges in the Amazons and the Andes was carried out on Bolivian, Peruvian, and Colombian territory with the complete involvement of these countries and their military and police forces, and with the cooperation of Venezuela, Ecuador, and Brazil, whose military intervention in logistics and intelligence was a surprise for the Brazilian population as it had indicated it did not want to be more involved in the war on drugs. See Brener, Jaime. "Maniobras radicales" in *Guerra antidrogas*, op. cit.

and fundamentalism finally tipped the balance of the power relations in the Southern Cone. This endangered any effort for regional cooperation. It also generated a synergy that prompted Brazil, and then other members of Mercosur, to join a special alliance on drugs with the hegemonic power so as not to be left on the sidelines in a game that encompassed the entire American space, North and South, with respect to satellite controls, radars and data interpreting centers connecting the US to every geographic point from the Mexican border to Tierra de Fuego.

Without forgetting the apprehension of the Southern Cone armies, which feared the growth of corruption as much as they feared distancing themselves from their traditional obligations, a new concept of continental security was probably taking shape, designed to include narco-trafficking, narco-subversion and narco-terrorism as threats to collective security as well as the penetration of narco-trafficking into the political, economic and social structures. This would allow a new kind of military alliance with the US And so the entire process repeated itself, like a smoke curtain hiding the penetration of narco-trafficking.[196]

The double-edged sword of narco-trafficking (participation in business and the repression that feeds business) would help to validate good relations with the superpower by guaranteeing the development of free enterprise and putting out revolutionary flames, stifling union demands and the cries of environmentalists worried about the extensive zone of forest decline. This justified the Armed Forces' new role as gendarmes and their increasing responsibility for controlling domestic security, as well as cases of fundamentalism/terrorism and subversion/delinquency associated with narco-

---

195. Brazil opted for a post on the UN Security Council and Argentina obtained the legitimacy of its armed forces after the disastrous dictatorship and the Falklands War, increasing its intervention in international conflicts as UN Peace Forces. V Rossi, Adriana, 1997,"*Argentina: ¿futuro gendarme de América?*" 1997, *Guerra antidrogas,*

196. During the Menem administration scandals have arisen because of the deep penetration of narco-trafficking in the Argentine political and economic structures, directly affecting Menem's personal circle. See Lejtman, Roman. *Narcogate. El dinero de la droga,* 1994, Eds Apóstrofe, Barcelona and A. ROSSI,1997, in *Crimen uniformado,* op. cit.

trafficking, just as in their day US strategists re-evaluated its role after the fall of the Berlin Wall.

C. Mexico and Central America

Mexico and Central America were brought into the war on drugs following a dynamic that is different from the Andean region and the Southern Cone.

In Mexico's case, the shared border of 2,000 miles, a shared history, and the implementation of NAFTA comprise a relationship that is far to many-dimensioned to be reduced to the drug problem alone, but that is the sole question that determined bilateral relations in the early 1980s.[197] When the Free Trade Agreement was signed, shared political and economic interests overcame the constant problems surrounding the drug issue. The incorporation of the Mexican military apparatus into the war on drugs has been problematic, and the role of US intelligence in applying increasing pressure to convince their Mexican counterparts of the need to assume the superpower's security framework has been controversial. The 1997 Rebollo case (the general who ran the top department for the fight on drugs, INCD) showed that high-level officials were protecting some narco-trafficking organizations while attacking others. It also exposed the involvement of large sectors of the Army — and the DEA's knowledge of (and hands-off attitude concerning) all these connections. This has raised serious doubts about US commitment to eliminating such connections, but even more so about its responsibility in spreading corruption to a sector considered vital to safeguarding sovereignty and territorial integrity such as the Army.[198]

---

197. Endemic Mexican corruption and the shared border allowed a constant flow of drugs and narco-traffickers. The case of Enrique Camarena, DEA agent killed in Mexico by important narco-traffickers protected by power, greatly complicated bilateral relations. There are significant allusions to this case in the 1986 Antidrugs Abuse Act which established the certification mechanism.

The gradual substitution of the Colombian cartels by Mexican cartels in illegal drug trafficking in Latin America[199] and the close connections of the latter with the Mexican Army leads to the notion that "the Rebollo case serves the US to prove to Mexico that it is not prepared to fight narco-trafficking. And if the Armed Forces were losing the fight with the drug barons, the White House could condition certification on a greater penetration of US military and police forces within their Mexican counterparts," as the Mexican expert on National Security, John Saxe Fernandez,[200] has said. He also stated that "there has been evidence for some time of the US need for armed forces in Mexico beyond the military barracks, to take care of domestic conflicts, as a key piece in a global design to control the country's geo-strategic resources, especially oil and uranium in the subsoil, through multinational companies."

This controversial strategy, repeated throughout the entire hemisphere, has been used to soften members of the military, "the third link," after political and economic ties, according to William Perry, Pentagon Chief at the end of 1995.[201] This softening has opened the way to a substantial increase in the number of US military advisors in Mexico, the training and preparation of members of the Mexican military in the US (in violation of Mexican law banning the training of troops outside of Mexico) and the increased presence of US military personnel and their right to bear arms and intervene inside Mexico. As a whole, the scandal has been very useful.

---

198. The Mexican army has been marked since the Mexican-American War (1846–48), when the US won a third of its territory, by anti-American nationalism, which has called for a progressive softening, obtained by the war on drugs with its different components (participation in the signaling, identification, marginalization and political pressure on the "corrupt" and guidance and intervention in the secret services and domination and handling of information.- DEA, CIA-)V.VAN KLAVEREN, Alberto, 1983, op. cit. (comp).

199. "Colombian Mafia denounced to the DEA the arrival of a drug plane", *Hoy* 3-4-1997 and "The Power of the Mexican Narco-Trafficking Supplants the Colombian in the US" *El Deber* 6-8-1997.

200. From the Universidad Nacional Autónoma de México, cit por Fazio, Carlos "México: el caso del narcogeneral," en VVAA *Crimen uniformado*, op. cit. 1997.

201. Fazio, Carlos: *El tercer vínculo*, editorial Joaquín Mortiz, México, 1996.

The US conditions imposed after the 1997 certification have been highly interventionist: the arrest of drug kingpins (i.e., Carrillo and the Arellano brothers), the extradition of 12 Mexican narco-traffickers using the new Extradition Treaty, diplomatic immunity for 39 DEA agents and permission for them to bear arms in Mexico, permission to sail US Coast Guard ships for tasks related to prohibition on territorial waters, the dismantling of the INCD and subsequent creation of a Mexican DEA — a special civilian investigative office with agents selected and trained by the FBI, the CIA and the DEA itself. The CIA also increased its power in Mexico: while Mexican intelligence services were dismantled, the CIA sent 200 agents, informants and analysts to address narco-trafficking, and permission was granted for 22 US anti-drug police officers to work on Mexican turf, added to the 45 DEA officers already there after the Alliance Against Drugs Accord[202] was signed by the US and Mexico. In addition to the employees of the DEA, CIA, FBI and the Department of the Treasury, US diplomats also increased, and all had the charge to investigate the penetration of narco-trafficking in all economic, political and governmental levels in Mexico.[203] By bringing the military into the war on drugs, and mounting multifaceted tactics, training and teams to control the rebel territories of Chiapas, makes Mexico's similar to Colombia's situation. The war on drugs is an example of low-intensity warfare, waged by attacking the guerrillas or at least reducing their social base.

In Mexico's case, anti-drug material, personnel and efforts have been used in counterinsurgency operations in Chiapas, Guerrero and Oaxaca, and wherever the authorities have detected the formation of a new Southeast Cartel operating in Chiapas, Campeche and Tabasco. As in Colombia, to avoid wear and tear on the Army, paramilitary groups are armed and encouraged, effectively privatizing the forces so

---

202. *El País*, 2-5-97, 7-5-97 y 8-5-97 y 8-2-98.

203. The first results came out of the Casablanca operation against the laundering of dollars, the first operation carried out completely by US organisms in Mexican banks without informing Zedillo's government. "Estados Unidos investigó a los principales bancos mexicanos sin informar al gobierno de Zedillo" *El País*, 20-5-98.

they can work with impunity. Paramilitary groups like the *Chinchulines*, and others, are responsible for the deaths or disappearances of up to 600 peasants between 1996 and 1997.[204] Chiapas has become a huge military zone with frequent mobilizations and intimidations on the part of the military in support of peasant paramilitary groups belonging to the then governing Institutional Revolutionary Party.[205]

With respect to Central America, as part of the vital zone for US security and hegemony, it was the scene where the Cold War was carried out in the late 1980s. The cocaine and crack boom was exploding throughout America. The fact that both phenomena coincided is not a matter of chance. Narco-trafficking was an extraordinary tool in the hands of the intelligence networks, which comprised the anti-subversion struggle in El Salvador, Nicaragua, Honduras, Guatemala and Panama. It would be impossible to understand the Central American crisis of the Reagan years if we did not consider the network of paramilitaries and narco-traffickers created with CIA supervision. Argentine advisors, experts in repression and dirty war and overseen by the CIA, connected Central American military apparatuses with Bolivian narco-traffickers to create a financing route that allowed for the hiring of mercenaries, and the establishment of paramilitary networks and arms trade.[206]

The end of the Cold War fed the criminal networks through the political displacement of large sectors of ex-fighters and mercenaries. Along with the economic crisis, high levels of unemployment, injustice and corruption, this made them easy targets for recruiters forming alliances with narco-traffickers and criminal organizations. The displaced continue pressuring for their interests and join in an informal economy which is illegal. There is, in all of these countries, an

---

204. Blixen, Samuel, 1997, *Guerra antidrogas*,op. cit.

205. Annual Summary 1998. Agencia Informativa Púlsar. http://www.amarc.org/pulsar.

206. The investigation revealed that drugs distributed in Los Angeles (attributed by the San Jose Mercury News to the origin of the crack boom in the African American population), was deposited in the Salvadoran air bases, and from there taken by small planes to Texas airports, with CIA protection. Between 1981 and 1988 up to 100 kilos of cocaine were brought in weekly. Blixen, Samuel. 1997, op. cit.

overlap between paramilitaries and former death squads, with heavily armed criminal structures that are responsible for kidnappings, extortions, bank robberies, auto theft and trafficking arms and drugs, the majority of which are linked to reactionary sectors of the Army and intelligence groups.[207]

In every case, the Armies have joined the war on drugs with no serious opposition. In Guatemala, the same members of the military who have systematically violated human rights have paradoxically received the mission to safeguard domestic order to fight the war on drugs. According to Nobel Peace Prize winner Rigoberta Menchú (1992), this is "counterproductive for democracy since the Army has power in parts of the country where no other State institutions exist and where, in the past 35 years, it has had absolute control over the population using systems of military proxies and other mechanisms of domination which were officially eliminated in the *peace negotiations*."[208]

As in other countries, enrolling the militaries into this war has been paralleled by a penetration of the Colombian cartels, as a result of which important links between narco-trafficking and militaries have been formed. While the confluence of narcos and the anti-subversive war created the distribution channels in the 1980s, today the same channels remain, paying the local narco-traffickers in cocaine. Cocaine has become a currency which can be converted to cash immediately.

While Costa Rica and Panama are fundamentally countries of transit and laundering, Guatemala, Honduras, and Nicaragua have become producers. In all of them the spread of consumption among the disenfranchised youth is alarming. In general, the extension of production is a consequence of formidable permissiveness and impunity from the seats of power.[209] A blind eye is turned to the fact

---

207. Jelsma, Martin. 1997, op. cit., in VVAA, *Guerra antidrogas.*
208. Leffert, Mike. 1997, "Guatemala: el narcotráfico y el ejército de posguerra" in VVAA Narcotráfico: obstáculo para la democratización y la desmilitarización en Centroamérica, Ed. TNI, Inforpress y CEDIB.
209. Celada, Edgar. 1997, in VVAA, *Narcotráfico: obstáculo*, Op. cit.

that narco-trafficking and the military sector have blended together, because the latter is pleased to accept their new role as police granted them by the war on drugs. They participate fully in the training of Special Forces organized by the US Southern Command, and they are generally satisfied with the increased US military commitment sponsored by the Pentagon[210] because, after the Cold War ended, it justified their existence with a new mission — a police mission.

The meeting of the hemisphere's military commanders, coordinated and led by the US, was foreseen as a Multinational Force resulting from US Pan-Americanism and the rhetoric of Drug-free Americas, in the planned (and, to date, failed) Multilateral Anti-Drug Center in the Republic of Panama. All diplomatic, political and military efforts, bilateral and multilateral, in America, were directed to the establishment of this operations center which was a vast strategic network uniting everything from Alaska to the Tierra de Fuego. Domestic US and Latin American opposition to the Multilateral Center, based on the fact that it violates the Carter-Torrijos treaty, and the anti-US sentiment revived by the new military base, have prolonged the negotiations.

Meanwhile, since the Howard Air Force Base in Panama (from which the US Southern Command had operated) was closed in 1999, the US has erected Forward Operating Locations (FOLs) at various points in Latin America (Ecuador, Aruba, Curacao and El Salvador). Puerto Rico has replaced Panama for forward basing headquarters in the region for the Army, Navy and Special Forces, while the SouthCom headquarters itself is located in Miami. It also operates some 17 radar sites in Peru and Colombia, all forming a cordon around Colombia. Furthermore, there are two older US bases in the region: Soto Cano (Honduras) and Guantánamo (Cuba).

The Pentagon has opted to subcontract part of the operations and maintenance personnel at these military bases to private companies. Dyn Corp, the most widely-known, has worked in the many operatives of the war on drugs since 1997. Its mercenaries have

---

210. Farah, Douglas. *Washington Post*, 13 July 1998.

been questions for their actions in the war in Yugoslavia and it has participated in the fumigation of illegal crops as well as in secret shipments of cocaine and the Colombian Dirty War.[211]

The host countries agreed to the establishment of the FOLs to facilitate military surveillance for the purpose of interdicting drug shipments. There is no evidence that the FOLs have made any discernible difference to the flow of illicit drugs to the USA, however, as even US military sources and the US General Accounting Office publicly acknowledge.[212] Analysts and experts underscore that illegal trafficking will not change at all because cocaine is now entering the US in huge, sealed containers, by sea or by land, and military radars and controls cannot detect them.[213]

In Colombia, the scheme functions based on aid for drug control (Tolemaida, Tres Esquinas, Apiay), but also on the aid to fight the FARC in Arauca (oil infrastructure protection). Around Colombia the armed forces of neighboring countries (Peru, Ecuador, Brazil and Panama) are the ones who provide containment, monitoring and border patrol.

If one notes the situation at the end of the 1970s, when the loss of US influence and the greater autonomy of the Latin American countries drastically reduced the number of US military advisors throughout the continent — going from more than 800 in 1968 to a

---

211. Mercenaries employed by Dyn Corp, acting in Bosnia, participated in the illegal trafficking of passports and weapons and were accused of trafficking young Russian and Romanian girls in Serbia and Croatia. In May 2000, a shipment of cocaine sent to the US by Dyn Corp was intercepted in the El Dorado Airport (Bogotá). This same company was contracted to train police in Iraq alter the fall of Baghdad. See V. Asociación Latinoamericana para los Derechos Humanos, http://www.tni.org/drogas/research/aldhu.pdf (accessed April 2004) and *El País*, April 1, 2003.

212. *TNI Drugs & Conflict Debate Papers*, No. 8, September 2003, Transnational Institute, at http://www.tni.org/reports/drugs/debate8.htm (accessed March 2004).

213. The Multilateral Center did not gel as an institutional measure and has been substituted by a scheme of hemispheric coordination, which on the bilateral plane translates into several memos of understanding, conventions and other instruments which obligates every country that interests the US to have: adequate laws (drug, organized crime, money-laundering and now terrorism), adequate institutions (within or without the police, but which must obey the policies and pursue the goals, at times, of the Embassy, the State Department or the Department of Defense) and similar political strategies. Communication from Ricardo Soberón. Comisión Andina de Juristas.

few more than 100 in 1980 (the majority of them concentrated in Central America), and then compares with the current situation according to *The Washington Post*, with 2,700 US special operations soldiers working in nineteen countries in Latin America and nine the Caribbean in 1998, and on any given day of the year, 250 military advisors operating in 15 different countries, one can easily deduce that weakened communism was not the most appropriate doctrine for strengthening continental ties and deepening and intensifying hegemonic control. Yet, the war on drugs, and more specifically the war on cocaine, has been very productive, at least from the US point of view.[214]

D. Eradication and Alternative Development

The international drug policy to control production which, through the 1931 Geneva Convention, authorized States and international organisms to police reductions control, has as its direct result the campaign of eradication and crop substitution, and the imprecise notion of "alternative development."

Justified by the 1950 UN Coca Leaf Report, which attempted to a priori eradicate crops and traditional consumption (*acullico*), the subsequent 1961 Single Convention on Narcotic Drugs granted 25 years maximum (starting in 1964) to eradicate crops by "uprooting wild cocaine and destroying illegal crops." The Vienna Convention, which in the end respects the rights of the traditional coca leaf consumer because of the demands of Peruvians and Bolivians, enshrines voluntary or forced eradication and alternative development as options for eliminating illegal coca. But basically the United Nations SCOPE proposal, intended to make coca and poppy crops disappear by 2008, justified the use of force and legitimized the militarization of the Andean region and the recovery of the US hegemonic impetus.

---

214. Lowenthal, Abraham. *Partners in Conflict - The United States and Latin America.* Baltimore, 1987, John Hopkins UP, p. 37. and Farah, Douglas in *Washington Post, 13-7-98.*

The popularization and extension of drug consumption among youth and adolescents beginning in the late 1960s moved US authorities to mount the first forced eradication runs with the aerial fumigation of Mexican and Colombian marijuana (1978–82), and the use of poisonous herbicides (*paraquat*). This was subsequently prohibited by the Environmental Protection Agency; but it was effective enough to push marijuana traffickers to try out cocaine, which was lighter to transport and more profitable.

As Colombians and exiled Cubans created the first distribution channels, with the complicity of Bolivian political and military authorities, cocaine spread and became very popular as a natural stimulant due to the progressive control of amphetamines. High level connections with the *cocaine regime* in Bolivia led repressive and prohibitionist forces to the weakest link in the chain, and pressure on small-time coca farmers began to be felt. After the Banzer and García Meza administrations, in the midst of a mining crisis and hyperinflation, the suspension of aid through the Hawkings Amendment was used to pressure Siles Zuazo's administration (1982–1985) to fulfill eradication quotas, hurting Bolivian government relations with the social sectors implicated.

The profound interconnectedness of political, economic and military sectors in narco-trafficking noticeably decreased Victor Paz Estenssoro's (1985–1989) ability to act. He attempted to reconcile the effort to crack down on illegal crops with a desire to recuperate the credibility of a nation based on an Andean culture that supports the use of coca leaf. These first attempts at crop eradication, averaging of 2% of planted acreage being destroyed, led to an annual rate of 10–20% new planting.[215] The coca leaf remained the most profitable and liquid crop, and compensations for voluntary substitution were insignificant ($369/hectare vs. the $34,221/hectare of coca for illegal cocaine). The trigger for current control and reduction of illicit crops

---

215. Garcia Sayan, 1989, op. cit. p.24, cfr. United States Department of State. Bureau of International Narcotic Matters (BINM) International Narcotics Control Strategy Report. Washington, 1989.

came with the 1986 US law establishing financing for eradication plans and the investigation of herbicides. Anthropologist Mauricio Mamani, Minister of Agriculture fired for defending the coca leaf, relates how he was contracted by the US State Department to try to grow coca leaf in Costa Rica and to test an herbicide. It was attempted with true interest but no satisfactory results.[216]

This was when the pressures of US public opinion, the growing consumption of cocaine and crack and the "electoralism" of drug issues led the US to exercise enormous diplomatic pressure on Andean governments to apply broad eradication and fumigation programs; in the end, these were more no effective than manual eradication and substitution. Around 1989, after almost a decade of forced eradication by burning and uprooting, the attempt was a total failure;[217] it was a slow task that required the extraction of the bushes one-by-one by a crew of workers. In Peru, for every acre eradicated, 15 to 20 were planted. In addition to the human effort involved, offensive action by the Shining Path guerillas also impeded manual eradication and there were not sufficient financial incentives for abandoning coca leaf or substituting it with something else.

Faced with failure, the US began to consider using Sumithion and Thebutirion, which had been rejected by governments and societies for their highly contaminating nature. Fumigation with the herbicide Spike, in the late 1980s, directly contributed to the extension and support of the Shining Path. The US idea to continue use of these herbicides in the 1990s, beginning in Alto Huallaga, was finally rejected because of the opposition of the Peruvian government and social leaders. From then on the US focused on proposals for alternative development, crop substitution, the banning of laboratories and small planes, etc., and abandoned forced eradication of any kind in Peru (to this day, only the seedbeds of new plants are confiscated and destroyed).

---

216. Chapter II.
217. Ugaz, José C. 1989 "Represión o prevención" pp. 307-317, Garcia Sayan, op. cit.

Yet in Bolivia, what began as union-controlled opposition to manual eradication soon became an ongoing confrontation between the Security Forces (supported by the DEA and the US Embassy) and the peasants who were well organized in union federations.

In 1998, the Bolivian Congress passed Law 1008 on the System of the Coca Leaf and Controlled Substances, which made many coca crops illegal and designated the largest coca zone, Chapare, as a transition zone where forced eradication would be implemented after a secret convention with the US passed by law in 1989. The nature of Bolivian narco-trafficking, intimately linked to the security forces and highest levels of the nation, dealt the hardest blows to small producers and peasants. The road from Cochabamba to Chapare was practically a military path between tall, green mountains leading to a tropical valley where small farming communities were located. In a space of 20 miles, people who have to give reasons for their travels pass through more than 15 military zones. Given such exhaustive controls over peasants and people who had nothing to do with the illegal economy,[218] it is surprising that there is illegal trafficking at all.

According to the people and to union members from the area, illegal trafficking is organized by the security forces (UMOPAR) themselves. In this valley with its modest constructions, motorcycles with large cylinders and gigantic tires abound while there is no sewage system, social or health services or even a little bar. Thanks to international aid in the drug war, the UN program for alternative development financed the paving of roads uniting some villages, and between tropical storms peasants and coca workers spread their leaves along the newly-blacktopped surfaces.

The rigor of the commitment to reduce coca, which spreads much, much faster than it disappears, made eradication and substitution into a military battle. The Sánchez de Losada administration compensated voluntary substitution at $2,500/

---

218. Personal trip to Chapare y Cochabamba, January 1998. From March on, the zone was completely militarized and access to the press, members of parliament, human rights organizations, and even the Bolivian human rights minister, was definitively closed.

hectare, but peasants used the money to finance new plants in fringe areas, and the plan for alternative development (which, according to Mamani, would fail because they were introducing crops that had no market in Bolivia and had no distribution mechanisms to bring them to foreign markets), was unsuccessful. They were pulling up bushes that were over ten years old and already useless.

Little government success in reducing coca forced Sánchez de Losada to withdraw his defense of coca leaf in international organisms, sign an extradition treaty with the US and develop a global plan for coca eradication. The government declared a near constant state of siege in Chapare and called for the arrest of union members. There were night military raids, which resulted in many wounded or dead, and the destruction of several villages to date. At the end of 1996, the Special Forces in the War on Narco-Trafficking (FELCN) certified the eradication of 7,512 hectares of coca and 84,238 meters of seedbeds. Soon thereafter, US satellites showed 7,200 new hectares of coca leaf had simultaneously been planted.

Constant human rights violations and military intervention increased denunciations by NGOs and other civic organizations. The US and Bolivian governments established a Convention protecting human rights,[219] but it has never even published in Bolivia, much less applied. Faced with confrontations with the Ecology Police, the Armed Forces and the UMOPAR began to organize self defense groups in 1997. According to union leader Rolando Vargas, it is very difficult to control those who have suffered violence and the murder of a relative. Thus it is not odd that, confronted with progressive militarization and increasing great demands, the self defense groups themselves have turned into armed groups and formed a new guerrilla movement.

The projected SCOPE plan for the destruction of all illegal coca and poppy crops attempted to eliminate some 90,000 acres by 2002,

---

219. In August 1996, after two visits by Human Rights Watch/Americas to Bolivia, the US Embassy and the Bolivian Minister of Government signed an accord, upon discovering human rights violations by some of its members, in which they agree not to assign US funds to anti-drug corps that do not take corresponding measures. See Roncken, 1997, *Guerra antidrogas*, op. cit.

and relocate 15,000 families, with an international fund directed by the UN (PNUFID). Since 1998 the farmers have received only $4,125/ acre ($1,650/hectare) eradicated, and this compensation was to disappear in 2002. To ensure the destruction of the old and new coca bushes, two sure alternatives are shuffled: chemical herbicides and new biological plagues.

The defenders of the plan alleged that the new biological agents were selective, but they can be even more destructive because of their ability to mutate genetically. No one knows what their ecological behavior will be or their consequences on the entire trophic chain.[220] Yet the strategies of destruction called attention to the damage that glyphosates did in Colombia. In Peru, the Fusarium Oxysporum mushroom has been every effective; it spread naturally throughout the Huallaga coca zone, though some unconfirmed rumors state that the DEA and Peruvian police also contributed to it.

In spite of the controversy of aerial fumigations, because of health and environmental concerns, Washington encourages it and it has been applied in the US, Mexico, Guatemala, Belize, Panama, Colombia (instigating a massive rebellion), Venezuela and (very recently) in Peru.[221] In the 1990s many fumigations were implemented in Colombia, feeding a strong and extensive social protest against glyphosates, which, according to the Environmental Ministry of Colombia, effectively destroyed 61% of coca and poppy lots, and which, according to human rights organizations, has been a determining factor in increased support for the guerrilla and rendering programs for alternative development absolutely useless.

No peasant wants to cooperate by experimenting with alternative crops and many abandon their property because fumigation burns and destroys, leaving the land sterile for more than a year.[222] The generalized protest against fumigants led to a

---

220. The US Department of Agriculture Research Service is investigating the manipulation of the genetic code of a mushroom against the coca. *Drogas y desarrollo*, monthly report nº 10, Sept. 98, ENCOD (European NGO Council on Drugs and Development, Belgium). *Biological Roulette: The Drug War's Fungal Solution? Covert Action Quarterly*, Spring 1998.

221. Jelsma, Martin. 1997, *Guerra antidrogas*, op. cit.

compromise by the government in 1994, to trade it for alternative development and apply it only on crops of more than 8 acres.

In any case, aerial fumigations in small planes could not access commercial plantations in the hands of the narco-landowners. The continuation of eradication tasks with health-damaging herbicides provoked the deaths of 50 people, and a baby, in 1996. According to area NGOs, it increased the "informal tasks" of paramilitary groups and the constant violation of human rights. For the peasants, fumigations in the Amazon (now home to small producers who have taken over parts of the jungle) meant para-state colonization of the big companies interested in oil and mineral wealth in the subsoil,[223] creating a situation very similar to that of Chiapas and other zones of armed struggle where strong paramilitary organizations are appearing.

Finally, the option for alternative development, which implies voluntary substitution of illegal crops and the funneling of millions of dollars to the coca zones, is resulting in an international fiasco. Since the international assumption of co-responsibility among producing and consuming countries in the early 1990s, the UNDCP World Plan of Action and the US and European governments have dedicated enormous amounts of money to development. Pilot projects train peasants and technical personnel in the production of determined food crops. This has created a sizable bureaucracy in the three Andean countries that depend on the Donor Tables organized in Europe and the US, which channel aid for development based on purely bureaucratic and barely economic criteria, all to maintain constant and sure financing (when it fails the project is stopped and the factory or crop disappears).[224]

Another problem which has vitiated governmental efforts for alternative development is the liberalization of Andean economies

---

222. Ricardo VARGAS, 1996, "The Impact...," op. cit.

223. *En busca de soluciones (co- operatives)* Informe Misión de Parlamentarios Europeos. 1998.

224. Estrategias nacionales de control de drogas, desarrollo alternativo y cooperación internacional. International Workshop, Cochabamba, Bolivia, 16-18 September 1997. AIDIA/GTZ. Lima, Perú.

and the opening of markets. In many cases, the advent of cheaper Chilean or Argentine products made any agricultural competition impossible. Alternative development is a trick that calms the consciences of post-industrial societies set on a sort of economic cooperation that does not question the roots of the problems.

Conclusion

The extension of narco-trafficking throughout the majority of Latin American countries with a perfect international division of work, and the collapse of the East-West confrontation paradigm, underscore the fact that relations between the North and the South are complex and interdependent. There is no one dimension that can encompass the relationship — not even drugs.

Illegal drug trafficking synthesizes the complexity of flux interchanges, and implies not only an economic process derived from the lack of development or the weak structure of some Latin American countries, but also the parallel existence of several subsystems embedded in power which feed narco-trafficking and the war on drugs. Narco-trafficking and policies designed to combat it are highly interdependent. Both are not merely a response to economic and social needs, but also to the priorities of a nation bent on hegemony, a nation that needs a harmonious and consensual base to re-establish its leadership in the region and the rest of the world. The war on drugs, and the particular and clear "war on cocaine" (which is almost entirely produced in Latin America), suggest a political intent that is much greater than the social prevention of drug use/abuse.

The cocaine war permits the recovery of dominance throughout the Western hemisphere and the renewal of the US role as internal actor, after the crises of the 1970s. The need to turn formal democracies into true democracies is the reason for Latin American reformism which, during the period of rivalry, so worried a US trying to prevent radical experiments like Cuba's. Since then, the great power has sought a doctrine to maintain all types of relations and allow economic expansion within certain margins of security. The war on drugs is configured as a framework which is useful for relations with Latin America, because it updates the Doctrine of National Security and incorporates everyone's armies in the struggle. Narco-trafficking, with its profound socio-economic interdependence, will be the new military target — like "terrorism," an uncertain, changing, contradictory and enormously flexible target impossible to hit.

Through the war on drugs, the revolutionary manifestation of the sharpest socio-economic tensions on the continent are avoided. Through the war on drugs the tensions of poverty are diluted: the disinherited alter their reality by consuming poisons or participating in the business. Nations suffer a similar illusion, called narco-dependency. Social demands are softened as are the just claims for equality on the international plane. US hegemony is re-established as military approximation is combined with economic approximation and this permits the diffusion of an elaborate philosophy according to North American views.

Given the impossibility of direct military confrontation, the Drug War is the banner under which the great power buys off the elites as well as the people, getting just a wink and a nod as it re-asserts ideological and military control though a renewed framework of the North/South confrontation.

The globalization of the crusade against drugs, currently led by the United Nations, and the US lead in setting the focus for international policies, leaves the Latin Americans little room for independent and realistic options. They are now silenced by economic aid and the many plans for alternative development.

A shift in the international order, say, the European Union playing a greater role with a strong, unified foreign policy, would allow the South to change the current direction. If reducing drug abuse were the goal, prohibitionist policies have been proven failures, anyway. In the end they have proven to encourage criminal activity and to spread Western-style drug consumption, mafias and corruption. In the absence of a sincere debate on drugs, the current exaggerated free market society relegates the issues to NGOs. NGOs with varied missions are, indeed, attempting to modify our world and bring the South closer to the North.[225] From their volunteerism and new, sincere and realist proposals, we have ways to substantially modify the war on drugs, treating a problem as human as drug consumption — legal and illegal, natural and synthetic, stimulants, sedatives and hallucinogens — from the side of prevention and reduction of possible damage, rather than from the side of police and military, diplomatic and political.

In the years to come, the widening gap between poor and rich countries and the strategy of the war on drugs, particularly the cocaine war, will dramatically worsen political conditions and human rights issues in the weakest democracies of Latin America. The excesses of opulence in the rich world and the contamination of poverty in the Third World require a new international position and a complete re-evaluation of the anti-drug policies in the heart of the UN, to allows us to turn the militarized framework of the war on drugs back to policies focused on consumption. This would put what has been in the hands of the police, throughout the 20th century, back into the hands of medical and pharmacology experts. It would also allow farmers in zones producing raw material, such as the coca leaf, to plant serious alternatives for development, in accordance with the capacities and characteristics of the cultural, ecological and human environment, to attain true sustainable development. This is certainly a challenge for a world in the advanced stages of "drug addiction."

Controlled Substances

---

225. In Europe, grouped in the Drugs and Development Coalition (ENCOD) and Transnational Institute, and in the US, the Lindesmith Center, also works for alternative and legalizing policies. For more information, see: www.tni.org ; www.lindesmith.org/.

The Commission on Narcotic Drugs produced eight schedules of "controlled" narcotic and psychotropic substances (four from the 1961 Convention and four from 1971), categorized according to their therapeutic value, risk of abuse, and associated health risks. Schedules I-IV appear on the following pages. Article 2 of the 1961 UN Convention introduces control measures for these schedules.

Schedule I contains, among others, methadone, opium, heroin, morphine, cocaine, cannabis. "The drugs...are subject to all measures of control applicable to drugs foreseen by the Convention."

In Schedules II and III, controls are less strict due to the therapeutic properties of the substances listed therein. Schedule II covers codeine, propiram, etc. Schedule III includes preparations based on opium, morphine, codeine, etc.

Schedule IV lists the most dangerous drugs that were already listed in Schedule I as being particularly harmful and having extremely limited medical and therapeutic value. Among others they include: acetorphine, cannabis, and heroin.[226]

---

226. Excerpted from "Reviewing legal aspects of substitution treatment at the international level," an ELDD Comparative Study, August 2000, by the European Legal Database on Drugs, available online at http://eldd.emcdda.org/.

SCHEDULES OF THE UNITED NATIONS OFFICE ON DRUGS AND CRIME
Revised Schedules including all amendments made by the Commission on
Narcotic Drugs in Force as of 5 March 1990

List of Drugs Included in Schedule I

Acetorphine	3-O-acetyltetrahydro-7-*alpha*-(1-hydroxy-1-methylbutyl)-6,14-*endoetheno*-oripavine
Acetyl-*alpha*-methylfentanyl	N-[1-(*alpha*-methylphenethyl)-4-piperidyl]acetanilide
Acetylmethadol	3-acetoxy-6-dimethylamino-4,4-diphenylheptane
Alfentanil	N-[1-[2-(4-ethyl-4,5-dihydro-5-oxo-1H-tetrazol-1-yl)ethyl]-4-(methoxymethyl)-4-piperidinyl]-N-phenylpropanamide
Allylprodine	3-allyl-1-methyl-4-phenyl-4-propionoxypiperidine
Alphacetylmethadol	*alpha*-3-acetoxy-6-dimethylamino-4,4-diphenylheptane
Alphameprodine	*alpha*-3-ethyl-1-methyl-4-phenyl-4-propionoxypiperidine
Alphamethadol	*alpha*-6-dimethylamino-4,4-diphenyl-3-heptanol
Alpha-methylfentanyl	N-[1(*alpha*-methylphenethyl)-4-piperidyl]propionanilide
Alpha-methylthiofentanyl	N-[1-[1-methyl-2-(2-thienyl)ethyl]-4-piperidyl]propionanilide
Alphaprodine	*alpha*-1,3-dimethyl-4-phenyl-4-propionoxypiperidine
Anileridine	1-*para*-aminophenethyl-4-phenylpiperidine-4-carboxylic acid ethyl ester
Benzethidine	1-(2-benzyloxyethyl)-4-phenylpiperidine-4-carboxylic acid ethyl ester
Benzylmorphine	3-O-benzylmorphine
Betacetylmethadol	*beta*-3-acetoxy-6-dimethylamino-4,4-diphenylheptane
Beta-hydroxyfentanyl	N-[1-(*beta*-hydroxyphenethyl)-4-piperidyl]propionanilide
Beta-hydroxy-3-methylfentanyl	N-[1-(*beta*-hydroxyphenethyl)-3-methyl-4-piperidyl]propionanilide
Betameprodine	*beta*-3-ethyl-1-methyl-4-phenyl-4-propionoxypiperidine
Betamethadol	*beta*-6-dimethylamino-4,4-diphenyl-3-heptanol
Betaprodine	*beta*-1,3-dimethyl-4-phenyl-4-propionoxypiperidine
Bezitramide	1-(3-cyano-3,3-diphenylpropyl)-4-(2-oxo-3-propionyl-1-benzimidazolinyl)-piperidine
Cannabis and Cannabis resin	and EXTRACTS and TICTURES OF CANNABIS
Clonitazene	2-*para*-chlorbenzyl-1-diethylaminoethyl-5-nitrobenzimidazole
Coca leaf	
Cocaine	methyl ester of benzoylecgonine
Codoxime	dihydrocodeinone-6-carboxymethyloxime
Concentrate of poppy straw	the material arising when poppy straw has entered into a process for the concentration of its alkaloids when such material is made available in trade
Desomorphine	dihydrodeoxymorphine
Dextromoramide	(+)-4-[2-methyl-4-oxo-3,3-diphenyl-4-(1-pyrrolidinyl)butyl]-morpholine
Diampromide	N-[2-(methylphenethylamino)-propyl]propionanilide
Diethylthiambutene	3-diethylamino-1,1-di-(2'-thienyl)-1-butene
Difenoxin	1-(3-cyano-3,3-diphenylpropyl)-4-phenylisonipecotic acid
Dihydromorphine	
Dimenoxadol	2-dimethylaminoethyl-1-ethoxy-1,1-diphenylacetate
Dimepheptanol	6-dimethylamino-4,4-diphenyl-3-heptanol
Dimethylthiambutene	3-dimethylamino-1,1-di-(2'-thienyl)-1-butene
Dioxaphetyl butyrate	ethyl-4-morpholino-2,2-diphenylbutyrate
Diphenoxylate	1-(3-cyano-3,3-diphenylpropyl)-4-phenylpiperidine-4-carboxylic acid ethyl ester

Dipipanone	4,4-diphenyl-6-piperidine-3-heptanone
Drotebanol	3,4-dimethoxy-17-methylmorphinan-6-*beta*,14-diol
Ecgonine	its esters and derivatives which are convertible to ecgonine and cocaine
Ethylmethylthiambutene	3-ethylmethylamino-1,1-di-(2'-thienyl)-1-butene
Etonitazene	1-diethylaminoethyl-2-*para*-ethoxybenzyl-5-nitrobenzimidazole
Etorphine	tetrahydro-7-*alpha*-(1-hydroxy-1-methylbutyl)-6,14-*endo*etheno-oripavine
Etoxeridine	1-[2-(2-hydroxyethoxy)-ethyl]-4-phenylpiperidine-4-carboxylic acid ethyl ester
Fentanyl	1-phenethyl-4-N-propionylanilinopiperidine
Furethidine	1-(2-tetrahydrofurfuryloxyethyl)-4-phenylpiperidine-4-carboxylic acid ethyl ester
Heroin	diacetylmorphine
Hydrocodone	dihydrocodeinone
Hydromorphinol	14-hydroxydihydromorphine
Hydromorphone	dihydromorphinone
Hydroxypethidine	4-*meta*-hydroxyphenyl-1-methylpiperidine-4-carboxylic acid ethyl ester
Isomethadone	6-dimethylamino-5-methyl-4,4-diphenyl-3-hexanone
Ketobemidone	4-*meta*-hydroxyphenyl-1-methyl-4-propionylpiperidine
Levomethorphan *	(-)-3-methoxy-N-methylmorphinan
Levomoramide	(-)-4-[2-methyl-4-oxo-3,3-diphenyl-4-(1-pyrrolidinyl)-butyl]morpholine
Levophenacylmorphan	(1)-3-hydroxy-N-phenacylmorphinan
Levorphanol *	(-)-3-hydroxy-N-methylmorphinan
Metazocine	2'-hydroxy-2,5,9-trimethyl-6,7-benzomorphan
Methadone	6-dimethylamino-4,4-diphenyl-3-heptanone
Methadone intermediate	4-cyano-2-dimethylamino-4,4-diphenylbutane
Methyldesorphine	6-methyl-*delta*-6-deoxymorphine
Methyldihydromorphine	6-methyldihydromorphine
3-methylfentanyl	N-(3-methyl-1-phenethyl-4-piperidyl)propionanilide
3-methylthiofentanyl	N-[3-methyl-1-[2-(2-thienyl)ethyl]-4-piperidyl]propionanilide
Metopon	5-methyldihydromorphinone
Moramide intermediate	2-methyl-3-morpholino-1,1-diphenylpropane carboxylic acid
Morpheridine	1-(2-morpholinoethyl)-4-phenylpiperidine-4-carboxylic acid ethyl ester
Morphine	
Morphine methobromide	and other pentavalent nitrogen morphine derivatives, including in particular the morphine-N-oxide derivatives, one of which is codeine-N-oxide
Morphine-N-oxide	
MPPP	1-methyl-4-phenyl-4-piperidinol propionate (ester)
Myrophine	myristylbenzylmorphine
Nicomorphine	3,6-dinicotinylmorphine
Noracymethadol	(±)-*alpha*-3-acetoxy-6-methylamino-4,4-diphenylheptane
Norlevorphanol	(-)-3-hydroxymorphinan
Normethadone	6-dimethylamino-4,4-diphenyl-3-hexanone
Normorphine	demethylmorphine or N-demethylated morphine
Norpipanone	4,4-diphenyl-6-piperidino-3-hexanone
Opium	
Oxycodone	14-hydroxydihydrocodeinone
Oxymorphone	14-hydroxydihydromorphinone
Para-fluorofentanyl	4'-fluoro-N-(1-phenethyl-4-piperidyl)propionanilide

PEPAP	1-phenethyl-4-phenyl-4-piperidinol acetate (ester)
Pethidine	1-methyl-4-phenylpiperidine-4-carboxylic acid ethyl ester
Pethidine intermediate A	4-cyano-1-methyl-4-phenylpiperidine
Pethidine intermediate B	4-phenylpiperidine-4-carboxylic acid ethyl ester
Pethidine intermediate C	1-methyl-4-phenylpiperidine-4-carboxylic acid
Phenadoxone	6-morpholino-4,4-diphenyl-3-heptanone
Phenampromide	N-(1-methyl-2-piperidinoethyl)-propionanilide
Phenazocine	2'-hydroxy-5,9-dimethyl-2-phenethyl-6,7-benzomorphan
Phenomorphan	3-hydroxy-N-phenethylmorphinan
Phenoperidine	1-(3-hydroxy-3-phenylpropyl)-4-phenylpiperidine-4-carboxylic acid ethyl ester
Piminodine	4-phenyl-1-(3-phenylaminopropyl)-piperidine-4-carboxylic acid ethyl ester
Piritramide	1-(3-cyano-3,3-diphenylpropyl)-4-(1-piperidino)-piperidine-4-carboxylic acid amide
Proheptazine	1,3-dimethyl-4-phenyl-4-propionoxyazacycloheptane
Properidine	1-methyl-4-phenylpiperidine-4-carboxylic acid isopropyl ester
Racemethorphan	(±)-3-methoxy-N-methylmorphinan
Racemoramide	(±)-4-[2-methyl-4-oxo-3,3-diphenyl-4-(1-pyrrolidinyl)-butyl]-morpholine
Racemorphan	(±)-3-hydroxy-N-methylmorphinan
Sufentanil	N-[4-(methoxymethyl)-1-[2-(2-thienyl)-ethyl]-4-piperidyl]propionanilide
Thebacon	acetyldihydrocodeinone
Thebaine	
Thiofentanyl	N-[1-[2-(2-thienyl)ethyl]-4-piperidyl]propionanilide
Tilidine	(±)-ethyl-*trans*-2-(dimethylamino)-1-phenyl-3-cyclohexene-1-carboxylate
Trimeperidine	1,2,5-trimethyl-4-phenyl-4-propionoxypiperidine; and

The isomers, unless specifically excepted, of the drugs in this Schedule whenever the existence of such isomers is possible within the specific chemical designation;

The esters and ethers, unless appearing in another Schedule, of the drugs in this Schedule whenever the existence of such esters or ethers is possible;

The salts of the drugs listed in this Schedule, including the salts of esters, ethers and isomers as provided above whenever the existence of such salts is possible

* Dextromethorphan ((+)-3-methoxy-N-methylmorphinan) and dextrorphan ((+)-3-hydroxy-N-methylmorphinan) are specifically excluded from this Schedule.

List of Drugs Included in Schedule II

Acetyldihydrocodeine	
Codeine	3-O-methylmorphine
Dextropropoxyphene	*alpha*-(+)-4-dimethylamino-1,2-diphenyl-3-methyl-2-butanol propionate
Dihydrocodeine	
Ethylmorphine	3-O-ethylmorphine
Nicocodine	6-nicotinylcodeine
Nicodicodine	6-nicotinyldihydrocodeine
Norcodeine	N-demethylcodeine
Pholcodine	morpholinylethylmorphine
Propiram	N-(1-methyl-2-piperidinoethyl)-N-2-pyridylpropionamide; and

The isomers, unless specifically excepted, of the drugs in this Schedule whenever the existence of such isomers is possible within the specific chemical designation;

The salts of the drugs listed in this Schedule, including the salts of the isomers as provided above whenever the existence of such salts is possible.

List of Preparations Included in Schedule III

1. Preparations of

Acetyldihydrocodeine,
Codeine,
Dihydrocodeine,
Ethylmorphine,
Nicodicodine,
Norcodeine, and
Pholcodine

when compounded with one or more other ingredients and containing not more than 100 milligrams of the drug per dosage unit and with a concentration of not more than 2.5 per cent in undivided preparations.

2. Preparations of Propiram containing not more than 100 milligrams of propiram per dosage unit and compounded with at least the same amount of methylcellulose.

3. Preparations of Dextropropoxyphene for oral use containing not more than 135 milligrams of dextropropoxyphene base per dosage unit or with a concentration of not more than 2.5 per cent in undivided preparations, provided that such preparations do not contain any substance controlled under the 1971 Convention on Psychotropic Substances.

4. Preparations of Cocaine containing not more than 0.1 per cent of cocaine calculated as cocaine base and preparations of opium or morphine containing not more than 0.2 per cent of morphine calculated as anhydrous morphine base and compounded with one or more other ingredients and in such a way that the drug cannot be recovered by readily applicable means or in a yield which would constitute a risk to public health.

5. Preparations of Difenoxin containing, per dosage unit, not more than 0.5 milligram of difenoxin and a quantity of atropine sulfate equivalent to at least 5 per cent of the dose of difenoxin.

6. Preparations of Diphenoxylate containing, per dosage unit, not more than 2.5 milligrams of diphenoxylate calculated as base and a quantity of atropine sulfate equivalent to at least 1 per cent of the dose of diphenoxylate.

7. Preparations of *Pulvis ipecacuanhae et opii compositus*
   10 per cent opium in powder
   10 per cent ipecacuanha root, in powder well mixed with
   80 per cent of any other powdered ingredient containing no drug.

8. Preparations conforming to any of the formulas listed in this Schedule and mixtures of such preparations with any material which contains no drug.

List of Drugs Included in Schedule IV

Acetorphine	3-O-acetyltetrahydro-7-alpha-(1-hydroxy-1-methylbutyl)-6,14-*endoetheno*-oripavine
Acetyl-*alpha*-methylfentanyl	N-[1-(*alpha*-methylphenethyl)-4-piperidyl]acetanilide
Alpha-methylfentanyl	N-[1-(*alpha*-methylphenethyl)-4-piperidyl]propionanilide
Alpha-methylthiofentanyl	N-[1-[1-methyl-2-(2-thienyl)ethyl]-4-piperidyl]propionanilide
Beta-hydroxy-3-methylfentanyl	N-[1-(*beta*-hydroxyphenethyl)-3-methyl-4-piperidyl]propionanilide
Beta-hydroxyfentanyl	N-[1-(*beta*-hydroxyphenethyl)-4-piperidyl]propionanilide
Cannabis and Cannabis resin	
Desomorphine	dihydrodeoxymorphine
Etorphine	tetrahydro-7-*alpha*-(1-hydroxy-1-methylbutyl)-6,14-*endoetheno*-oripavine
Heroin	diacetylmorphine
Ketobemidone	4-*meta*-hydroxyphenyl-1-methyl-4-propionylpiperidine
3-methylfentanyl	N-(3-methyl-1-phenethyl-4-piperidyl)propionanilide; *cis*-N-[3-methyl-1(2-phenylethyl)-4-piperidyl]propionanilide; *trans*-N-[3-methyl-1-(2-phenylethyl)-4-piperidyl]propionanilide
3-methylthiofentanyl	N-(3-methyl-1-[2-(2-thienyl)ethyl]-4-piperidyl)propionanilide
MPPP	1-methyl-4-phenyl-4-piperidinol propionate (ester)
Para-fluorofentanyl	4'-fluoro-N-(1-phenethyl-4-piperidyl)propionanilide
PEPAP	1-phenethyl-4-phenyl-4-piperidinol acetate (ester)
Thiofentanyl	N-[1-[2-(thienyl)ethyl]-4-piperidyl]propionanilide; and

The salts of the drugs listed in this Schedule whenever the formation of such salts is possible.

BIBLIOGRAPHY

AIDIA/ GTZ *Estrategias nacionales de control de drogas, desarrollo alternativo y cooperación internacional.* International Workshop, Cochabamba, Bolivia, 16-18 September 1997. Lima, Perú.

Aguilo, Federico S.J. "El complejo Coca-cocaína". *Economia y Sociedad* nº 11 26-8-87. Iese "Facultad de Ciencia Económica y Sociología. Cochabamba, Bolivia, 1987.

Albo, Xavier. "El mundo de la coca en Coripata, Bolivia" pp. 253-295, *América Indígena* XXXVIII, México, 1978.

Alfonso Garcia, Raúl. "El debate sobre la coca en América Indigena. Bibliografía comentada 1945-1978," pp. 973-1021, *America Indigena,* vol. XXXVIII, nº4 oct-dic 1978. México.

APEP. 1990. *Cocaína: Problemas y Soluciones andinos.*Asociación Peruana de Estudios e Investigaciones para la Paz, Lima, 357 páginas.

Azcui, Mabel. 1990. "Bajo la sombra de la sumisión" in *Criterio* Nº142, 31 marzo, La Paz, Bolivia.

Bagley, Bruce Michael "Colombia and the war on drugs" pp. 70-92, *Foreign Affairs,* vol 67 nº 1, fall 1988. (Versión en español: "Colombia y la guerra contra las drogas" en Tokatlian et al.: *Economía y Política del Narcotráfico,* 1990, Cerec, Bogotá). Las notas de todo el trabajo se refieren a la publicación inglesa.

Bagley, Bruce Michael. 1988. "La ley antinarcóticos de 1988 en EEUU y su impacto para Colombia" pp.3-7, Colombia Internacional nº 4 Oct-Dec; Centro de Estudios Internacionales de la Universidad de los Andes, Bogotá.

Bagley, Bruce M. 1989. "Cuatro posibles soluciones al problema del narcotráfico" pp. 411-415. *Sintesis* nº9, sept-dec, Madrid.

Bagley, B. et. al. (eds.) 1991. *La Economía Política del Narcotráfico. El caso ecuatoriano.* FLACSO Ecuador. North-South Center de la Universidad de Miami.

Bagley, Bruce M. 1991. "La política exterior estadounidense y la guerra de las drogas: Análisis de un fracaso político" en "Bagley, B.et. al.(eds.): *La Economía Política del Narcotráfico. El caso ecuatoriano.* FLACSO Ecuador. North-South Center de la Universidad de Miami.

Bagley, Bruce M. 1992 "Myths Of Militarization: Enlisting Armed Forces In The War On Drugs" pp. 129-150 in P. H. Smith (Ed.): *Drug Policy In The Americas.* University Of California. San Diego. Westview Press.

Benitez, Raúl. 1988. "Narcotráfico y Terrorismo En Las Relaciones Interamericanas" pp. 2-21, *Polemica* Nº 5, 2¦ Epoca, Flacso, San José De Costa Rica.

Beristain, A.Y De La Cuesta, J.L. 1986. *La Droga En La Sociedad Actual. Nuevos Horizontes En Criminología.* Vitoria. Caja De Ahorros De Guipúzcoa.

Bitar, Sergio. 1985. "La Desconcertante Recuperación De La Hegemonía De Estados Unidos" in Maira, L. (Ed.) *Una Nueva Era De Hegemonía Norteamericana?* pp. 129-149, Rial, Gel. Buenos Aires.

Bonilla, Adrián. 1991. "Ecuador: Actor Internacional En La Guerra De Las Drogas" in Bagley, B. et al. (Eds.): *La Economía Política Del Narcotráfico. El Caso Ecuatoriano,* pp. 9-45. Flacso Ecuador. North-South Center, University of Miami.

Boron, Atilio A. 1984. "La Crisis Norteamericana y La Racionalidad Neoconservadora" pp. 90-123, Maira, L.: EEUU. *Una Visión Latinoamericana.* Fce. México.

Botero, Ana Mercedes. 1988. "EEUU, Nueva Ley Antidroga," pp. 27-29; *Nueva Frontera.* Nº 709 November 14-20. Bogotá.

Buenahora, Pedro. 1990. *El Problema De La Droga* Editorial El Mañana Internacional, Quito, 52 páginas.

Burchard, Roderick E. 1974. "Coca y Trueque de Alimentos". In Alberti,G. Y., Mayer, E. *"Reciprocidad E Intercambio En Los Andes Peruanos"* pp. 209-251, Instituto De Estudios Peruanos, Lima, Perú.

Burchard, Roderick E. 1986 "Una Nueva Perspectiva Sobre La Masticación De La Coca". Caceres, B. Et Al.: *La Coca. Vision Indigena De Una Planta Satanizada,"* Primera Edición 1978 América Indígena XXXVIII, Instituto Indigenista Interamericano(I.I.I.). México.

Bustamante, Fernando. 1986. "La Política Del Narcotráfico: Prioridades y Limitaciones Del Enfoque Estadounidense" pp. 1-4, *Cono Sur*, Vol 5 Nº4, Ag-Sept.

Bustamante, Fernando. 1990. "La política de EEUU contra el narcotráfico y su impacto en América Latina," pp. 240-276. *Estudios Internacionales* nº90, abr-jul. Univ. Chile.

Bustos Ramirez, Juan. 1990. *Coca-Cocaína: Entre El Derecho y La Guerra (Política Criminal De La Droga En Los Países Andinos)*. 147 Páginas, Promociones y Publicaciones Universitarias, Barcelona.

Caballero, Antonio. 1986. "Hay Que Legalizar La Coca" in *Texto y Contexto*, pp..69-78, sept-dic 1986, nº 9, Universidad de Los Andes, Bogotá.

Cabieses, Hugo, "Notas sobre la revalorización y despenalización de la hoja de coca. Propuestas conprotesta," Consejo Permanente en Defensa de los Productores de Hoja de Coca en los Países Andinos, 1995.

Cabieses, Fernando, 1989. *Coca, ¿dilema trágico?*. Ed. By ENACO, Lima, Peru.

Caceres, Baldomero. 1986. "La Coca, El Mundo Andino y Los Extirpadores De Idolatrías Del Siglo Xx". Caceres,B. Et Al.: "*La Coca. Vision Indigena De Una Planta Satanizada*", Instituto Indigenista Interamericano (I.I.I.), México.

Camacho Guizado, Alvaro. 1989. "Colombia: Violencia y Narcocultura" pp. 191-206, Garcia Sayan, Diego (ed.): *Coca, Cocaína y Narcotráfico. Laberinto en los Andes* pp. 191-205, Comisión Andina de Juristas, Lima, Perú.

Camino, Alejandro. 1989. "Coca: del uso tradicional al Narcotráfico" pp. 91-108, Garcia Sayan, Diego (ed.):*Coca, Cocaina y Narcotráfico. Laberinto en los Andes* pp. 91-108, Comisión Andina de Juristas, Lima, Perú.

Campodonico, Humberto. 1989. "La Política Del Avestruz" pp. 226-258, Garcia Sayan, Diego (ed.):*Coca, Cocaína y Narcotráfico. Laberinto en los Andes* pp. 226-258, Comisión Andina de Juristas, Lima Perú.

Carothers, Thomas. 1990. "The United States and Latin America after the Cold World," *Latin American Program. Working Papers* nº 184. The Wilson Center, Washington DC.

Caro Baroja, Julio. 1986. *Las brujas y su mundo*, Alianza Editorial.

Carter, William and Mauricio Mamani, 1986. *Coca en Bolivia*, Editorial Juventud, La Paz, Bolivia.

Carter,W.E.Y. Mamani, M. 1986. "Patrones de uso de la coca en Bolivia" pp.207-249, Caceres,B. et al.:*La Coca. Vision Indigena De Una Planta Satanizada*. Primera Edición 1978 América Indígena XXXVIII Instituto Indigenista Interamericano (I.I.I), México.

Castillo,Fabio 1989. "Made in Colombia," *Nueva Sociedad* nº102, jul-ag, Caracas.

Castro de la Mata, Ramiro, and Noya T., Nils D., 1995. *Coca: Erythrozylum coca, Erythroxilum novogranatense, bibliografía comentada*, Seamos, Drogas: Investigación para el Debate, number 11, La Paz.

CEPEI *Narco-Trafficking: the Current Situation and Perspectives for Action*, Peruvian Center for International Studies (CEPEI), 1995.

Cirules, Enrique. *El imperio de La Habana*, Habana: Ediciones

Casa de las Américas, 1993.

Club de Roma (1972–1976) and Informe Meadows de la Sociedad Sostenible, in Meadows O. and Randesers, J.D., *Más allá de los límites del crecimiento*, Editorial El País, 1993.

Cole, Wayne S. 1968. *An interpretative History of American Foreign Relations*. Dorsey Press, Illinois.

Coleman, Kenneth M. 1984. "La política exterior comparada: comentarios sobre el ensayo de Van Klaveren" pp. 50-61, H.Muñoz y J.Tulchin en *Entre la autonomía y la subordinación. Política exterior de los países latinoamericanos*, GEL. Buenos Aires.

Collet, Merril. 1989. "El fantasma de la narco-guerrilla", *Nueva Sociedad* nº 102, jul-ag. Caracas.

Comisión Andina de Juristas. *Drogas y control penal en los Andes. Deseos, utopías y efectos perversos*. Lima, 1994.

Covington, Paula. 1990. "Cubrimiento del comercio colombiano de la droga por parte de la prensa de Estados Unidos" p. 389-420 en TOKATLIAN et al.: *Economía y Política del Narcotráfico*, Cerec, Bogotá.

Craig, Richard. 1985. "Illicit drug traffic and US Latin american relations", *Washington Quarterly*, nº 8, 1985.

Chavez Alvarez, Manuel Gonzalo. 1989. "Narcotráfico: um novo item nas relacoes entre os EUA e América Latina" pp. 40-52, *Politica E Estrategica*,vol VII,nº1 jan-mar, Sao Paulo.

Dobson, Andrew. 1995. *"Green Political Thought"* Routledge Ed.

Donelly, Jack. 1992. "The United Nations And The Global Drug Control Regime" pp 282-305, Smith P. H. (Ed.): *Drug Policy In The Americas*, University Of California. San Diego, Westview Press.

Drekonja, Gerhard. 1983. "Contenidos y Metas De La Nueva Política Exterior Latinoamericana" pp. 1-23, in Drekonja y Tokatlian, J.G. (Eds.): *Teoría y Pr ctica de la Política Exterior Latinoamericana* CEREC, Bogotá .

Eddy, Paul. *"Cocaine Wars."* WW. Norton &Company, 1988.

ENCOD (European NGO Council on Drugs and Development, Belgium). *Biological Roulette: The Drug War's Fungal Solution? Covert Action Quarterly*, Spring 1998.

Enrico, Roger. 1986. *The Other Guy Blinked, How Pepsi won the Cola Wars*. Bantam Books.

Escohotado, Antonio. 1990. *El libro de los venenos*, Mondadori.

Escohotado, Antonio. 1989. *Historia De Las Drogas*. 3 Volúmenes. Vol. 1: 397 P Gs., Vol. 2: 425 P Gs., Vol 3: 440 Pags. Alianza Editorial. Madrid.

Escohotado, Antonio. 1998. *Historia General De Las Drogas y Fenomenología De Las Drogas*, Espasa Calpe.

European Union, *Report on Drugs in Latin America*. Mission of Experts, September–October 1996.

Fazio, Carlos. 1996. *El tercer vínculo*, editorial Joaquín Mortiz, México.

Flores, Miguel Angel. 1990. "Ayuda Europea A Bolivia", in *Criterio* Nº142, 31 Marzo 1990, La Paz, Bolivia.

Forney, Mary Ann. 1990."Extradition And Drug Trafficking" pp. 327-338in INCIARDI, J.A. (Ed.): *Handbook Of Drug Control In The U.S.*"Greenwood Press, N.Y.

Fraga, Gaspar in "Colombia: Uribe for President" Revista *Cáñamo* nº 54. June 2002, Barcelona.

Gagliano, Joseph A. 1963. "The coca debate in colonial Perú" pp. 43-63, *The Americas*, XX, julio 1963, Academy of American Franciscan History, Maryland.

Gagliano, Joseph A. 1965"The popularization of peruvian coca", *Revista de Historia de América* nº59, pp.:164-179, en-junTacubaya, México.

Gagliano, Joseph A.1986. "La medicina popular y la coca en el Perú: un Análisis histórico de actitudes" Caceres, B. Et Al.: *La Coca Andina. Visión Indígena De Una Planta Satanizada*" 1¦ Ed.:America Indigena México.

Garasino, Alberto M. 1989."Droga y Politica" pp. 13-40, *Revista Argentina De Estudios Estrategicos* año 6 nº 11, Buenos Aires.

Garcia Sayan. 1989. "Narcotráfico y región andina: una visión general" pp. 20-49, Garcia Sayan, Diego (ed.): *Coca, Cocaína y Narcotráfico. Laberinto en los Andes*, Comisión Andina de Juristas, Lima Perú.

Garcia Sayan, D. (comp.). 1990.*Narcotráfico: Realidades y Alternativas*. Conferencia Internacional. Lima 5-7 feb 1990. Comisión Andina de Juristas, Lima.

Garcia Sayan, Diego (comp.). 1989. *Coca, cocaína y narcotráfico*. 392 pags. Comisión Andina de Juristas, Lima.

Garcia-Tornel, Carlos. 1989. "Apuntes sobre el problema de la droga en 1989" pp. 247-255 *Anuario Internacional Cidob* 1989, edita Fundación CIDOB, Barcelona.

Garzón, Baltasar y Megías, Eusebio, *Narco*, Celecció Gregori Mayans, Editorial Germanis, Valencia, 1997.

Gilbert, Félix. 1961. *To the Farewell adress. Ideas of Early American Foreign Policy*. New Jersey, Princeton University Press.

Gomez Buendia, Hernando. 1990. ""Cuál es la guerra?, Colombia, EEUU y la droga", pp. 28-36, *Nueva Sociedad* Nº 106 mar-abr, Caracas.

Gonzales Manrique, José E. 1989."Perú: Sendero Luminoso en el Valle de la Coca" pp. 207- 223 Garcia Sayan, Diego (ed.): *Coca, Cocaína y Narcotráfico. Laberinto en los Andes*" Comisión Andina de Juristas, Lima Perú.

Gonzalez, Guadalupe. 1989. *El narcotráfico como un problema de seguridad nacional*, 39 páginas. Seminario"Los nuevos desafíos a la soberanía y la seguridad de América del Sur" 11-13 jul Comis. Sudam. de Paz, Santiago de Chile, ILET.

Grinspoon, Lester and Bakalar, J.B., *Cocaine: A Drug and its Social Evolution*. Basic Books, 1985.

Grinspoon. L., and Bakalar, J., *Marijuana, the Forbidden Medicine.* Yale UP, 1993.

Greising, David *I´d like the world to buy a coke. The life and leadership of Roberto Goizueta*, Joan Wiley and Sons, 1998.

Gironda, Eusebio *Coca Inmortal*, Plural Editores, 2001.

Haining, Peter 1976 *El Club del Haschish. La droga en la literatura* TAURUS Madrid

Henman, Anthony Richard 1989"Tradición y represión: dos experiencias en América del Sur"pp. 109-130, Garcia Sayan, Diego (ed.): *Coca, Cocaína y Narcotráfico*. Laberinto en los Andes Comisión Andina de Juristas Lima Perú

Hirst, Mónica (comp.) 1987 *Continuidad y cambio en las relaciones América Latina- EEUU* GEL, Buenos Aires

Hulshof,Joseé1986 "La coca en la medicina tradicional andina"Caceres, B. et al.: *La coca andina. Visión indígena de una planta satanizada* Ed.:AMERICA INDIGENA I.I.I., México.

Hurtado Pozo, José1986"Terrorismo y tráfico de drogas"en Beristain *La droga en la sociedad actual* Vitoria. Caja de Ahorros Provincial de Guipúzcoa.

Ianni, Octavio 1985"Diplomacia e imperialismo en las relaciones interamericanas" pp. 35-66 en Maira, L (Ed.): "*Una nueva era de Hegemonía Norteamericana?*.Programa de Estudios Conjuntos sobre las Relaciones Internacionales de América Latina. Grupo Editor Latinoamericano. Buenos Aires

Informe de la mission de parlamentarios europeos a la region andina *in busca*

de soluciones (cooperatives), Informe Misión of European Parliament members, and representatives of NGOs for the Andean Region Colombia, Peru and Bolivia), March 1998.

Informe Del Dialogo Interamericano 1989"Drogas: tomar en serio oferta y demanda" pp. 35-45, *Las Americas en 1989: Consenso para la Acción*.Aspen Institute. Washington

Informe Del Interamerican Working Group 1988"*Collective Security in the Americas: New Directions*". World Peace Foundation. Boston.

IRELA 1991 *América Latina y Europa frente al problema de la droga: "Nuevas formas de cooperación?* 64 pags. Dossier nº 32 mayo 1991, Madrid.

Jaramillo Restrepo, Carlos 1988 *Comentarios al Estatuto Nacional de Estupefacientes* Editorial Temis; Bogotá

Jimenez Herrero, Luis M 1989 *Medio Ambiente y Desarrollo Alternativo*. 400 p gs. IEPALA. Madrid.

Jordan Pando, Roberto et. al.1989"Coca, cocaismo y cocainismo en Bolivia" pp. 79-171 en I.I.I (VVAA):*La coca...tradición, rito, identidad*I.I.I., México.

Kaplan Marcos 1990*Aspectos sociopolíticos del Narcotráfico*. 245 páginas. Instituto Nacional de Ciencias Penales, México, D.F.

Kaplan, John 1988 "Taking drugs seriously" pp. 32-51 en *The Public Interest*, n° 92, summer 1988, Washington D.C.

Kleiman, M. and Saiger, A. 1992 "Taxes, Regulations, and Prohibitions: Reformulating the Legalization Debate" pp. 223-241 en P. H. Smith (Ed.) *Drug Policy in the Americas*, University of California. San Diego, Westview Press

Kramer, Michael 1993Clinton's Drug Policy is a bust"*Time*, 20 dec, 1993

Kryzanek, Michael J. 1987 *Estrategias políticas de EEUU en America Latina*, GEL, Buenos Aires.

Kurth, James R. 1990 "The rise and decline of the Inter-American System: a U.S. view"en Bloomfield R.J. (ed.) : *Alternative to intervention; A new US-Latin American Security Relationship*. World Peace Foundation Study, Lynne Rienner Publishers.

Lee, Rensselaer W. Iii 1990 "Tráfico De Drogas y Países En Desarrollo" pp. 15-31 in Tokatlian Et. Al *Economía y Política Del Narcotráfico*, Cerec, Universidad De los Andes, Bogotá .

Lejtman, Román. *Narcogate. El dinero de la droga*, Editorial Apóstrofe: Barcelona, 1994.

Lerner, R. and Ferrando, D. 1989 "El Consumo De Drogas En Occidente y Su Impacto En El Perú," pp. 51-90, Garcia Sayan, Diego (Ed.): *Coca, Cocaína y Narcotráfico. Laberinto en los Andes* Comisión Andina de Juristas, Lima, Perú.

Libermann, Kitula and Godinez, Armando (coord.) 1992 *Territorio y dignidad. Pueblos indígenas y medio ambiente en Bolivia*. 174 páginas. Instituto Latinoamericano de Investigaciones sociales ILDIS - Bolivia, Editorial Nueva Sociedad.

Liga Internacional Antiprohibicionista 1989"El prohibicionismo: un fracaso" Resolución política Congreso fundacional 30 mar 89 Roma*Nueva Sociedad* N° 102Caracas, Venezuela

Lowenthal, Abraham 1987*Partners in conflict - The United States and Latin America*, 237 pags. John Hopkins University Press, Baltimore and London.

Lowenthal, Abraham F 1990"Rediscovering Latin America"pp. 27-41, *Foreign Affairs* vol. 69 n°4 fall 1990

Lowenthal, Abraham F. 1992 "The Organization of American States and Control of Dangerous Drugs" pp. 305-313 en SMITH, P.H. (Ed.): *Drug Policy in the Americas*. University of California. San Diego, Westview Press.

Maira, Luis (Ed.)1984 *EEUU. Una Visión Latinoamericana*. Fce. México. 523 Pags.

Maira, Luis. 1984."Perspectivas y Opciones De La Sociedad Norteamericana," pp. 17-43 in Maira, L.(Ed.) *EEUU: Una Visión Latinoamericana* Fce, México.

Maira, Luis 1985(Comp.): *"Una Nueva Era De Hegemonía Norteamericana ?"* 359 páginas. Rial Gel, Buenos Aires.

Maira, Luis 1985: "Introducción: Una Mirada Histórica A Los Márgenes De Hegemonía Internacional De Estados Unidos" pp. 15-37 in Maira, Luis (Comp.): *" Una Nueva Era De Hegemonía Norteamericana ?* Rial Gel, Buenos Aires.

Maira, Luis 1988*Los Intereses Políticos y Estratégicos De EEUU En América Del Sur.* 55 P Gs. Documento De Trabajo.
Comisión Sudamericana De Paz. Santiago De Chile.

Mamani, Mauricio. "El Jilaqata En El Coqueo En Los Andes" In *Revista Del Museo De Etnografía y Folklor*, Number 4, 1991.

Mares, David R.1992 "The Logic Of Inter-American Cooperation On Drugs", pp. 329-342, in Smith P. H. (Ed.): *Drug Policy In The Americas*, University Of California. San Diego, Westview Press.

Marti, José, *Caso 1/1989 El Fin De La Conexión Cubana.* Editorial José Martí, La Habana, Cuba, 1989.

Martin, Lisa L 1992 "Foundations For International Cooperation" pp. 249-265 in Smith P. H. (Ed.): *Drug Policy In The Americas*, University Of California. San Diego, Westview Press.

Maxwell, Augusto 1989 "Una Ley Contradictoria" pp. 327-338Garcia Sayan, Diego (Ed.): *Coca, Cocaína y Narcotráfico. Laberinto En Los Andes*comisión Andina De Juristas;Lima, Perú.

Mayer, Enrique 1986 "El Uso Social De La Coca En El Mundo Andino: Contribución A Un Debate y Toma De Posición"Caceres, B. Et Al.: *La Coca Andina. Visión Indígena De Una Planta Satanizada* 1¦ Ed.:America Indigena ,México.

Medina-Mora, M.E. and Mariño, M.C. 1992"Drug Abuse In Latin America"in Smith, Peter H. (Ed.): *Drug Policy In The Americas.* pp. 45-56 University Of California. San Diego, Westview Press.

Ministerio De Justicia y Del Derecho y Dirección Nacional De Estupefacientes *Guía Bibliográfica Sobre Drogas*, Santa Fe De Bogotá, 1996.

Morison, S.E. Et. Al 1980 *Breve Historia De Los Estados Unidos* 967 P Gs. Fce, México.

Muñoz H. and Tulchin, J. 1984*Entre La Autonomía y La Subordinación. Política Exterior De Los Países Latinoamericanos.* Gel 1984. Buenos Aires.

Muñoz, Heraldo 1986 "The Latin American Policy Of The Reagan Administration" pp. 5-40 in R. Wesson and H. Muñoz (Eds.): *Latin American Views Of U.S. Policy.* Stanford University.

Muñoz, Heraldo 1987a "Las Relaciones Entre EEUU y América Latina Bajo El Gobierno De Reagan: Divergencias y Ajustes Parciales" pp. 501-522, *Foro Internacional* N° 108 Abr-Jun. Colegio De México, México.

Muñoz, Heraldo 1987b "El Estudio De Las Políticas Exteriores Latinoamericanas, Temas y Enfoques Dominantes" pp. 406-434 *Estudios Internacionales* (20) 80, Oct-Dic 1987, Chile.

Muñoz, Heraldo 1988 *Agenda De Seguridad in Las Políticas Externas Sudamericanas.* Documento De Estudio N° 5. Comisión Sudamericana De Paz. Santiago De Chile

Musto, David F 1992, "Patterns In US Drug Abuse And Response" pp. 29-45, Smith P. H. (Ed.): *Drug Policy In The Americas* University Of California, San Diego.

Musto, David F. 1993 *La Enfermedad Americana. Origenes Del Control Antinarcóticos En Eu.* Tercer Mundo Editores, Edición Aumentada, 377. Pags, Bogotá , Colombia. Original: Musto, David F. *The American Disease: Origins Of Narcotics Control.* NY: Oxford UP, 1987.

Nadelmann, Ethan A. 1986. "Latinoamérica: Economía Política Del Comercio De Cocaína," pp. 27-49 Revista *"Texto y Contexto"*, Sept-Dic 1986, N° 9 Univ. Los Andes, Bogotá Colombia.

Nadelmann, Ethan A. 1988a "U.S. Drug Policy: A Bad Export". pp. 83-108, *Foreign Policy* N° 70, Spring 1988.

Nadelmann, Ethan A. 1988b "The Case For Legalization" pp..3-31, *The Public Interest* N° 92, Summer, Washington D.C.

Nuñez R., Georgina. 1986"Propuesta Para El Diseño De Un Mapa De Toma De Decisiones De E.U. Hacia México: Migración y Narcotráfico. in Estados Unidos. Perspectiva Latinoamericana. N° 20. Cide. México 2$ Semestre 1986. *Cuadernos Semestrales.*

Olmo, Rosa Del. 1989a "Drogas: Distorsiones y Realidades" *Nueva Sociedad* N° 102 Jul-Ag. Caracas.

Olmo, Rosa Del. 1989b "Leyes Paralelas" pp. 277-306, Garcia Sayan, Diego (Ed.):"*Coca, Cocaína y Narcotráfico. Laberinto En Los Andes*" pp..277-306.Comisión Andina De Juristas; Lima Perú.

Oporto Castro, Henry. 1989. "El Complejo Coca-Cocaína" pp. 171-190, Garcia Sayan, Diego (Ed.) *Coca, Cocaína y Narcotráfico. Laberinto En Los Andes* Comisión Andina De Juristas, Lima Perú.

Ossio, Juan Et Al. 1989, *La Coca...Tradición, Rito, Identidad*, 429 Páginas. Instituto Indigenista Interamericano, México.

Ossio Acuña, Juan et. al. 1989. "Cosmovisión Andina y Uso De La Coca" pp. 231-309 in Ossio Et. Al. : *La Coca...Tradición, Rito, Identidad.* Instituto Indigenista Interamericano, México.

Palomares, Gustavo. 1991. "La Politica Exterior De Las Últimas Administraciones Republicanas De Los EEUU Con Centroamerica". *Centroamérica, Balance De Una Década* Cedeal, Madrid.

Palomares, Gustavo. 1992. "La Organización De Estados Americanos En La Solución De Conflictos y En La Defensa De La Democracia" pp..56-63Revista *Tiempo De Paz*, Nº 24-25, Otoño 1992.

Pardo, Rodrigo. 1991. "Los Intereses Nacionales De Colombia y La Cooperación Internacional Frente Al Narcotráfico". *Revista Cancillería De S.Carlos* Nº 6, Marzo 1991, Bogotá Colombia.

Pendergast, Mark. "*For God, Country And Coca-Cola*". Revised New Edition. Basic Books 2002.

Peña Begue, Remedios. 1971. "El Uso De La Coca En América Según La Legislación Colonial y Republicana" pp..179-204, *Revista Española De Antropología Americana*, Vol 6, Fac. Filosofía y Letras U. Complutense; Madrid.

Peña Begue, Remedios De La. 1972. "El Uso De La Coca Entre Los Incas" pp. 277-304 *Revista Española De Antropología Americana*, Vol 7:1, Fac. Filosofía y Letras, U. Complutense, Madrid.

Perez De Barradas, José. 1957. *Plantas Mágicas Americanas*, Csic, Madrid.

Perez Gomez, Augusto. 1986. "En Busca De Las Explicaciones Del Consumo De Cocaína"pp. 9-24, *Texto y Contexto*, Nº 9, Sept-Dic 1986. Universidad De Los Andes, Bogotá.

Perl, Raphael Francis. 1986. "Narcopolítica: La Ley Norteamericana Contra El Abuso De Drogas y Las Relaciones EEUU-México *Cuadernos Semestrales* Nº 20, 2º Semestre. México.

Petro, Gustavo, "La Economía De La Mentira", In *Papeles De Cuestiones Internacionales*, Number 62, CIP, Madrid, 1997.

Poitras, Guy. 1988. "Un Post-Mortem Prematuro. La Doctrina Reagan y América Latina", pp. 364-378 in *Nueva Sociedad*, Nº 98, Nov-Dic, San José De Costa Rica/Caracas, Venezuela.

Portales, Carlos 1986"Sudamérica: Seguridad Regional y Relaciones Con EEUU" pp. 279-334, *Estudios Internacionales*, Jul-Sept 1986, 19 (75)Santiago De Chile

Quiroga, José Antonio. 1989. "Paradojas De Una Responsabilidad Compartida" pp. 169-172 *Nueva Sociedad* Nº 102 Jul-Ag ,Caracas

Rabey, Mario. 1989. "Legalidad E Ilegalidad Del Coqueo En Argentina" pp. 35-79 in I.I.I.: *La Coca...Tradición, Rito, Identidad*. I.I.I., México

Reid, Michael. 1989. "Una Región Amenazada Por El Narcotráfico" pp. 135- 170, Garcia Sayan, Diego (Ed.):"*Coca, Cocaina y Narcotráfico. Laberinto En Los Andes*" Comisión Andina De Juristas; Lima Perú

Rementería Ibán De, *La Elección De Las Drogas. Examen De Las Políticas De Control*, Editorial Fundación Friederich Ebert, Lima, 1995.

Rementeria, Ibán De. 1989. "La Sustitución De Cultivos Como Perspectiva" pp. 361-388 ,Garcia Sayan, Diego (Ed.): *Coca, Cocaína y Narcotráfico. Laberinto En Los Andes* Comisión Andina De Juristas, Lima Perú.

Reuter, Peter. 1988. "Can The Borders Be Sealed?" pp. 51-65 in *The Public Interest*, Summer 1988, N° 92; Washington.

Rico, Carlos. 1985. "Crisis y Recomposición? De La Hegemonía Norteamericana. Algunas Reflexiones En Torno A La Coyuntura Internacional En La Segunda Mitad De Los Ochenta," pp..37-59 En Maira,L. (Ed.) *"Una Nueva Era De Hegemonía Norteamericana?*Rial. Grupo Editor Lainoamericano. Buenos Aires

Rojas Marcos, Luis. 1992. *La Ciudad y Sus Desafíos. Héroes y Víctimas*. Espasa Calpe, 5¦ Edición. Madrid

Rojas Aravena, and Solis, F. 1988. *"Subditos O Aliados? La Política Exterior De EEUU y Centroamérica*. 53 P Gs. Flacso Costa Rica

Romano,Ruggiero 1986. "Coca Buena, Coca Mala? Su Razón Histórica En El Caso Peruano," pp. 299-351,Caceres, B. et al.: *La Coca Andina. Visión Indígena De Una Planta Satanizada*, America Indigena, I.I.I., México.

Roncken Theo, "Bolivia: La Impunidad y El Control De La Corrupción En La Luchaantridrobas", in *Guerra Antidrogas, Democracia, Derechos Humanos y Militarización En América Latina*, Editado Por Tni, Cedib, Inforpress Centroamericana, Guatemala, 1977.

Roth, Erik. 1989. "Actitudes De La Población De La Paz Ante La Hoja De Coca" in I.I.I.: *La Coca...Tradición, Rito, Identidad.*I.I.I., México.

Roux, Carlos Vicente De 1989 "El Bien Jurídico Protegido" Garcia Sayan, Diego (Ed.): *Coca, Cocaína y Narcotráfico. Laberinto En Los Andes*" Comisión Andina De Juristas, Lima Perú.

Sabbag, Robert, *Ciego De Nieve. Traficando Con Cocaine*, 1976 (Edición Española,Compactos Anagrama, 1990). New Edition In English: *Snowblind: A Brief Career In The Cocaine Trade*, Grove Press, 1998.

Schnitman, Luis Eduardo. 1990. "La Teoria Sobre La Causa Del Consumo En El Enfoque De La Guerra Contra Las Drogas" pp. 141-147 in Tokatlian, J. Et. Al: *Economía y Política Del Narcotráfico*, Fondo Editorial Cerec, Universidad De Los Andes, Bogotá .

Smith, Peter H. (Ed.) 1992. *Drug Policy In The Americas*, 347 Pags., University Of California. San Diego, Westview Press.

Smith, Peter H. (Ed) 1992. "The Political Economy Of Drugs," pp. 1-23 in

Smith P.H. (Ed.): *Drug Policy In The Americas* University Of California. San Diego, West-view Press.

Soberón, Ricardo And Others, *Crimen Uniformado, Entre La Corrupción y La Impunidad*, Cedib, Cochabamba, Bolivia, 1997.

Soberón, Ricardo, "Entre Cuarteles, Culetas y Fronteras: Fuerzas Armadas y Lucha Antidrogas," In VVAA, *Guerra Antridrogas, Democracia, Derechos Humanos* Y

Militarización En América Latina, Ed. Tni, Cedib, Inforpress Centroamericana, Guate-mala, 1997.

Soria Medina, Samuel. 1986. "La Economía Clandestina En Bolivia," En *Correo-Los Tiempos*, 30 Oct, Entrega Especial,Cochabamba, Bolivia.

Steinsleger, José. 1989. "Los Paraisos Financieros. El Caso De Panam ", pp. 259-274, Garcia Sayan, Diego (Ed.): *Coca, Cocaína y Narcotráfico. Laberinto En Los Andes* Comisión Andina De Juristas, Lima Perú.

Sterling, Claire. *"Thieves' World. The Threat Of The New Global Network Of Organized Crime.* NY: Simon & Schuster, 1994.

Szasz, Thomas. 1989. "Contra El Estado Terapeútico. Derechos Individuales y Drogas" pp. 173-182, in *Nueva Sociedad* "La Alquimia Política De Las Drogas" N⁰ 102, Cara-cas Julio-Agosto 89.

Tokatlian, Juan G. 1988. *Seguridad y Drogas: Su Significado En Las Relaciones Entre Colombia y EEUU.* 44 Páginas. Seminario Internacional "Seguridad Democrática Regional: Una Concepción Alternativa De Seguridad", 23-26 Marzo 1988, Comisión Sudamericana De Paz, Santiago De Chile.

Tokatlian, Juan G. 1989 *Drogas y Seguridad Nacional: ¯La Amenaza De La Intervención?* Comisión Sudamericana De Paz, Santiago De Chile.

Tokatlian, Juan G. 1989 "Las Drogas y Las Relaciones EEUU- América Latina" pp. 74-78 *Nueva Sociedad* N⁰ 102 (Especial Drogas), Jul-Agosto 1989. Caracas.

Tokatlian, J.G. and Bagley, B.M. (Comp.)1990 *Economía y Política Del Narcotráfico*, 422 Páginas, Fondo Editorial Cerec, Universidad De Los Andes, Bogotá .

Tomassini, Luciano 1988"La Cambiante Inserción Internacional De América Latina En La Década De Los 80" pp. 13-29, *Pensamiento Iberoamericano* N⁰ 13. Enero-Junio 1988. Madrid.

Torre, Rosario De La, 1988. Inglaterra y España En 1898, Editorial Eudema, Madrid.

Tulchin, Joseph S. 1988 "The United States And Latin America In The 1960s'" pp. 1-36, in *Journal Of Interamerican Studies*, 30, #1 (Spring) University Of Miami, Florida.

U.S. Government, *National Strategy For Drug Control*, 1989 and 1991

Ugaz, José C. 1989. "Represión O Prevención" pp. 307-317, Garcia Sayan, Diego (Ed.): *Coca, Cocaína y Narcotráfico. Laberinto En Los Andes*, Comisión Andina De Juris-tas, Lima, Perú.

Van Klaveren, Alberto 1983 "El Lugar De Estados Unidos En La Política Exterior Latinoamericana" pp. 121-141 in Drekonja Et. Al: *Teoría y Práctica De La Política Exterior Latinoamericana*. Cerec. Bogotá .

Van Klaveren, Alberto. 1984. "El Análisis De La Política Exterior Latinoamericana: Perspectivas Teóricas" pp. 14-49 H.Muñoz and J.Tulchin *Entre La Autonomía y La Subordinación. Política Exterior De Los Países Latinoamericanos* Gel. Buenos Aires.

Van Klaveren, Alberto 1986"The United States And The Inter-American Political System" in R. Wesson and H. Muñoz (Eds.): *Latin American Views Of U.S. Policy*. Stanford University.

Van Klaveren, Alberto. 1987. "Las Relaciones De Los Países Latinoamericanos Con EEUU: Un Ejercicio Comparativo." Hirst, Mónica (Comp): *Continuidad y Cambio En Las Relaciones Al-EEUU* Gel, Buenos Aires.

Van Klaveren, Alberto. 1989. "Las Relaciones Internacionales De América Latina En La Década De 1980: Cambio y Continuidad," pp. 1-40, in PNUD - CEPAL: *"América Latina y Europa Occidental En Los Umbrales Del Siglo Xxi"*. Proyecto De Cooperación Con Los Servicios Exteriores De América Latina. Doc. De Trabajo Nº 4.

Varas, Augusto 1987 "Cooperación y Paz En América Latina" pp. 11-28, Vv.Aa: *La Situación Estratégica De América Latina. Estados Unidos y La Seguridad Regional*. Cladde-Rial.

Vargas Meza, Ricardo, "The Farc: War And State Crisis." *Nacla Report*, Vol XXXI, Nº5 1998. En Español "Las Farc, La Guerra y La Crisis Del Estado" *Nacla Report*, Volume Xxxi, Number 5, March – April, 1998.

Vargas, Ricardo. "The Impact Of Drugs Control Policies At The National Level In Colombia. Drugs Control Policies In Colombia 1986-95: Prohibition, Institutional Crisis And The Absence Of Civil Society," *Releasedrugs Edition*, Issue 11, March 1996.

Vazquez Carrizosa, Alfredo 1990"La Conferencia De Presidentes De Cartagena Para La Lucha Antinarcóticos" in *Analisis Politico*, Nº 9, Bogotá En-Abr.

VVAA. 1989. "La Alquimia Política De Las Drogas"*Nueva Sociedad* R-10, Nº Especial Drogas Nº 102, Jul-Ag Caracas

VVAA, *Centroamérica: Gobernabilidad y Narcotráfico*, Transnational Institute And Heinrich Boll, Foundation, Guatemala, 1997.

VVAA, *Guerra Antidrogas, Democracia, Derechos Humanos y Militarización En América Latina*, Editado Por Tni, Cedib, Inforpress Centroamericana, Guatemala, 1997.

VVAA. *Narcotráfico: Obstáculo Para La Democratización y La Desmilitarización En Centroamérica*, Ed. Tni, Inforpress y Cedib.

Wagensberg, Jorge, *Ideas Sobre La Complejidad Del Mundo*, Metatemas, Tusquets, 1994.

Wagner, Catherine A. 1986 "Coca y Estructura Cultural En Los Andes Peruanos" Caceres, B. Et Al.: *La Coca Andina. Visión Indígena De Una Planta Satanizada* 1¦ Ed.:America Indigena Xxxviii 1978 Boldó I Climent, I.I.I., México.

Walker Iii, William O. 1992 "International Collaboration In Historical Perspective" pp. 265-282, in Smith P. H. (Ed.): *Drug Policy In The Americas*, University Of California. San Diego, Westview Press.

Wacquant, Loic. "El Encierro De Las "Clases Peligrosas" En Estados Unidos," *Le Monde Diplomatique*. August — September, 1998.

Wola (Office Of Latin American Affairs In Washington), 1991, *Clear And Present*

Dangers. The US Military And The War On Drugs In The Andes. Spanish Version *"Peligro Inminente? Las Ffaa De Estados Unidos y La Guerra Contra Las Drogas."* 250 P Gs.Tercer Mundo Editores. Bogotá Colombia.

Wola, *Explorando La Guerra Contra Las Drogas*, By Jacqueline Williams. Ed. Washington Office On Latin America, Translated By The Asamblea Permanente Derechos Humanos Cochabamba, 1997.

Youngers, Coletta and Walsh, John. 1989. "La Guerra Contra Las Drogas En Los Andes: Una Política Mal Encaminada" pp..346-360 Garcia Sayan, Diego (Ed.) *Coca, Cocaína y Narcotráfico. Laberinto En Los Andes* Comisión Andina De Juristas, Lima Perú.

Zorrilla, Javier 1986El Hombre Andino y Su Relación Mágico Religiosa Con La Coca" Caceres, B. Et Al.: *La Coca Andina. Visión Indígena De Una Planta Satanizada*" America Indigena, I.I.I., México